Performing Drama / Dramatizing Performance

THEATER: Theory/Text/Performance

Enoch Brater, Series Editor
University of Michigan

Around the Absurd: Essays on Modern and Postmodern Drama
edited by Enoch Brater and Ruby Cohn

Tom Stoppard and the Craft of Comedy: Medium and Genre at Play by Katherine E. Kelly

Performing Drama/Dramatizing Performance: Alternative Theater and the Dramatic Text
by Michael Vanden Heuvel

The Plot of the Future: Utopia and Dystopia in Modern Drama by Dragan Klaić

Shaw's Daughters: Dramatic and Narrative Constructions of Gender by J. Ellen Gainor

How Dramas End: Essays on the German Sturm und Drang, *Büchner, Hauptmann, and Fleisser*
by Henry J. Schmidt

Critical Theory and Performance edited by Janelle Reinelt and Joseph R. Roach

The Actor's Instrument: Body, Theory, Stage by Hollis Huston

Acting as Reading: The Place of the Reading Process in the Actor's Work by David Cole

Presence and Resistance: Postmodernism and Cultural Politics in Contemporary American Performance
by Philip Auslander

Ionesco's Imperatives: The Politics of Culture by Rosette C. Lamont

The Theater of Michael Vinaver by David Bradby

Rereading Molière: Mise en Scène from Antoine to Vitez by Jim Carmody

O'Neill's Shakespeare by Normand Berlin

Postmodern Theatric(k)s: Monologue in Contemporary American Drama by Deborah R. Geis

The Player's Passion: Studies in the Science of Acting by Joseph R. Roach

Theater at the Margins: Text and Post-Structured Stage by Erik MacDonald

To Act, To Do, To Perform: Drama and the Phenomenology of Action by Alice Rayner

Tom Stoppard in Conversation edited by Paul Delaney

After Brecht: British Epic Theater by Janelle Reinelt

Directing Beckett by Lois Oppenheim

Susan Glaspell: Essays on Her Theater and Fiction edited by Linda Ben-Zvi

The Theatrical Gamut: Notes for a Post-Beckettian Stage edited by Enoch Brater

Staging Place: The Geography of Modern Drama by Una Chaudhuri

The Aesthetics of Disturbance: Anti-Art in Avant-Garde Drama by David Graver

Toward a Theater of the Oppressed: The Dramaturgy of John Arden by Javed Malick

Performing Drama / Dramatizing Performance

Alternative Theater and the Dramatic Text

Michael Vanden Heuvel

Ann Arbor

THE UNIVERSITY OF MICHIGAN PRESS

First paperback edition 1993

Published in the United States of America by
The University of Michigan Press
Manufactured in the United States of America

1999 1998 1997 1996 5 4 3 2

Library of Congress Cataloging-in-Publication Data

Vanden Heuvel, Michael, 1956–
Performing drama/dramatizing performance : alternative theater and the dramatic text / Michael Vanden Heuvel.
p. cm. — (Theater—theory/text/performance)
Includes bibliographical references and index.
ISBN 0-472-10240-0 (cloth : alk. paper) — ISBN 0-472-08248-5 (paper : alk. paper)
1. Drama—20th century—History and criticism. 2. Experimental theater. 3. Experimental drama. 4. Postmodernism (Literature) 5. Theater—History—20th century. I. Title. II. Series.
PN2193.E86V36 1991
792'.022—dc20 91-10888
CIP

British Library Cataloguing in Publication Data
Vanden Heuvel, Michael
Performing drama/dramatizing performance : alternative theater and the dramatic text.—(Theater : theory/text/performance).
1. Drama
I. Title II. Series
792.028

ISBN 0-472-10240-0
ISBN 0-472-08248-5

For Joan and Norbert Vanden Heuvel, and all the sibs

Acknowledgments

Many friends and colleagues have helped to shape this book as it emerged over a period of time. And though I assume responsibility for the final form of the ideas presented within, I cannot take credit for developing them entirely on my own.

My first debt is to Michael Hinden, who encouraged my initial interest in experimental theater and who later remained staunchly behind me as I careened gracelessly through the research. To Joseph Wiesenfarth and John Lyons, who read early versions of the manuscript, I extend warm thanks for their helpful comments. Enoch Brater pointed out errors of fact and judgment and provided many helpful insights, while, at the University of Michigan Press, LeAnn Fields, Linda Berauer, and Chris Milton helped steer the project to its conclusion.

For the support, encouragement, and criticisms I received from colleagues and friends during preparation of this study, I owe a large debt of thanks. Ernest Suarez helped to brew up some important insights when inspiration was lagging and unfailingly yanked me back to original purposes and aims. I thank William Demastes for many enjoyable hours of conversation and debate over things theatrical out on the Union terrace, where things got done when nobody expected them to, and for staying in my corner, no matter how many I've painted myself into. Finally, to Susan in her Absence and to Tracy for her Presence, I offer these pages.

Contents

Robert Wilson/Philip Glass, *Einstein on the Beach*.
Sheryl Sutton, Lucinda Childs. Directed by Robert Wilson, Brooklyn Academy of Music, 1976. Photo © 1976 Babette Mangolte. All rights of reproduction reserved. Photo courtesy of the Brooklyn Academy of Music.

Introduction: Drama, Performance, and the Emergence of a New Dialogics of the Theater

> In brief, relativity, uncertainty, complementarity, and incompleteness are not simply mathematical idealizations; they are concepts that begin to constitute our cultural languages.
>
> —Ihab Hassan

We live, says Herbert Blau, in an age with a "now-established Tradition of the New" (Blau 1982a, 25). And although we have become used to dramatists making extravagant claims for originality in their work, it is still disarming to see today how often critics flock as well to new banners of the avant-garde (and even "post-avant-garde") to proclaim a new style or approach or author utterly resistant to previous influences and to categorization. But despite the sometimes stunning originality apparent in contemporary theater, little work is actually produced sui generis. Modern variety and postmodern eclecticism notwithstanding, almost everything we see in today's theater, mainstream or experimental, is traceable to a surprisingly restricted set of traditions. Our theater assumes the appearance of endless innovation and diversity for two reasons. First, as a reflection of modernism's combustive and oedipal attitude toward tradition, modernist artists have often insisted upon their radical departure or separation from the past. More recently, we have witnessed a reaction against this often destructive exploitation of the resources of tradition, and a consequent tendency in contemporary art to recycle self-consciously a wide variety of existing traditions in order to reconstitute them as new hybrid forms. Even this new "Green" attitude toward the past and its artistic traditions, however, lends itself to exploitation, as it denies real artistic heritage—in its bourgeois or Marxist sense—in favor of what Patrice Pavis calls "*memory* in the technical sense of the word, as an immediately available and reusable memory bank" (Pavis 1986, 1). Both attitudes generate a tendency to create novel alternatives without much regard for the integrity of discrete traditional forms and practices.

In the contemporary period, with its art-history sensibility and aesthetic attitude toward history, we have seen, in theater especially, an increased rubbing together of disparate traditions—of different acting methods, various dramatic modes and genres, a wide diversity of global theatrical styles, and competing theoretical positions—and a tendency toward self-conscious amalgamation. Critics have often hastily concluded that such blending by itself heralds the arrival of a "postmodern" theater, but they do so without considering important distinctions that appear as truly new forms of theater slowly emerge from a long process of distillation.[1] Much theatrical experimentation over the past forty years has revealed, despite claims that undesired vestiges of modernism have been shed, a distinctively high-modernist agenda. Even when its modernist bases were significantly altered or subverted, early experimental theater often simply reinscribed modernist practices and strategies. It is only in the last fifteen years or so that the various threads of America's vital experimental theater have wound together to produce a viable and lasting form of expression that shows the potential for significant evolution through and beyond the modernist heritage. And that result was achieved only after the most radical experimentation—with what are usually described as essential postmodern ideas such as decenterment, the demystification of reason, the liminality of language, and so on—had exhausted itself, and artists had turned again toward assimilating theatrical and humanistic traditions within their work in newly modified hybrid forms.

Over the past four decades, a primary catalyst for initial experiments within avant-garde theater, as well as for the more recent recuperation of tradition within contemporary work, has been the dynamic—sometimes antagonistic—relationship between what I will call "drama" and "performance." Since I am seeking to explore the wide and fluid space between the two, I have chosen to adopt rather strict definitions of both in order to extend artificially the expanse that separates them.

By *drama* I mean generally that form of theatrical expression that is constituted primarily as a literary artifact, according to particular "dramatic" conventions, and empowered as text. Dramas, of course, do not remain merely literary and textual; they are often performed. Nevertheless, the specific fields of pleasure they induce or refuse, and the source of their power to move or distance the spectator, are mainly textual, rooted in literary conventions of narrative, language, scene, character, and semiosis. This does not mean, however, that there exists a single paradigm of the text that manifests the same affects among its readers or spectators. Umberto Eco (1979) has shown how every text postulates its own receiver, and recent reader-response criticism has effectively theorized the means by which texts are authenticated by various institutions ("model reader," "informed reader," "community of readers," and so on).[2]

The definition of text, then, has been substantially repositioned in the wake of structuralist and poststructuralist theory, as well as in semiotics, where it now resides as a methodological field, a version of *ècriture* containing naturalized literary conventions and codes. So, as used in this study, text/drama is best understood as representative both of those conventions and of a larger cognitive activity of imposing structure or meaning on reality. That is, drama and text define first a manner in which such structures are perceived by readers and spectators. I restrict my focus here not to what Barthes would call the *scriptible,* or interrogative, text that resists the spectator's conventional reading strategies and expectations, but rather to the thoroughly conventional and *lisible,* or readerly text of classic realism. This latter text is characterized by such qualities as its conformity to prevailing discourses and reading strategies, its emphasis on illusionism, its syntactically organized vision of a universal and transcendent reality, its use of relatively transparent language, and its overarching gesture toward hypotaxis and intelligibility.[3] The usual emplotment of such texts takes the form of an argument ("the argument of the play"), and helps to constitute a construction of reality grounded in contest, struggle, and resolution. Other concrete qualities associated with such dramatic texts would include the entire range of affects Derrida ascribes to the "theological stage": recognition of the integrity of the author's vision, of authorial mastery over signs and their signifieds, and of the playwright's adherence to a conjunctive form constituted by stable constructions of character, plot, and language (Derrida 1978, 235).

The social function and desirability of the *lisible* text have been rigorously questioned in recent theory because the strategies of such texts are thought to divert the reader from differences and to re-mark existing, naturalized ideologies and signifying systems by representing them and by endowing them with Presence. As Marcuse has demonstrated, bourgeois culture detours revolutionary values to the imaginative realm and thus denies their real-world realization. Further, in dramatic forms tightly bound to the traditional text, such as realism, the mobility and dynamism of the various theatrical sign-relationships is severely limited: spectators anticipate that the signified class will be represented by signs that are immediately recognizable as a "realistic" member of it. Thus semiotically constrained, such work appears to some critics (Theodor Adorno, Augusto Boal, many feminist critics) impotent to expose contradictions that exist within the socially constructed and hegemonized reality of dominant discourses. The theological stage itself, in collusion with the traditional organic text, is accused of promoting the illusion of a reality that is stable and a social order that is sufficient and valid. As a result, these critics feel that such dramatic styles tend to replicate existing discourses and acculturate attitudes of conciliation, assimilation, and adaptation.

This critical aversion to textuality suggests that, beyond mere literary concerns, textuality also describes a process of endowing the perceived world with the attributes of a traditional text—the activity of fabricating master emplotments of history, for example, or of constructing holistic integrative frames of reference between people, events, and objects, or synthetic relationships between language, objects, and desire. These transactions between self and world form an aggregate logocentric attitude or cognitive activity that can also be termed "textualizing." And in virtually all applications of textuality—literary and cognitive—the seminal desire is mastery, or what I define in theatrical terms as Presence, the totalizing pathology described by Nietzsche in *The Will to Power* as the "hyperbolic naivete of man: positing himself as the meaning and measure of the value of things." Such desire is expressed in theater through the medium of the theological stage, from which in Western culture the author projects his or her illusion of control, Presence, and potency over meaning and interpretation.

Performance, similarly, is traditionally defined in our culture as the staging of the literary artifact and is thus implicated in the reconstituting of determinate meaning and authorial power. The term is certainly no longer restricted to that activity, however. The experimental work I am concerned with in this study, in fact, has done much to destabilize the common definition of the word and to open up our understanding of how performance functions in a variety of contexts. Through various discourses and their theories, we have been advised that performance can be ludic, liminal, liberating; that it can infiltrate the text, dispossess it, and displace its power along with that of the inseminating author. Further, we are informed that performance, in only one of its many paradoxes, can deconstruct Presence utterly, and empower Absence or powerlessness. Since it is activated by nonperiodic, nonlinear activities—improvisation, play, transformation, parataxis, game structures—performance breaks down the illusion of rational control and power over meaning (and the structural metaphor of argument underlying the text), and substitutes a dispersal of order into disorganization. Its primary gesture is thus toward chaos or indeterminacy.

This should not suggest that performance by nature yields no structure or system of reference at all, but rather that, as in chaos theory, the structure comprises a moderated randomness so complex that its underlying order cannot be recuperated entirely within rational systems. Instead of building itself, like the text, in the form of an argument, performance is constructed in terms of networks that may appear disorderly but that contain unique forms of internal order. Similar nonlinear structures in nature may, for instance, reveal spatial order but temporal disorder; some exhibit disorderly patterns that nevertheless contain structures that are self-similar on different scales or that eventually evolve into steady states or oscillating ones. Like such natural chaotic systems, then, performance makes its first gesture toward breaking down rational order. Performance deconstructs authorial power and its illusion of Presence, and disperses its quanta of energies among the performers and the spectator as a potential source of a deferred, hypothetical, and immanent power. Performance is therefore initially the displacement of Presence, or power, and the affirmation of Absence and powerlessness. In some instances, however, the deconstruction of an orderly system (like the text) by the intervention of disorder or turbulence can initiate evolution toward a higher order of complexity; and so as a secondary effect, performance has the potential to open up new systems, sometimes new levels, of meaning.

For my purpose, performance refers first to a theatrical medium that has traditionally acted to translate the dramatic text, but which in recent years has been ordained as an autonomous art form, as an alternative to "literary" drama, and, finally, as the privileged mechanism for deconstructing the theological stage and conventional dramatic semiosis. The specific strategies of performance within theatrical events will be introduced throughout the study, but they generally operate as a means to mark and organize a structure of resistance to logocentrism, *Gestell,* authorial Presence, and the conventional reading strategies of textuality. Like drama and text, however, the term has wider applications as an *épistémè* (in Foucault's sense of the term), that is, a system of cognitive activities, similar in many respects to those associated with poststructuralist theory. The "performative consciousness," it has been theorized, is acutely conscious of difference and contradiction, and is characterized as one whose desires are not directed toward Presence or origins. Processual in nature, refusing to be anchored within a stable system of referents, the performative self exists in an indeterminate and pluralistic state, joyously transforming and diffusing itself into "ludic diffractions of the self" (Hassan 1987, 65). The activity of deconstructing identity and the various master texts of culture in order to disperse them becomes an affirmative response to a reality and a language defined by slippage, leaks, gaps, and indeterminacy.[4] As Richard Schechner (1982, 6) described it, "the beauty of 'performance consciousness' is that it invites alternatives: both 'this' and 'that' are both operative simultaneously. . . . [P]erformance consciousness is subjunctive, full of alternatives and potentiality. . . . [It is] a celebration of contingency."

The last element in the triangle within which this study is positioned is theater itself. I will restrict my use of the term to mean the event—inscribed within a text or improvised by performers—that is enacted before a spectator. The narrow use to which I apply the term, however, should not conceal the dynamic space that theater occupies today in our culture. From my view, theater has become the privileged site of difference in a culture increasingly given to simplified dichotomies. In opposition to culture's flattening out of difference, theater has maintained itself as an arena where potentially conflictual, even antithetical, issues and value perceptions about the world—including those values and cognitive activities associated with text and performance—are transformed into interactive energies that can be made to sustain, rather than dominate, one another. As David George has written, theater "is in many ways a more authentic representation [of reality] because it recognizes and enforces a conception of reality as plural and parallel, indeterminate and hypothetical, the co-creation of spectators-players—in a word, potential" (George 1988, 174). Thus, theater by its nature gives voice to difference, and provides the matrix for the fruitful interactions between opposed categories like textuality and performance that motivate the work analyzed in these essays.

In fact, these changing relationships between drama and performance have helped to produce some of the most interesting experiments in recent theater, as well as much of the significant theory outside theater. The results of such recombinative activities have expanded the very field of theater, allowing spectators and critics to accept within the mainstream theatrical canon new work that emphasizes alternative, sometimes nontextual, qualities or effects as criteria for judging the status of a given work or oeuvre. In some cases, incongruous combinations between "literary" drama and nontextual, performance-oriented work have shown us that today, more than ever, the relationship between drama and performance is not as stable as we might have once believed. No longer can we accept a linear, Newtonian model that describes the text and its affects as the absolute reference for measuring theatrical work, and performance as merely an "illustration," "translation," or even "fulfillment" of that text (Carlson 1985, 6). Instead, we are forced to look for new metaphors to describe a more complex relationship, a new language that captures the dynamics between drama and performance.

Still, critics today often attempt to understand and describe this nonlinear phenomenon (the relationship of text to performance in new theater work) by reference to an outdated, though stable, model. That model is satisfactory because it has worked well for so long as a paradigm for the way theater ought to be constituted. But paradigms should do more than set laws; they should also record inconsistencies and make possible new discoveries when the model's periodic order is disrupted by the onset of an unexpected breakdown or turbulence. The growing movement in contemporary drama and performance toward deconstructive aesthetics centered on the disruptive potential of performance, and the creation of hybrid theatrical forms that problematize our traditional methods for creating meaning in the theater, have created just such a chaotic motion. In addition to producing some very provocative theater work, these experiments have disclosed theater as a decidedly schizophrenic entity that no single or stable hierarchical relationship between text and performance can describe adequately.

Francis Fergusson noted forty years ago that the "centerless diversity" of twentieth-century dramatic forms—absolutely meager by today's standards—may be modern theater's greatest source of strength. But while the explosion and cross-indexing of dramatic styles and idioms, and the shifting relations of power between text and performance, have certainly enriched modern theater and provided audiences with a range of choices greater than ever before, they have made large-scale critical studies of drama in general difficult and often frustratingly incomplete. Critics of drama have long faced the choice either to hazard generalizations, the wide applicability of which necessarily attenuates their power to recognize and conceptualize important differences among different kinds of plays, or else to follow the trend toward variety and concoct various "Theater-of-X" categories. The latter usually illuminate a limited number of plays by revealing similarities often merely thematic or stylistic, without regard to what Austin Quigley calls a play's "use of theater space . . . a use that links texture, structure, and theme to the mode of performance that is characteristic of a particular kind of play in a particular kind of theatrical space" (Quigley 1985, 6–7). As a result, these categories artificially pigeonhole works that belong together tonally or thematically at best.

The problem has been compounded in the last thirty to forty years by the irruption of new "image" theaters and versions of performance art within the once-sacrosanct domain of orthodox, text-centered drama, works whose use of performance space is radically different from, and often deconstructive of, that of conventional literary drama. These developments and the stylistic and conceptual changes they have wrought—in the creation of new types of dramatic language, the use of nonlinear narrative structures, the development toward more physical acting styles, and innovative experiments in the use of theatrical time, space, and the mise-en-scène—have expanded theater's capacities for expression by opening up the art to new theoretical perspectives drawn from anthropology, behavioral psychology, speech act theory, semiotics, poststructuralist and feminist literary theory, and other disciplines. But the amazingly efficient recuperative mechanisms of late capitalist culture have also brought these once-radical innovations into contact with the mainstream of contemporary drama. What were only several decades ago subversive experiments (often taking place outside mainstream theater) in "antidrama," "nonmatrixed performance," and performance art, shared usually among a coterie of avant-garde practitioners and their theoretically radicalized high-art audiences, are now

Samuel Beckett, *Endgame*.
Directed by JoAnne Akalaitis, American Repertory Theatre, 1984.
Photo by Richard Feldman/American Repertory Theatre.

used alongside conventional dramatic elements in popular scripted theater work by playwrights (many with previous connections to experimental performance theater) like Sam Shepard, Maria Irene Fornes, David Rabe, Megan Terry, Lanford Wilson, Jane Wagner, and David Mamet in America, and by British authors such as Caryl Churchill, Pam Gems, and Tom Stoppard, to name only a significant few. At the same time, we see the other swing of the gate—that is, the increased marshaling of traditional dramatic elements within avant-garde performance theater—in pieces by contemporary experimental performance groups like The Wooster Group and Squat, by autodramatists and performance artists like Spalding Gray, Laurie Anderson, and Ping Chong, and by director/auteurs like Robert Wilson, Richard Foreman, and JoAnne Akalaitis.

Such a blending of seemingly antithetical theatrical modes, I will argue, has introduced exciting new work into world theater. It has also, however, made problematic a cohesive picture of what was formerly termed "drama." It seems hardly possible today for books to be written with titles like *The Elements of Drama*, much less *The Idea of a Theater*. The encroachment of avant-garde performance theater and its own values (holistic/therapeutic, deconstructionist, political action, formalist) and uses of performance space (environmental theater, "holy" theater, structuralist theater, theater anthropology, theater of sources, feminist theater, to name only a few) into the mainstream of world theater and culture over the past forty years has significantly challenged our perceptions of how theater can and ought to function. In the same way, the recent retrenchment of avant-garde performance theater within a more recognizably dramatic framework has altered our notions (developed and somewhat exaggerated in the heyday of experimental performance) of the limited range and power of the autonomous act of performance itself.

From a longer perspective we can trace the inevitable process of this uneasy rapprochement between the dramatic text and the art of performance. The dominant forms of drama over the last century (realism, expressionism, epic theater, and formalism) have been at one time or another challenged, and the result has been a growing sense that none, by itself, has worked consistently to produce a dramatic idiom appropriate for arresting the flow of spirit, in T. S. Eliot's phrase, "before it expands and ends its course in the desert of exact likeness to the reality which is perceived by the most commonplace mind." Realism, the dominant Western theatrical mode in the twentieth century, has of course been challenged from its inception in the late nineteenth century, and every student of theater history knows that its greatest innovators—Ibsen, Strindberg, Chekhov, Shaw—at some late date in their careers became disenchanted with the form and experimented with more expressionistic styles, whether dream play or "Fantasia in the Russian manner." Still, expressionism in its myriad guises (symbolism, surrealism, Dada, certain kinds of recent experimental theater) has never really gathered itself into a coherent theatrical style, but instead has too often devolved into simply an alternative or supplement to realism without ever carving out a unique space of its own. Epic theater, which appeared so promising after Brecht's work and theory were introduced in the west, is still often described today as an important "first step" toward a viable new theater. Increasingly, however, epic theater is being perceived as an essentially obsolete strategy for the representation of the complex and indeterminate realities of the postmodern world. A contemporary German playwright like Heiner Müller, for instance, views his own relationship to Brecht not as fraternal but as "parricidal." Müller's work, along with that of revisionist Brecht productions by feminist directors and dramaturgs, although obviously influenced by Brecht's notions of *gestus* and the mise-en-scène, attempts to overcome the linear narrativity (which Müller refers to as "A-B-C dramaturgy") and overly didactic stance of Brecht's plays with a new "antistructure" that utilizes a deconstructionist dramaturgy to "blow up" the Brechtian docudrama. As for formalism, which in its minimalist form perhaps reached its zenith in just the last decade, it has already come under fire for its insistent ahistoricism and for what one critic calls its "great unexamined assumption . . . that [it] can stimulate some implicit, perceptual change in consciousness" (Coe 1985, 18).

Lacking a dominant dramatic literary form, modernist and contemporary theater artists have thus ventured outside literary tradition to seek new energy from nonliterary disciplines: the surrealists' flirtation with Jungian dream-therapy, Beckett's use of vaudeville, Kaprow's visual art concerns, for example. In one of the most simple, yet most challenging responses to the loss of significant literary form in modern theater, some artists began to look beyond the horizons of new textual expression, and sought instead to revise the conventional relationship between drama and performance. Instead of leaving performance as the handmaiden to the text, they reversed the hierarchy and ordained performance as the true locus of power within—sometimes hoping to extend it beyond—theatrical representation.

In doing so, early performance-theater artists produced unique events, which they claimed were closer to what theater was meant to be before the literary text and its author began to dominate the spectacle. Yet, for all the singular qualities of expression that were engendered, these artists really only succeeded in maintaining the dialectical tendencies of Western culture by substituting one authoritarian locus of power for its opposite. In its purest form, performance art privileges the spontaneous and physical activity of performing as an autonomous form of artistic expression. That expression is said to differ from literary, textual, or "closed" forms in that it does not impose a preformed hierarchy of discourses or meaning upon the spectator. In the earlier years of performance art, the emphasis was in fact often on the deconstructive power of the performance to infiltrate and displace the constraints of textuality. Within simple versions of performance art, for instance, the performer claims not to control the audience or to impugn any determinate meaning or interpretation at them. Yet certainly the power of the performance to induce pleasure, identification, the *jouissance* of deconstructive dispersal, catharsis, or any other spectatorial response still resides within the performer, who has simply displaced the author. The only way such a style of performance art can possibly free itself from such closure and control is for the performance artist to allow himself or herself to be displaced in turn, perhaps by a spectator.

In fact, the power and Presence imbued in performance art is, if anything, increased because the spectator is aware that the performance is singular, that it will occur *this way* only this time. The spectator's response may be unique at such an event, but it is no less enclosed or hypostatized for all that; it is rather more narrowly confined simply because the spectator feels a sense of particular ownership of the response or interpretation of what he or she has seen. If, says Patrice Pavis, "we accept the idea that the modern text's meaning is only what can be reconstituted by the hypotheses and open tracks of the reading process, then this text can be read according to a schema entirely constituted by the recipient, and then both difficulty and polysemy vanish forever" (Pavis 1986, 3).[5] So, too, in performance art. In truth, performance as a purely autonomous form of expression does not displace the dramatic text and its Presence, but simply mimics and restates it while only marginally dispersing its power. Seeking to break down the text's transcendental signifieds, performance often inadvertently proposes itself as a new transcendental signifier. As Arlene Raven succinctly puts it, "Performance is an act of empowerment and an exercise of power. It demands response and wants historical place" (Raven 1988, 215). In fact, most of the murmuring against "textual imperialism" has been simple cant, easily exposed by critics like Blau and Jonathan Kalb, the latter of whom notes that the slogans directed against the author are actually a "form of projection, since those who shout them are really asserting . . . simply a differently ordered aristocracy" (Kalb 1989, 149).

A more fruitful approach would ignore the noisy propagandizing of authors, performance artists, and directors, and conclude that text and performance, when one dominates without the mediating influence of the other, tend to confirm and endorse Presence and to give a self-confirming illusion of power. The essential difference is that the text does not mask its Presence, while performance art uses a more subtle strategy to mystify its relationship to the spectator, one akin to the lesson of the fifty-eighth Tao: "One who excels in employing others humbles himself before them. / This is known as the virtue of non-contention; /This is known as the making use of the efforts of others; / This is known as matching the subliminity of heaven."

The failure to produce a theater event that could break through this illusion of power and produce a new, nondominant response through the medium of either text or autonomous performance has induced many prominent theater artists to attempt a break from a stable or narrowly dialectical relationship between the two.[6] Sharing a tendency found in other recent art forms, contemporary theater artists reveal a distrust of imposed orders and a desire to dissolve the rigid, dichotomous thinking inherent in Western culture. One result has been an exploration of a new dialogics for the theater, built upon an open-ended and speculative relationship between the dramatic text and its claims to objectivity, its human reference, and its satisfying sense of closure on the one hand, and the emphasis on interiority, deconstructive dispersal, and liminality inherent to performance on the other. Like contemporary architecture, recent theater has adopted a kind of "adhocism," which characteristically "double-codes" or consciously juxtaposes elements, idioms, and functions to create ironic and transformative space between them.[7] In the case of theater, the space exists between the poles of text and performance, which are often perceived and theorized as antithetical modes of theatrical presentation and spectatorship. Indeed, the two modes of presentation are often understood to represent competing ideologies, marking differences regarding the production, exchange, and reproduction of meaning, the proper function of language, and politically appropriate attitudes toward culture, history, and praxis.

Having established by experiment and practice that neither the traditional text nor deconstructive performance captures or defers Presence wholly, many theater artists now seem content to explore the fertile space between the two in order to consider how they might supplement one another in a given theatrical event. The direction is away from the monologism and anxiety that infiltrate thought built on rational dichotomies, toward a pluralistic investigation of less overarching and self-affirming narratives and performances. Though the art remains profound, sometimes disturbing, a sense of accommodation and acceptance is common. "I have reached no conclusions, have erected no boundaries," concludes the speaker of A. R. Ammons's "Corsons Inlet": "shutting out and shutting in, separating inside from outside: I have / drawn no lines . . . / Scope eludes my grasp." Instead, like particle physicists who link conjugate variables such as waves and particles, position and trajectory, and discontinuity and continuity in complementary relationships, these artists often seek the indeterminate fields within which performance and drama create fruitful friction and harmony, rather than trying to find a means to absorb or annihilate one or the other set. "So it is with us all," remarks the Russian double (triple?) spy and particle physicist in Tom Stoppard's *Hapgood:* "we're not so one-or-the-other. . . . [P]erhaps in the moment before unconsciousness—we meet our sleeper—the priest is visited by the doubter, the Marxist sees the civilizing force of the bourgeoisie, the captain of industry admits the justice of common ownership" (Stoppard 1988, 72). So, too, the meeting of the performance/text "double."

This new impulse toward repositioning the relationship between text and performance often redirects theater back toward its sources, toward the *theatron* or "seeing place," where it traditionally functioned to allow spectators to develop a means to interpret and speculate about the world in which they lived. Since speculation itself is a processual activity with finite limits, theater works best when it advocates to the spectator this sort of complementary relationship between the affects of drama and performance, rather than when it seeks to infringe the vision of a single author or text upon the audience or when it appears to disempower artistic interpretation at all. The pluralistic space such theater opens up is, like Einstein's four-dimensional universe, "closed but unbounded," and receptive to—perhaps generative of—new modes of perception and interpretation.

The New Languages of Theater

> *Tortoise:* . . . [H]ave you ever considered that such chaos might be an integral part of the beauty and harmony?
> *Achilles:* Chaos, part of perfection? Order and chaos making a pleasing unity? Heresy!
>
> —Douglas Hofstadter

Critics confronting this "new" version of theater, when they have noticed it at all, have generally attempted to accommodate it within the genre of drama and to interpret it from a more or less literary perspective. Doubtless such interpretation remains useful, yet essential differences exist and must be considered regarding exactly what forms of performance and drama are combined for what function. It hardly suffices to say that literary dramas by, for instance, Sam Shepard and David Mamet function similarly to performance works by The Wooster Group or to the autodramas of Spalding Gray. Yet all to a degree have blended traditional dramatic elements with more experimental performance strategies in their work. Beyond the simple fact that each shares similar elements and stylistic concerns, then, lies the more important question of the manner in which those elements and concerns are used to create certain kinds of theater events, literary "drama" or otherwise.

Many looking at the current state of affairs, however, seem unwilling to accept the deeply chaotic, even contradictory nature of a theater built on an unstable and shifting relationship of difference between literary drama and performance. For most, there is still an implicit faith that if *the* idea of a theater (built upon the privileged dramatic text) no longer exists, at least *an* idea can, even if the idea does not hold up to the reality of the situation. And so the tendency still predominates to seek unifying elements that might somehow lend a bit of continuity and order to what is happening in contemporary theater, even though what we are faced with is an essentially unstable set of phenomena and an art better understood in terms of difference.

A popular universalizing approach in recent years, in America at least, has been to suggest that the dominant dramatic form (realism in any of its several definitions) has joined with others (absurdism, expressionism, and avant-garde theater, as well as nondramatic sources like new dance, photography, and film) and has subsequently become "entwined" or "braided" with them.[8] The results, it is felt, are peculiarly effective concoctions for expressing the form and pressure of the "postmodern condition."

Behind this critical agenda lies the notion that orthodox realism and traditional naturalism by themselves lack the necessary structural, linguistic, and ideological flexibility to voice accurately contemporary society's sense of chaos, uncertainty, and alienation—are unable, that is, to "accommodate the mess," in Beckett's phrase—and are impotent to privilege the contemporary urge for process, dispersal, deferment, and play. If, as it is often suggested, the arrival of the postmodern indicates a substantial change in the way we envision culture, history, and consciousness, then, as Robert Corrigan suggests, "the challenge confronting the theater is to create forms that will both represent and make sense of the emerging new world that the transformation of consciousness is heralding" (Corrigan 1984, 161).

But because textual drama (especially realism) retains certain alluring features—an open but generally verifiable system of semiotic codes (linguistic, symbolic, etc.), narrative structures with which the audience can be comfortable, psychologically developed characters who engage the spectator's active sympathies, and a cumulative method of knowledge acquisition (as opposed to a discontinuous and therefore disquieting one)—the form is thought not to have lost altogether its attraction and usefulness. And, as Jill Dolan (1989a) has noted, a playwright's recourse to realism is still intimately tied to a play's economic life and its acceptance into the mainstream critical canon. Such spectatorial and materialist factors are certainly important, though we must also realize that on another level realism retains its stature simply because, as Samuel Bernstein writes, it has managed to sustain a capacity to "put one in touch with the resources of one's own humanity, with the ethos of a nation, and with the dynamics of the human experience" (Bernstein 1980, x).

So in order to maintain the best of realism while at the same time revising it to accommodate new realities, critics have heralded a "new realism." The congenial blending of these qualities of realism with more adventurous styles, that express—through altered or ironized dialogue, self-conscious theatricality, or expressionistic staging—a felt sense of the difference and contradiction that informs contemporary experience is said to promise playwrights an effective method for dealing with the changing consciousness of our time.

Critics approaching recent theater from this perspective have certainly provided many important new insights. Their initiatives have provided a better understanding of the function of Albee's and Bond's sometimes disorienting plots and language, a sense of Shepard's true dramatic roots, and a surer grasp of the peculiar craft that produces the oddly appropriate "physical" dialogue and the eccentric imagery we find in essentially realist works by Mamet, Rabe, Tina Howe, and others. We have, too, another perspective from which to consider better what were once thought to be slight, mainstream realist works by Beth Henley, Marsha Norman, Ed Bullins, and other prominent playwrights. In each case, realizing that these and other text-oriented playwrights have for some time been tapping into nonliterary forms in order to develop ironic idioms suitable for expressing the ethos of contemporary

Western culture and for demystifying the power of the dramatic text has broadened our perspectives and opened up new and fruitful critical approaches.

There remains a sense, however, that such approaches have likely purchased their continuity at the expense of plenitude, comprehensiveness, and *différance*—in Derrida's sense of a condition of dynamic possibility that resists ultimate hypostatization—itself. Critics who point to the various entwinings with realism in contemporary drama still consistently overemphasize what they obviously consider to be the "source" or privileged form of drama, realism, at the expense of all others. Too often this approach masks implicit positivist assumptions, such as the one that suggests that realist, text-oriented drama has somehow "mated" with and then outlasted the encroaching species of experimental performance, drawn what was useful from the latter's dwindling gene pool, and passed it on to new generations of hybrid realists (a similar genetic history is already in place to describe the move from melodrama to realism in American theater). The same linear, Lamarckian logic would suggest that all theater is progressing toward the greater refinement of realist drama. In addition to its historical inaccuracy and cultural chauvinism (realism being only a very recent and isolated development in world drama), such an emphasis makes improper the analogies to braiding, entwining, and the making of hybrids, since each of these refers to an ongoing process involving the joining or recombination of two essentially equal parts or gene pools to form new entities.

I mention this not only out of a concern for metaphorical propriety, but also because it overlays a serious critical fallacy. The exclusion in recent critical studies of theater work produced by nonliterary artists, especially work that eschews the use of a fixed and unified dramatic text as the basis for production (a propensity brought to its highest degree of efficiency in realist drama), is evidence of consistent textual and "literary" biases, which are likely connected to matters of gender, class, and ethnicity as well. Playwrights have for centuries, of course, cast a cold eye on both performance (Ben Jonson comes to mind) and the text (here it is Brecht), but critics and academics responsible for forming the almost exclusively "literary" dramatic canon have consistently come down squarely on the side of the written word. Unless there is a dramatic text to analyze, it is thought, there is no theatrical event to consider, that event usually being construed simply as the illustration or translation of the privileged text. But one of the most far-reaching innovations of recent experimental theater has been the critical intervention of deconstructive performance *against* the unified text; and, though we may sometimes have strong reservations about the effects that have followed, such a significant phenomenon cannot simply be ignored.

In truth, we need a new language to describe what takes place in modern theater, an idiom that captures some of the inconsistency, indeterminacy, and downright counterintuitive strangeness of the unstable relationships that form between and then deconstruct literary and performative modes of expression. Perhaps the logic of the metaphors we use to animate our understanding of contemporary theater and how it develops should come from contemporary physics (rather than Lamarckian biology), where interaction is analyzed in terms of the fields or spaces that exist between elements and that mutually interact to generate, not solid objects, but unstable events.[9] In the curved space-time universe of relativity and in the subatomic realm of quantum mechanics, such dynamic interanimative fields or intervals and their indeterminate outcomes are, paradoxically, more important than the elements themselves in terms of creating new entities, for it is here that transformative energy and force are released. "In science" says Natalie Crohn Schmitt (1990b, 231),

> it has come to be understood that the event is the unit of all things real—that energy, not matter, is the basic datum. In the increasingly widespread perception of reality as endless process, performance, not the art object, becomes primary. The overt presence of the actor and the audience in or at the performance makes clear its nature as event rather than object.

Just as important, those interactions are understood as unpredictable, as are the laws that govern them. Knowledge of such events can be described only in terms of probabilities and possibilities, not as consistent predictions of the results. The so-called wave function, Erwin Schröedinger's description of observable reality, simply makes it possible to predict the likelihood that at a given place and time we can measure the velocity or position of a particle—and never both simultaneously, according to Heisenberg's uncertainty principle. Equally disorienting in this description of reality is the fact that any measurement of the object will unavoidably alter and restrict the accuracy of the experiment, so that every observation is necessarily disruptive. As Niels Bohr remarked, we must become conscious of our status as actors, and not merely observers, on the stage of life.

When used to describe what occurs when the dramatic text confronts another valency like performance, and when the spectator actively confronts and re-stages the consequent unstable event, such dynamic metaphors describe more accurately the interaction and the indeterminate results that follow than do the homier, linear metaphors to which we have become accustomed. If we conceive of theater itself as a form of wave function, and performance and drama as waves or particles within that function, we can observe the paradoxes and inconsistencies that keep them in a state physicists call complementarity: mutually exclusive descriptions of reality that are inconsistent if applied simultaneously but each essential at different times if we are to have a complete description of the universe. The *épistétèmes* of textuality and performance, then, and the values and affects they produce, are not mutually exclusive, but dynamic and fecund. In addition, the notion of what George (1988) terms a "quantum theater" allows us to speak more directly to the growing realization that theater is characterized not by the imposition of meaning by a determinate text upon a stable and passive spectator, but by a dynamic transaction between observer and the observed. When spectators enter the hermeneutic space of the theater, its wave function is "collapsed," and what is observed is rendered uncertain, shifting, contextual, and multiple, rather than simply ambiguous yet enclosed.

One cannot help but notice the significant similarities between the functions and effects of such metaphors drawn from quantum physics and the general predicates of poststructuralist theories of reading. Like poststructuralism, quantum science doubts the usefulness of general laws and complicates the opposition between subject and object upon which objective perceptions of reality rest. Just as any reading is theorized by Derrida to be contaminated by the traces of language and the subjects' own patterns of desire, so any observation of quantum mechanics is tainted by the observer's need to isolate either the velocity or the path of a given subatomic particle. Finally, Derrida's deconstructions of the structure of binary oppositions lead him to a linguistic version of the principle of complementarity, wherein terms that appear to be contradictory and in opposition to one another are actually, like waves and particles, accomplices of one another.

When we think, then, about the profound effects that follow when drama and performance interact dynamically, we might keep in mind an analogy McLuhan draws: "Two cultures or technologies can, like astronomical galaxies, pass through one another without collision; but not without a change in configuration. In modern physics there is, similarly, the concept of 'interface' or the meeting and metamorphosis of two structures" (McLuhan 1967, 149). Such an interface between the paradigms of performance and drama in contemporary theater need not be construed as a conflict, with an anticipated resolution or deterministic synthesis, but as an ongoing and formative process. As Gerald Holton has written, with quantum theory "the search has turned to a more direct confrontation of complexity and derangement, of sophisticated and astonishing relationships among strangely juxtaposed parts" (Holton [1973] 1988, 96). By seeking out such complexity and recognizing the derangement from which it often springs, and by thinking about theater in this way, the interaction between literary drama and experimental forms of performance becomes understandable in terms of the "interface" of the interdependent forces governing *each* body; and this in turn allows us to consider more equitably the subsequent dynamical metamorphoses of both.

Therefore, if we want to study the truly productive mechanics that makes possible the dynamic and fluid relationship between textual drama and nontextual performance—instead of being satisfied with simply evaluating a portion of the results (e.g., new-generation realist dramatists)—then we have to overcome biases and nostalgia concerning the priority and power of textuality and of the cultural history that produces the illusion of such priority. In doing so, we naturally sacrifice a great deal of the continuity usually mapped out in contemporary drama, because of the greater number of elements and the consequent wider field—drama, performance, and the variable spaces between them—that open up for analysis.

But as I have noted, such well-made criticism is an illusion derived from an overly linear perspective. The new approach entails viewing the current situation in terms of both typology and difference; that is, by reference to the properties that remain unchanged when drama and performance "interface" and are deconstructed and deformed, as well as in terms of the differential development of related properties after they have begun to evolve in their own manner. For theater studies this means, first, including analyses of nonliterary, sometimes nontextual theater pieces and performances that, for all their radical departures from textual drama, still include vestigial traces or transformations of the complementary form. Second, it means looking more closely at contemporary literary drama to see how performative elements have been given new emphases within scripted work in order to unchain signification and redefine the limits of textuality. Finally, although the complete history of the dynamics of text and performance lies well outside the frame of this study, some attention must be paid to recent historical processes that have initiated this new form of interface, determined the nature of its metamorphoses, and directed further growth in new directions.

Such initiatives are under way in recent studies that approach contemporary theater from a variety of critical perspectives. Herbert Blau recasts the debate over the postmodern in theater and culture by teasing out and then subverting the bases of poststructuralist thought, playfully "blooding" text, performance, and theory to reveal them as matrices of play and desire, common only in that they each tend entropically toward an eventual remission. His essays, launched in a self-deconstructing style appropriate to the subject of the quantum transformations enacted between performance and drama, themselves express the dynamic rhythm of performance as it engages textuality. And, in its recognition of the amortizations of performance (in theater, as in theory), Blau's writing virtually enacts the interface between text and performance that is the subject of this study. Other critics, usually associated with the New York theater scene and various manifestations of poststructuralist and feminist inquiry—critics such as Richard Schechner, Philip Auslander, Bonnie Marranca, David Savran, Jonathan Kalb, Gerald Rabkin, Jill Dolan, Robert Coe, Elin Diamond, and Elinor Fuchs, among others—have similarly contributed a new vitality to the investigation of experimental theater and performance. Their revaluations of contemporary artists have proceeded without the usual animus toward a type of performance that is not dependent upon—indeed, that often confronts and critiques—the traditions and demands of the dramatic text.

Building upon their promising foundation, I hope to describe a significant impulse within contemporary theater, that is, both within mainstream, text-oriented "drama" and among the nontextual alternatives found in various kinds of "performance." To provide historical contexts that shape these recent developments, I begin with a brief, more or less objective sketch that traces the initial movement away from the kind of text-based dramatic realism that predominated in American and British theater in the fifties and early sixties (a realism related to, but quite different from, say, Ibsen's realism), toward the radically subversive and sometimes anarchic experiments with performance in the sixties. After clarifying important terms and concepts that grew out of these experiments, I provide an overall evaluation of the successes and shortcomings of this first-generation American avant-garde performance theater. From there, transitions are suggested that lead to experimental performance work of the seventies, work that recuperates many significant initiatives from the sixties while moving into more rarefied conceptual forms and an increasingly aggressive theoretical atmosphere. I analyze this second phase of avant-garde performance theater and its attempts to displace the text with performance, and conclude the historical and conceptual background with suggestions as to why the eighties offered an especially appropriate matrix for the development of dynamical systems of theater that combine what was once considered a lifeless mainstream literary drama with what is often seen as a waning experimental tradition of performance. This initial chapter is intended as a general overview of the pertinent historical and theoretical material previously mined by the critics already acknowledged, material that has positioned my understanding of recent trends in drama and performance.

In subsequent chapters, examples of work from representative performance groups, auteurs, performers, and playwrights are introduced. Their work is described in terms of a shared process of interfacing traditional modes of drama with alternative varieties of performance in order to produce a dynamic performance drama.[10] I begin by positing the canon and authorial career (as well as the critical reception) of Samuel Beckett as a paradigm of the contemporary search for an end to textuality and of the eventual return to a radically modified text. The next three chapters investigate representative work by a performance collective (The Wooster Group), an auteur (Robert Wilson), and a literary playwright (Sam Shepard) in order to speculate about the ways each has developed interfaces between drama and performance to produce significant forms of theater. The emphasis here is not on placing one artist's work in any kind of aesthetic or ideological proximity to another's, but on describing various ways that performers and writers have proceeded through their own interfacial phases and have come eventually in unique ways to combine elements of performance and conventional drama in order to achieve a variety of aesthetic and ideological ends.

The common denominator that positions all these artists as what

Foucault would call "nodes in a network" and that expresses a prominent concern in contemporary culture is the ultimate repositioning of their work within a text. This does not mean, however, that textuality and drama have somehow "defeated" or outlasted performance as the dominant principle in today's theater. Since the artists and groups enact unique modifications on their own "texts," we should not be surprised to find a plurality of new textual forms rather than a reactionary return to the traditional paradigm of the narrowly *lisible* or deterministic text. In the work of each artist considered in this study, the insurgency of performance against the closure of the text has effected significant, sometimes radical changes in the function and affects of textuality itself. What separates this from earlier experiments in antiform or "nonsemiotic" theater (a term coined by Michael Kirby) is the artists' willingness to negotiate with the dramatic text, to approach its temporal, linguistic, and semiotic structures with an eye toward carving out a mutualist space between it and the deconstructive potentialities of performance. The result is an emphasis on what Anne Ubersfeld (1977) calls the *troué* characteristic of the dramatic text, its open and indeterminate nature.

But determinism itself still applies to reality, even in our quantum universe. Significantly, however, such determinism can now be rendered only statistically, and always contains within it the seed for potential change. "Let us not forget," said the sociologist Edgar Morin,

> that the problem of determinism has changed over the course of a century. . . . In place of the idea of sovereign, anonymous, permanent laws directing all things in nature there has been substituted the idea of laws of interaction. . . . [T]he problem of determinism has become that of the order of the universe. Order means that there are other things besides "laws"; there are constraints, invariances, constancies, regularities in our universe. . . . In place of the homogenizing and anonymous view of the old determinism, there has been substituted a diversifying and evolutive view of *determinations*. (Prigogine 1988, xxii–xxiii)

Thus indeterminacy (performance) and certainty (the text) need not be irreconcilable, but instead can combine to contribute to a higher system of order, complexity, and understanding of the nature of reality.

It is, after all, the growth of similar but often contradictory forms and their peculiar distribution within American culture that make the contemporary theater scene so vital. The promised end of this study is an evaluation of a small part of that work and of the space it occupies in that culture.

Chapter 1

The Avant-Garde Urge and the Margins of Performance

The Background

Much of what passed for experimental theater during the late fifties and the sixties appears now rather naive and improbable. This familiar assessment is accurate to a point, but it does not take into account that, given the often tired and unimaginative use of conventions in American mainstream theater after the last posthumous O'Neill plays were presented and after the output of superior material from the leading playwrights (Miller, Williams, and later, Albee) began to dwindle in the late fifties and early sixties, experimental theater was by choice directed toward subverting the probability, rigid focus, and overly illusionistic qualities of a mainstream theater that had seemingly lost its dramatic velocity and its power to address a changing audience.

Avant-garde theater artists of the late fifties and early sixties, when they were reacting to the present state of drama at all (which was not entirely the case for, say, Happenings, which were essentially extensions of concerns from visual and spatial art), were reacting against realism, but realism of a particular kind. Historically realism is, in Carol Gelderman's words, "a moralizing art and, quintessentially, an art of opposition" (Gelderman 1983, 357). In America, however, especially after World War II, the realism of playwrights like Inge, Williams, and to a lesser extent Miller showed signs of losing its confrontational, if not always its moralistic, character. Their response to the historical and social pressures of the time was a theater too often characterized not by a true moral rigor and a critical stance toward society, but by themes of individual loss, alienation, and the collapse of an idealized American community. It was also a nostalgic drama particularly disdainful of a prevailing ideology or stance toward history. Such theater reflected a growing philosophical relativism accentuated by postwar ennui and the belief that the American positivist agenda, with its trust in perception and reason, its desire to strip away illusion, and its faith in progress and a moral imperative, had failed without providing an appropriate method for responding effectively to history.

Thus, unlike Ibsen's and Shaw's, American realism of the fifties usually contained no recognizable moral agenda and very little in the way of a confrontational stance toward society and history. And, unlike American drama of the thirties (that of the Group Theater and Federal Theater, the early unproduced plays of Miller, Williams, and others), it had no political basis. If a suggestion of ideology was to be found, it usually appeared as a form of either the watered-down existentialism of Martin Buber or the diluted Marxism of Erich Fromm, or else in the political-sexual transcendence theorized by Herbert Marcuse and expressed in Beat poetry and in Alan Watts's domesticated versions of Zen Buddhism. These related transcendentalist urges appear in many American plays of the period, especially in the works of Inge, Williams, and Miller, but only in their attenuated form, as sources of loss, pain, and sexual guilt. Albee, moving to Broadway from the new Off-Broadway milieu, managed to invest his early plays with a more materialist critique of American society and (especially in *Who's Afraid of Virginia Woolf?*) of the making of history itself. Still, his call for a new commitment to moral responsibility, like Miller's, is predicated upon an initial personal transcendence that only vaguely points to effects in the social sphere. So although the personal transformations of character give such work an undertone of political consciousness, it does not constitute a politics; instead, the politics lies hidden, often in ironies buried in the playwright's stage directions and character descriptions. Not until the next decade are such ideas reconstituted in an attempt—certainly with its own share of evasions—to form a coherent, positive therapy for contemporary feelings of isolation, alienation, and the disgust felt by many toward America's civil rights problems, the wars in Korea and then Vietnam, and the rampant materialism that characterized American politics and society.

Realism shorn of its essential adjuncts of moral and oppositional impulses is prone to turn eventually into a recognizable set of conventions that, unless used imaginatively to adjust its rhythms to history and culture, can make for a sentimental and lifeless theater. It becomes a category of what Karen Malpede calls "bourgeois realism," which is antithetical to any social purpose because of its implicit assumption that neither human nature nor society can be fundamentally changed (Malpede 1972, 7). This in turn suggests that the playwright's reactionary task is simply to express or reflect feelings of alienation and nostalgia for a lost world of moral certainty and self-authentication. Such realism has in American theater traditionally been associated with Method acting, which is itself conservative because it limits the actor or actress to portraying his or her own emotional past, an approach that effectively limits performers from objectively critiquing or commenting on the reality they are presenting. "In order to develop freely," writes Malpede (echoing Brecht), "the actor has to be rid of the limits of his or her emotional past. . . . Abandonment, receptivity, repetition—in place of recall—make this experience possible" (Malpede 1974, 15).

Certainly this potentially apathetic realism does not characterize all work produced in America during the late forties and the fifties. Miller and Williams infused their best works with a highly charged irony that rendered more powerful their deepening sense of unease with a culture that increasingly alienated the individual from choosing real commitment. Albee's work, too, in its critique of a debased language and its insistence upon stripping away illusion, often attained a fitful articulateness that powerfully castigated the still-quiet generation of the early sixties. And even Inge's traditionally limned portraits of quietly desperate characters elicited a genuinely effective pathos. Such work, however, was perceived by an emerging counterculture generation of theater artists to be incapable of questioning or transforming the bourgeois status quo. The tendency of American playwrights to leave their characters to suffer the indignities of their economic situation, their psychological or sexual pathologies, and their social deprivations seemed to deny any possibility for positive social or spiritual change. When a reconciliation or transformation did take place, it was almost always within the individual, and usually transient. Certainly the world was seldom made aware of its effects, but continued unregenerate and inhospitable.

As the political and moral insularism of the fifties gave way to the more activist social agenda of the New Frontier, the emerging civil rights movement, and the growing unrest over America's role in Vietnam, the bourgeois realism of Miller, Williams, and Albee seemed to some inadequate for addressing immediate pressures and concerns. Their drama was perceived by many in the burgeoning counterculture movements to speak movingly of the loss of individual dignity and social values, but to be incapable of taking an active role in effecting change. And in the decade that proclaimed that if you weren't part of the solution you were part of the problem, it seemed a time for questions and action rather than irony and nostalgia.

The majority of the quiet generation of the fifties was not especially inclined to pose such questions, and theater of the period to some degree followed suit. Even the regional experimental theaters and Off-Broadway groups formed early in the decade (Circle in the Square and the San Francisco Actor's Workshop, among others) produced rather mainstream works, with only occasional attempts at something more radical.[1] "There weren't many ideas to pick up on," remembered Blau of his years with the Actor's Workshop, "but nobody told us you were supposed to have them" (Blau 1982b, 57). And when new ideas were being tested, American artists and audiences seemed disinclined to pay much attention. In only the most glaring instance of a consistent artistic parochialism, the cultural insularism that prevailed during the period, combined with American distaste for a philosophy that denigrated individual integrity and traditional teleology, greatly reduced the influence of absurdist theater in America (Esslin [1961] 1969, 266). Such was also the case at the time with other provocative new continental ideas from Artaud, Jean Vilar, Fernando Arrabal, Beckett, and other artists and theoreticians.

Such provincial attitudes on the part of playwrights and audiences remained potent until a shift in cultural aesthetic standards began to permeate American art in general. Perhaps the earliest and most far-reaching of these in America came out of John Cage's collaborative and interdisciplinary experiments at Black Mountain College (with Charles Olsen, Buckminster Fuller, Merce Cunningham, and others) in the early fifties and his subsequent championing of Artaud (*The Theater and Its Double* was translated in 1958). Other new directions were initiated by Blau, who returned from Europe in 1959 convinced that crucial new directions in theater had been discovered on the continent, and that American alternative theater, if it was to survive at all, would have to reckon with these new initiatives. This view was adhered to by many in Blau's Actor's Workshop, some of whom (Ronnie Davis, Lee Breuer, Ken Dewey) went on to form their own alternative theater companies at the end of the decade.

Indeed, 1959 is often considered an important transitional year in

American alternative theater. In addition to Blau's return from Europe and his consequent exciting productions of Beckett, Ionesco, and Genet, the year marks Ronnie Davis's founding of the San Francisco Mime Troupe and The Living Theater's pivotal production of Jack Gelber's *The Connection,* one of the first Off-Broadway works to attract much mainstream critical attention. In the same year, Albee's *Zoo Story,* the first theatrically intelligent attempt at adapting absurdist idioms to American themes, also premiered Off-Broadway, and within a year Ellen Stewart had opened Cafe La Mama in New York City. It was, according to C. W. E. Bigsby,

> perhaps no wonder that suddenly there was a feeling that the American theater had found itself. The collapse of political consensus at the end of the 1950s had its theatrical correlative. There were now many audiences, some defined racially, some politically, some aesthetically, and Off-Broadway, Off-Off-Broadway (which also began to emerge in 1959), and a newly constituted regional theater were ready to address them. At the beginning of a new decade, with a new young President for whom the arts represented more than an occasional western novel, change seemed in the air. (Bigsby 1985, 21)

Generally, the movement was held together by the common bonds of an antiauthoritarian attitude and a related willingness to trash tradition in favor of experiment. The changes that resulted, however, as might be expected from the ferment of revolutionary political, social, and artistic change in the air, followed for a time no formulated agenda or coherent set of impulses. Yet, despite turbulence and critical confusion, a powerful vitality was stirring and confusion was but one aspect of significant and exciting change. The tremendous energy of the alternative theater of the period, in fact, is best appreciated by recognizing the diversity of experiments, in acting styles (especially those begun by Jerzy Grotowski at his Polish Laboratory Theater, and continued and modified in the United States by Blau, Richard Schechner, and Joseph Chaikin), production environments (found spaces, lofts, art galleries, created "Environments" and "Assemblages"), dramatic functions (as agit-prop theater, ritual theater, live poetry, dance theater, theater therapy, and theater anthropology, to name only a handful), and dramatic styles.

Because of this great diversity and because the purpose of this chapter is to present a conceptual overview and evaluation of the important work generated during this period (rather than a historical summary), what follows is a redaction of some of the essential ideas and experiments that characterize the work of the period as a whole. For more detailed commentary on specific groups, individuals, and productions, the reader is directed to the footnotes and to the final bibliography.

The Experimental Theater Agenda

> The actor is a human being who has dis / covered and un /covered himself so much that he re / veals [= unveils] something of man. He is a miracle.
>
> —Jerzy Grotowski

The critical claim that American avant-garde theater, especially that of the sixties, lacked concentrated reflection and theoretical potency is accurate, but this is partly because, first, the period was indeed one of experiment, and such periods are not usually conducive to prolonged theorizing and reflection. But more important, much avant-garde work of the period was directed consciously away from the kind of potency implicit in reflection. The work was a calculated attempt to circumvent the rational, intellectual aspect of traditionally "literary" drama and to replace it with a more intuitive, visceral, body-oriented performance theater that would act as a celebration of life rather than a cerebralized slice of it. What theater experiment of the period provided was a working through of an impulse that seems to lie at the heart of theater—simply to become something other than theater.[2] In reaction to the worn-out, unimaginatively imposed conventions that predominated in American realist theater of the forties and fifties, and in support of a new political activism stemming from the rising political consciousness of minority groups and women, of new pop culture and psychology, and so on, theater experimenters of the sixties did not simply try to alter existing dramatic or literary frameworks and styles. What was intended was a totally new kind of theater event that would function in a new kind of way; not as an art built on its distinction from life, or between artifice and experience, but as life itself as it was meant to be lived before the meddling human intellect drew distinctions between the two:

> This theater sought to liberate the instincts, to destroy repression and revert to that stage of erotic and sensual spontaneity which is characteristic of childhood in the individual, and primitive and largely pre-literate physicality in the race. . . . Its adherents were not concerned with delineating the moral burdens implied by necessary sublimations but with liberating the individual and art from social and mimetic constraints. For them the theater was no longer to be a part of that system which placed the mind over the body, the reality principle over the pleasure principle. It was to be a revolutionary force returning man to a prelapsarian state of grace. It was not to be a reflection of life; it was to be life itself. (Bigsby 1985, 68)

The foci of these changing notions were not restricted to work in theater alone, but characterized a great deal of experiment in a variety of artistic disciplines. Cage's early experiments with music and theater were essentially directed toward subverting, even breaking down completely, the traditional distinctions between life and art. The point of the groundbreaking performance of "4′33″" was simply that, without the intrusion of premeditated and prefabricated sounds, "music" could be achieved by sequencing common sounds (coughing, movement of chairs and bodies) in an utterly random way. No "art" is used to arrange the piece in a tidy narrative, psychological, or formal pattern, so life and art meet on common ground. Cage's interests in subverting the psychological basis of art extended to the use of chance procedures borrowed from the *I Ching,* which stresses the order concealed in the contingent and which teaches that meaning is found in process rather than in a finished product. These concerns with indeterminacy, chance, and process later find important expression in avant-garde performance experiments as well.

Similar innovations were introduced into dance, where the rigidly choreographed and conventionalized movements of ballet were giving way to the more abstract and self-expressive style of Martha Graham. Other dance artists felt that Graham's narrative structures and expressive gestures had themselves become fixed and melodramatic, and so even sparer and more abstract styles were developed by Balanchine, Merce Cunningham, and Alwin Nikolais. These choreographers endorsed the use of movement disassociated from any psychological or narrative context, where the medium of movement becomes the work's message. Such dance shows little concern with relating a determinate story or expression of recognizable emotional states, but stresses instead the beauty and geometry of pure movement.

In the visual arts, too, Alan Kaprow's Happenings introduced spectators into environments where various unrelated everyday activities were carried out. These works used what Richard Kostelanetz calls a "compartmented" structure based on the arrangement and contiguity of self-contained units, units that remain hermetic because they do not pass on information to others, as is the case in traditional theater (Kostelanetz 1968, 8–9). Lacking the conventional information structure, Happenings can operate without the entire matrix of time and place—cause and effect structure of plot, the "clichés" of exposition, character development, conflict, and so on—that characterizes most literary drama. And without such a matrix, the spectator is exposed, as in Zen exercises, to the peculiarity of particular objects, acts, or environments. The emphasis here, as in Cage's experiments, is placed upon the processual experience of creating meaning, and not upon the constitution of stable meaning itself.

While various aesthetic and political concerns were at the root of these widespread movements in the arts, there were common interests as well. In most, the underlying motive was a perceptual one; like pop existentialism, Zen, and the psychosexual radicalism of Norman O. Brown and Herbert Marcuse, early experiments in the fifties such as these all addressed the same contemporary sense of alienation and fragmentation that is the subject of plays by Miller, Williams, Inge, Albee, and others. But while these playwrights produced work that offered the spectator the opportunity to feel the pathos of loss and, less often, to study the causes of alienation, avant-garde artists were looking for a means to transcend these feelings and to bridge the gaps between the individual and society and the individual and authentic experience. The chance procedures and valorization of the actual over the mimetically re-presented favored by Cage, Cunningham, Kaprow, and other avant-garde artists, as well as their rejection of traditional dramatic elements, were not simply in reaction to an enervated tradition of drama. They also formed a potent base from which to undermine the authority of the implicitly Cartesian nature of Western thought, perception, and culture as a whole.[3] What they offered in its place, following Artaud, was an art that often functioned as therapy (or Plague, which to Artaud was one form of therapy) for the deeply ingrained and repressive oedipal urges they saw as undermining the natural and instinctive life of man. The therapeutic approach was, in each case, directed at subverting the rationalizing and psychologizing impulse sublimated into Western art and life and replacing it with new perceptual attitudes built on notions of spiritual or political transcendence. Such enlightenment was to be discovered through the media of ritual, chance and the unconscious, Dionysian body mysticism, the political concerns of the collective, and the Presence (or "aura," in Walter Benjamin's sense) of the polymorphous performing body.

Though the artists shared an urge to be radical, there were still distinctions between the radical left and radical right.[4] The former included groups and performers characterized by a structured or ideological political commitment (Davis's San Francisco Mime Group, El Teatro Campesino, The Bread and Puppet Theater), while the latter's work was therapeutic on the level of individual consciousness (The Performance Group, The Open Theater). These distinctions are useful, but it is important to keep in mind that none of the groups mentioned remained static, and plenty of cross-lapping was bound to occur (The Living Theater and The Bread and Puppet Theater are cases in point). Indeed, it is still the slow shifts between these poles that characterize much of the contemporary interaction between experimental performance, with its more flexible theatricality and its accent on transformation and transcendence, and traditional realist drama, with its emphasis on a historical matrix, strong human reference, and a moral and oppositional stance toward society.

In theater itself, these revolutionary ideas designed to break down the barriers of art and life and thereby provide transcendental therapy for the audience's political and spiritual lack took many forms: new acting styles, especially in Grotowski's search for an intensely physical and authenticating style that would elicit a total act of "self-penetration" from the performer, and which could stand as an example of human spiritual capacity; innovative theater environments and actor/spectator relationships, most often in some form of interaction or participation that would suggest the power (political or spiritual) of the commune or collective; and various radicalized uses of traditional dramatic elements like language, the mise-en-scène, and the actor's charismatic Presence, all of which would help the spectator escape the constraints of a closed social and perceptual system, and would open up new avenues for attaining awareness and heightened consciousness. Such consciousness-raising was achieved primarily through the liminal act of performance itself, and by the medium of "play" as the concept was elaborated by Brown, Marcuse, Victor Turner, and Jonathan Huizinga.[5]

This emphasis on play as an ontological and epistemological model for transcendence led eventually to the single most radical and potentially subversive change effected in experimental theater, the rejection of the dramatic text and the consequent valorization of performance, the common (but, it was often thought, not essential) adjunct of the drama. Performance, it was theorized, promised the perfect antiauthoritarian response to the repressive authority of the text and to the power structure that controlled the rationalist language within it. It was also the quickest path to subverting the intellectual bases of drama, with their mind/object distinction, quantified sense of time, and psychological development of character. And aside from its potential for disrupting the essential structures, political bases, and production processes of bourgeois drama, performance also promised an alternative to traditional aesthetics built on conventional notions of semiosis.

Conventional realist drama—indeed, most text-based drama as a whole—like all representative art, presupposes what Maria Minich Brewer calls

> a static relationship between subject and object, viewer and viewed, spectatorship (narration, reading) and scene. Narrative, authorial, and critical points of view exist in a mimetic relationship (of assent) that frames out whatever falls out of their perspectival "point" of view. Here the theatrical apparatus reins the text and excludes modes of rhetoric, language, and writing that cannot be ordered by the intentionality of a subject desiring to dramatize its own consciousness. (Brewer 1985, 15)

Such presuppositions of course derive from classic realism (which is not coterminous with the rise of literary realism or dramatic naturalism) and Renaissance humanist ideology, both predicated on notions of humankind's homogeneity. "Human nature," positioned within such ideologies, is conceived as universal and unchangeable in its essence, however various its forms. Art precipitated by such predicates is characterized by an emphasis on illusion, and usually proceeds via narrative structures that lead to a determinate closure or closed field of signification, based on an authorially established hierarchy of discourses that generates the "truth" of the story. The texts produced are similar to those Barthes calls *lisible* or "readerly," that is, determinate representations of what is perceived to be an intelligible world built on stable relationships between integrative frames of reference. While such readerly texts do not preclude ambiguity and a certain *plaisir* derived in the act of reading, the uncertainty is only relative, and is constrained by the mode of writing that produces it.

Performance, on the other hand, is said to "desemiotize" drama and to provide a means of subverting repressive, determinate structures built on authorial intention and its logocentric impulse. As Blau says,

> in this mission, the enemy is mimesis, which breeds the lie of humanism, with its myth of individuation. What we see rather in the image of man is the grotesque offspring of the theater's self-perpetuating enormity: ego, self, personality, a mere reproductive subject, slave to the ideological apparatus of reproduction, who must learn to free himself from false acting by true performance. (Blau 1987, 166–67)

Thus free from the mechanical and meretricious motions of acting, and from the confining apparatus of the text, the performer, like Wallace Stevens's Ludwig Richter, presumably loses "the whole in which he was contained. / Knows desire without an object of desire / All mind and violence and nothing felt" ("Chaos in Motion and Not in Motion"). The typical spectatorial response to such open-ended structures is termed by Barthes *jouissance,* by which he seems to define a kind of psychic abandonment or libidinal bliss.

Instead of relating a story built upon a coherent illusion of plot and character development, a cogently symbolic mise-en-scène, and (especially) discursive or expressive language, performance disrupts, displaces, and deconstructs these codes by revealing what Barthes calls the "encroachments, overflows, leaks, skids, shifts, slips" that occupy the seams between them (Barthes 1974, 69). Performance theorists originally argued that, with the negation of the rational (but illusory) superstructure of the dramatic text and the exposure of a new desemiotized space, performance could be freed to create energy "flows" and new holistic models of praxis discovered in the experience or process of the performance itself. The "true performer" might, for instance, reveal to the spectator improvisatorial acting techniques and transformation exercises as a model for escaping the social constraints of playing a fixed and static role. In another fashion, performers might blur the distinctions between the actor/character and spectator in order to expand the stage environment to develop participatory relationships and interactions. Actors also often objectified their bodies (sometimes in the nude), used scatological language or drugs, or asked the spectators to help them escape their fictive role by accompanying them out of the theater—all in order to reveal ways of transcending the constraints imposed by an overly cerebralized and puritanical society. On a more sophisticated level (already anticipated by Beckett, but fulfilled by Grotowski and later somewhat trivialized by performance artists like Chris Burden), the "archetypal actor" would transform his or her physical discomfort and body discipline, as well as the spiritual freedom that such a *via negativa* promises, into the aqueduct through which energies are channelled through the performer and then toward the audience. In Grotowski's famous phrase, "Impulse and action are concurrent: the body vanishes, burns, and the spectator sees only a series of visible impulses."

Since the models of perception and praxis proposed in the sixties usually turned out to be spiritual (Grotowski's "secular holiness") or psychic (Artaud's Plague) alternatives allied loosely to a Zen-inspired transcendentalism, the means to acquire a liberated consciousness naturally emphasized an awareness of the physical qualities of the real. This in turn meant objectifying the actor (the body, movements, and voice), subverting the functional use of theatrical language in order to obscure its connections to discursive communication and to bring out its tonal, sonic, and physical qualities, and using forms of montage and bricolage as structural principles that disrupt the traditional cumulative information structures of conventional realist theater. The creation of such new valences within the theatrical event would thereby force the spectator to concentrate on finding new relationships and contingencies within the space of the performance itself, apart from the narrative skein of the text and the psychological development of "character." By destabilizing such "literary" structures as dialogue, character, plot, and a unified theme, performance would valorize nontextual, improvisatorial competencies like the performer's manipulation of the body and of various performance spaces, his or her interaction with the spectator, and the displacement of textures of sound, light, and movement. The possibility of using these performative attributes to realize Artaud's dream of a gestural theater of plague and cruelty that would open up disruptions in the fabric of illusion appealed strongly in a number of ways to experimental artists in the theater of the sixties. Its nonnarrative and nonrepresentational character rendered it a viable alternative to the intellectualized drama of Miller and Williams, which avant-garde artists saw as incapable of effecting the kind of transcendence they desired.

The desire to give o'er the play and thereby escape from author-ity and the domination of the text found its inevitable outlet in avant-garde performance and initiated a variety of interesting—though often misguided—experiments in theatrical form, theatrical language, manipulations of the mise-en-scène, and performance styles. After a time, somewhat surprisingly, performance and its ideological attributes of process, play, deferral, and desemiotization became the self-reflexive operational principle in other disciplines: as a primary agenda for poststructuralist and radical feminist theory; as a model for revisionist Freudians, proponents of speech act theory, and reception aesthetics; and as an analytical subject for semiologists and deconstructionists. For a time it seemed that theater, historically the artistic form most recalcitrant to aesthetic innovation and most immune to ideological provocation, had by its proximity to performance assumed the forefront of avant-garde theory and practice. Performance theories (usually allied with other theories from anthropology, psychoanalysis, semiotics, or literature) sprung up in a variety of journals and manifestos, and radically innovative performances were staged in nontraditional spaces, using nonprofessional performers instead of actors and only the barest minima of almost absent texts. Numerous theater practitioners, dancing in the flames of the revolution, predicted the death of the text, its author, and the audiences of traditional bourgeois drama.[6] In their place was to appear a new kind of theater, pointing the way to a new kind of life for a new kind of spectator, one unbridled by the "mind-forg'd manacles" that had kept the instincts hostage for centuries.

Critical Response to the Avant-Garde Agenda: Experimental Performance Theater of the Sixties

But if theater is usually slow to seek out innovation, it is also a form peculiarly sensitive to margins—to those ingrained in its own ontological form, in the culture that produces it, in the languages that express it, and in the mind that possesses it—all of which increasingly appear to be nothing *but* language. Theater, which more and more reflects the unredeemable desiring of the mind itself, can elicit the most enticing and inspiring kinds of dreaming: to escape the reality principle, to free oneself from the claims of the ego, to recapture something of the primitive and spontaneous, and to reconstitute feeling and subvert man's most deeply embedded oedipal instincts. But the dramatic text and, it appears, performance too, for all their promise of transcendence and transubstantiation, have their own "seams," or margins, as well. And, confronted with such ontological imperatives, theater has never really found a way to make the jump from artifice to life, no matter how ingenious the experiment, no matter whether the vehicle is the dramatic text or the performing body, and no matter how loudly ecstasy is proclaimed.

Yet the reversion in theater to the immanent point of arrest is not caused by a lack of ingenuity or daring—all the avant-garde artists mentioned so far have these in abundance—but by the limits of the mind itself. Herbert Blau, for whom the limits of performance have become the focal point for a provocative critique of Western culture, feels that the search for transcendence through the medium of performance was bound to come up short of its goal:

> Yet if, by whatever devious means, old forms return, it's because they were never absent to begin with. . . . [T]he disturbing truth appears to be we are the same old performers of the hour. Things come around. Human needs being what they are, we find that new needs are a recycling of old denial. What was not absent was just strategically ignored, scrupulously overlooked or refused validity on what can only be a trial basis. We look for breathing space, exemption, a new geography. The new perspective on the return of the will is a familiar coign of vantage, an open landscape which, we discover, has its margins, as every continent a land's end. Then, the turning back, the turning in: last year's freedom is another structure. It was already said in the mind. (Blau 1982b, 268)

Most of the new breathing spaces opened up in theater during this period via the most radical experiments in "nonmatrixed" and "nonsemiotic" performance, in alternative uses of language, in the valorization of the performer's Presence, and so on, advocated by avant-garde artists of the sixties seem already outmoded and, for all their underlying radicalism, uncomfortably naive and pretentious. "Performance drama," says Bigsby, "is very much a phenomenon of the 1960s and early 1970s, with its concern for free expression of the senses, its communitarian impulse, its search for personal transcendence, its optimistic and even naively sentimental presumption about the essential goodness and even holiness of human nature" (Bigsby 1985, 73). Jonathan Kalb has even suggested that the entire avant-garde enterprise of deprivileging the dramatic text was nothing more than a coup d'état of directors looking to systematize their already considerable dominance in theatrical production (Kalb 1989, 150).

Such historical and infratheatrical contexts serve to illuminate many of the limitations of a theater event based primarily on the power of performance, but do not address important extrahistorical reasons for the waning of performance theater. Our hindsight from the verge of this decade's "land's end" reveals several reasons why avant-garde theater of the sixties finally realized its own limitations and disappeared under the weight of its own radical theory and agenda. Many of the difficulties stemming from such a displacement of the orthodox relationship between performance and drama are, of course, simply pragmatic. Others are ontological. Even so devoted a performance theorist as Richard Schechner (1982), despite his belief in the efficacy of what he terms a "deconstructive-reconstructive" process between tradition and the new, and between text and performance, has in the last few years revealed anxieties about the margins of the experimental theater he helped to bring into prominence, and about its emphasis on performance. Schechner's critique locates the real crisis in avant-garde performance theater's very resistance to culture and tradition. He argues that experimental theater resists by its nature "recapitulation" and "repetition," that the creation of unpublished "performance texts" and collective, improvisational performance work, as well as highly self-referential autodrama, cannot be re-presented and therefore inscribed within a viable tradition out of which new work and talent can emerge. The impasse he reaches calls into question the very aims of earlier experimental theater: "My generation failed to develop its own means of training—of getting performance texts across to the future. For this reason alone the work of the last thirty years may prove sterile" (Schechner 1982, 36).

More far-reaching than even such important practical concerns regarding the development and decline of sixties performance theater are the conceptual problems with the notion of ordaining performance at the expense of textuality. In the haste to radicalize and subvert existing dramatic conventions (and sometimes to do without them altogether), experimental theater artists of the sixties often did not pause to consider the validity or ideological weight of those conventions. Everything we call conventional in theater was, after all, at one time an innovation introduced as a necessary adjunct to an ideological or artistic pressure; and in contrast to the urge for the tradition of the new, Blau suggests soberly that if we are to understand what we have not yet imagined, we must first take strict account of what we have forgotten:

> Indeed, it is (in our own time) not the new but the conventional which is strange and even awesome when you think it over, what we *do* take for granted. The mere raising of a curtain, for instance, is a theater event of major consequences if it is remembered that it was once not there, and you are forced to ask what possible disjunctures of evolutionary desire—what rudimentary perversions of the old unitary communion—had realized itself when it was. (Blau 1982a, 38)

But if avant-garde artists of the period were not willing to take thoughtful measure of existing conventions, it was due partly to their deeply rooted desire to reconstitute theater in a completely new form. The problem was that they attempted to do so while simultaneously trying to retain certain essential elements of drama, such as the presence of an actor, a performance space, some gesture toward language or semiotic address, and an audience. Schechner and others, for instance, working from principles established by anthropologists like Roy Rappaport and Victor Turner, saw the very structures of theater and ritual as comparative subclasses of human behavior that they termed "performance."[7] Because the two subsets were conceived as roughly equal, Schechner assumed that one could encompass the other within the context of the larger class of performance, and that within an essentially theatrical context an actual ritual could take place. Studies (and one's own experience of various so-called ritual theaters) have shown, however, that it is in fact extremely rare for any group to perform an actual ritual within such a context. Moreover, the same research suggests that those groups who do achieve ritual are actually no longer performing theater.[8] The inherent difficulties in forming the assembly into a congregation rather than an audience of spectators removed from the ritual action (a problem encountered by Peter Brook's performers as well during their polyglot performances in Africa in 1980), in making performances efficacious instead of affective or merely entertaining, and in creating a reiterative context instead of an imitative one proved impossible to circumvent for groups as diverse as Schechner's Performance Group, El Teatro Campesino, and The Bread and Puppet Theater. All were part of the larger movement that was pushing performance to do something that, within its ontological limits of representation and illusion, it simply could not do.[9]

Unhindered by reflection, a significant group of avant-garde theater artists took as their primary aim the dismemberment of drama, and in doing so they neglected the complementary relationship that exists between it and performance. Seeking in performance a therapy for everything they found pathological in drama, they also neglected to consider the eventual margins of performance, and continued to seek in it a transcendental ecstasy and therapy for themselves and their audiences. This entailed, first, the breaking down of what were perceived to be repressive structures (the text, representation, etc.) in order to "wake the body," in Josette Féral's phrase, "the performer's and the spectator's—from the threatening anaesthesia haunting it" (Féral 1985, 174). This in turn inspired a variety of further experiments: the use of rehearsal exercises in actual performances in order to express more vividly the sense of life felt as a continuum, the doing and not the product of the doing; the emphasis on performance as a liminal state of pure play instead of a mechanical reproduction of a lifeless text ("a perpetual present," says Barthes, "upon which no *consequent* language can be superimposed"); the Zen-inspired strategies to unite word and object, sound and desire, in the howls and chants of The Living Theater, culminating in the synthetic language created by Ted Hughes in Brooks's *Orghast;* the experiments with foreign performance styles (Noh, Butoh, Bunraku, Kathakali) as a means of discovering a universal performance grammar that, itself, would stand as testimony to a possible transcultural *communitas;* the acting styles developed by Grotowski and carried on by Blau, Schechner, and Chaikin, intended to elicit a total act and transcendent freedom for the performing body;[10] the stress on movement and sound divorced from their traditional kinesic and communicative functions, rendered instead as products of an uninhibited libido; and, most important, in order to satisfy the desire to experience life unmediated by the artifices of drama, the use of real time and space in the performance to create "actuals" and events that are there, present, not re-presented textually as an absent source: "With neither past nor future, performance *takes place.* It turns the stage into an event from which the subject will emerge transformed" (Féral 1985, 177).[11]

For these and other equally radical desires, performance insinuated itself as a means of gratification and therapy and took on affective functions that traditional theater—itself a ritual mode of expression that occurs after rituals no longer retain their original efficacious functions—had never attempted. That performance also provided a strategy for circumventing the typical production process and its allegiance to capitalist market venturing only made it more attractive to dissident artists working in garages, lofts, the street, and other unfunded performance spaces.

This avant-garde agenda produced some remarkable theater work in the sixties. To this day we have nothing that matches Grotowski's Polish Laboratory and its disciplined corps of ascetic actors, The Living Theater's artistic and social integrity, the sheer visceral dramaturgy of The Open Theater's Jean-Claude Van Itallie, and the energy, commitment, and dedication of countless unremembered avant-garde performers, directors, writers, and theorists. The agenda and the work engendered, however, were limited not only by historical circumstance and pragmatic concerns, but also by their recurring dream of discovering in performance a cure for the sense of loss and alienation that characterized the postwar period. Whereas for Miller this loss could be traced to a historically determined failure of American moral initiative, for theater experimenters of the sixties it sprang from more metaphysical origins. Like various German romantic philosophers, many avant-garde writers saw their work as a means to rediscover a lost source of being, or at least as a mechanism to assuage the feeling of the primordial breach that initiated reflexivity and self-consciousness. Their work tried to recapture that original state of wholeness experienced in some *locus amounesis* before primordial individuation took place, and attempted to regain the Buddhist nirvana sought by Fichte and Schopenauer or the Dionysian ecstasy described by Nietzsche.[12] "The same Fall," says Blau (1982b, 252), "which brought consciousness into the Garden also brought the first actor"; and in the work and theory of Grotowski, Chaikin, Schechner, and Beck, it was this actor (penitently striving to become an authentic performer or "holy actor") who would heal the breach and bring us back to the Garden.

Artaud's influence on this work is generally acknowledged, and ever since he was "discovered" and translated in 1958, this holistic dream has often been associated with theater, especially but not exclusively the theater of cruelty. The notion that performance, by rejecting the closed codification and signifying systems of the text and its hierarchies, could present unmediated experience and therefore reclaim the lost source or old *communitas* (in the shape of a *Paradise Now!,* a communal sharing of bread and puppetry, or the ritual of a group caress) motivated a great deal of avant-garde theater's most provocative and moving works.

In this century, theater that has strived for the experience of or return to these irredeemable originary memories of wholeness and Presence has usually posited performance in some form as the agent for desystematizing the closed symbolic order or "codes" of theater (and often, by extension, of a repressive society) and for opening up psychic aqueducts from which "flows" of unconscious and unmediated desire may run. Yet in the rush to proclaim performance as the latest species of transcendence, much that was self-limiting in performance itself was often ignored. By suggesting that performance allowed the experience of the unmediated, theorists and practitioners of the period merely assumed that such self-affirming mastery of the self and reality were in fact attainable. From a poststructuralist perspective, such a function of performance acts (ill-advisedly) as an extension of the shadow of the *logos,* the innately human desire for self-sufficiency, for the unqualified and unmediated, and for the need of the conscious entity to be present to itself and therefore self-confirming. What was truly radical in avant-garde theater of the sixties, however, was not just that it sought this confirmation by escaping the closure and constraints of theater and literary drama (an agenda already suggested by earlier artists like Artaud, Pirandello, Brecht, and Gordon Craig, and to some degree an element in any transcription of text into performance), but also that it subscribed to the belief that this alteration or freeing of the theatrical structure could be used to effect a similar change in group or even social consciousness. This therapeutic function of performance within experimental theater is usually associated with what Christopher Innes (1981) calls "holy theater," and represents the fruits of over two centuries of American transcendentalist thought and art.

But this attempt to restore the elemental, to purify the words of the tribe and dance us back the tribal morn, is beyond the margins of theater and performance. Speaking from his position within avant-garde performance theater and theory, Herbert Blau has articulated the most thoroughgoing critique of its practices: "There is nothing more illusory in performance," he asserts, "than the illusion of the unmediated. It is a very powerful illusion in the theater, but it *is* theater, and it is *theater,* the truth of illusion, which haunts *all* performance, whether or not it occurs in the theater" (Blau 1987, 164–65). Performance is never a source of self-confirming communion or *communitas,* but rather "a testament to what separates," the product of a "rub" within theater that always encourages the unrealizable desire for a realized original experience instead of the re-presentation of it in theater (1987, 165). Thus Blau is markedly ambivalent about many of the attempts to escape representation and textual mediation in the experimental theater of the sixties. Within *all* performance, he argues, there is the trace, what he calls a "ghost," of whatever was present before individuation and consciousness precipitated man into performance (1982a, 84). But performance cannot itself give free scope to play or bring the ghost into being; rather, performance always "amortizes" play within its own necessarily limited sphere of illusion and representation. The power of drama and performance thus can be found only *in* their illusion-making power, for it is only by way of illusion and re-presentation of the primordial breach that the ghost is made bodily present, though it remains always an opacity beyond the barrier of actual precipitation. As with Lacan's notion of the unconscious coming into being at the moment when language cannot name desire, performance is precipitated at the moment when origins are lost and cannot be reclaimed or reconstituted, but remain to haunt the unconscious (and performance itself) as a schism.

These limitations, or amortizations, of performance and play undermine in a number of crucial areas the avant-garde agenda of the sixties. The entire therapeutic and ritualistic function of performance theater is called into question, as are many of the strategies used by performers to heal themselves and their audiences. For instance, experimental theater's concern with the physical Presence of the performer and with "the actor's freedom" (to quote the title of Michael Goldman's influential book) has increasingly been undermined by an awareness of Absence (mimesis, textuality) and its own peculiar power. To avant-garde directors and performers of the sixties and early seventies, the potency of Presence lay in the performer's ability to capture and enact spontaneously the totality of reality and to make it available to the spectator. By seeming to comprehend one's deepest intuitive levels of being and therefore create and express one's genuine grasp of reality, the performer became the paradigm of the ideal authentic self ("Presence," says Derrida, "forms the matrix of every idealism").[13] Conceived of as the "center," the performer acts as the reagent for attaining a moment of pure Presence and self-awareness. Thus the disciplined performing body is exhibited as the empowered source whose physical aura can capture and guarantee Presence and once again recuperate reality in all its spatial, temporal, and psychic fullness.

But the power of such Presence, says Elinor Fuchs,

> was staked on the revelations of the self and a corresponding suspicion of the text. To the positive value assigned improvisation, audience participation, myth, ritual, and communion they opposed a view of the author's script as a politically oppressive intruder, demanding submission to author-ity. The speech that bubbled up from the inner depths was more trustworthy than the alien written word, and many of them experimented with efforts to slip the constricting knot of language altogether. The desire was to come closer and closer to a center of human experience through a self-exploration of such intensity that it redefined the self. "I have reached into my entrails and strewn them about the stage in the form of questions," writes Beck. (Fuchs 1985, 164)

The valorization of theatrical Presence as theater's most dominant physico-spiritual power, propagated by avant-garde directors and performers, was, as Fuchs says, essentially a "rearguard action" of the sixties (1985, 164). The idealization of Presence during the period represents only a more vociferous advocacy of the actor's primacy over the author than had been advanced earlier, and signifies on one level the growing power of the director and the performer in modern theater. But the revelations of Presence also grew out of the body-orientation philosophies of the period, and were staked on something akin to the fear of which Donne speaks in his mourning valediction: "Dull sublunary lovers' love / —Whose soul is sense—cannot admit / Absence, because it doth remove / Those things that elemented it." Artists whose souls were sense, like Chaikin, Schechner, and Beck, were still carrying out a transcendentalist agenda that had as its goal the intensely physical and holistic realization (the "elementalizing") of that psychological self who could possess entirely a unitary present, a full reality and confirmation of self.

Apart from the fact that such an agenda does not seek to displace textuality, but simply to recuperate its illusion of Presence in another guise, the notion that such a pure and unitary present exists at all has since been rigorously critiqued, especially by Derrida. For Derrida, the present is always something reconstituted, the impure residue of an experience that can never be wholly present. Every attempt to enter fully into an unconstituted present is "always already" contaminated by the trace, which originates in the conceptual opposition between traditional dualisms like speech and writing. In traditional "logocentric" metaphysics, for instance, the human voice is privileged as a source of essential truth over the written word, the latter of which is presumably contaminated, as T. S. Eliot writes in "The Hollow Men," by the Shadow that infiltrates the space between "the motion / And the act . . . . Between the emotion / And the response." Speech, as unmediated expression, is conventionally characterized as a spontaneous link between sound and sense, an immediate realization of meaning and transparent understanding. Writing, on the other hand, is devalued and marginalized as a warped mirror of the true understanding that flows naturally from speech, and is defined as a suspect supplement to the authentic utterance.

Derrida's critique of Western metaphysics erodes this conceptualization by pointing out that speech is always preceded by *écriture,* by which he means not only the written word but the superordinate linguistic frame that motivates speech and thought as well. In this larger sense, writing reveals the essential "made up" quality of knowledge and acts to displace determinate meaning and to emphasize the differential character of language and our ideas. And, given that no assurance of the stable bond between thought and speech really can exist, there can be, says Fuchs, "no single moment at which utterance originates; and if no originary principle can be identified, then such a thing as a self-same Presence is merely a self-serving illusion" (1985, 166).

Under the pressure of Derrida's poststructuralist critique of Western metaphysics, the entire donnée of much performance theater and theory of the sixties is rendered problematic. And while it is not possible or fruitful to conclude that poststructuralist theory caused the demise of early performance theater, there is good reason for suggesting that it helped re-orient the experimental theater work that followed in the next decade. In fact, it can be said that the enthusiastic reception of poststructuralist theory in America made necessary the next phase of performance theory and practice, one that attempted to join deconstructive aesthetics with experimental performance. And as we shall see, it was the deconstructive excesses of this second wave of experiment that have in turn made possible an eventual rapprochement between "pure" performance and the literary drama it had set out to dispossess.

Performance of the Seventies: The Movement toward Abstraction and Ahistoricism

> The inhabitants of the earth had grown too enlightened to define their faith within a form of words, or to limit the spiritual by any analogy to our material existence. . . . Therefore, as the final sacrifice of human error, what else remained to be thrown upon the embers of that awful pile except the book which, though a celestial revelation to past ages, was but a voice from a lower sphere as regarded the present race of man?
>
> —Hawthorne, "Earth's Holocaust"

By the early seventies many of the initial impulses motivating the aspirations and innovative performance techniques of experimental theater had come under close critical scrutiny. This, joined with the new wary political quiescence of the later seventies, made the sometimes unreflective and rash agenda of the previous decade less attractive for new artists. Also lost in this period of transition, however, were the moral seriousness and spiritual yearning that had given the counterculture of the fifties and sixties its energy and direction. In the arts, groups like The Living Theater, composers like Cage, painters like Jasper Johns and Jackson Pollock, and choreographers like Cunningham defied the materialist, consumerist values of Eisenhower's America and worked with few of the inhibiting anxieties that are part of the drive for popular success. By the late fifties and early sixties, the historical avant-garde's opposition to the status quo deepened through a new alliance with alternative politics and lifestyles, which aided in the birth of an Off-Off-Broadway theater movement. This context allowed experimental performance ensembles like The Open Theater, and the Judson Poets (and later Dance) Revolution, the multimedia extravaganzas of Cage and Cunningham, Kaprow's Happenings, and other art performances to flourish. All of these artists and groups sustained the historical avant-garde's provocative affront to bourgeoise values.

Experimental theater of the mid-to-late seventies, on the other hand, was more apt to develop from the aesthetic experiments of the sixties rather than from its social engagement. Generally, this second wave of avant-garde theater art takes the form of a restrained formalism, as seen in the early theater work of Robert Wilson, Richard Foreman, and the Mabou Mines and Wooster Group performance collectives, as well as in the performance art pieces of Meredith Monk and the postmodern dance of Lucinda Childs. Such performances continued the self-reflexive exploration of theater's formal languages begun in the sixties, but without the explicit opposition to prevailing culture that characterized earlier avant-garde theater. Replacing this unprogrammatic but potent social engagement was an increasing interest in the temporal and spatial aspects of performance, and in developing "deconstructive" spectacles built around qualities of dislocation, play, and the deferral of thematic closure.

Yet the popular and critical response to this theater, initially enthusiastic, waned rather quickly as formal concerns and often insipid conceptual approaches overtook matters of significant content in the work. In the best examples of the period, as in, for instance, Robert Wilson's "theater of vision" operas (*The Life and Times of Sigmund Freud, Deafman Glance*), time and movement are distended interminably in order to present disorienting gestalten that might generate new forms of perception and mentation. Still, although Wilson's experiments in such unique perceptual fields at first elicited a great deal of critical interest, even his exciting spectacles hardly gathered anything beyond a devoted coterie audience. One reason was that these and later productions (*The Life and Times of Joseph Stalin, A Letter for Queen Victoria,* and others), though marked by an extraordinary visual and acoustic beauty as well as by carefully crafted compartmental structures, induced, in one critic's estimation, a "meditational atmosphere without providing the traditional content of meditation—ideas and emotions" (Rouse 1987, 56). These theater pieces, continuing some of the trends of the sixties, were anti-intellectual, antiverbal, and antitextual; but, following the collapse of the radical left, they were also utterly apolitical, almost antipolitical, if not without their own disturbing ideology.

The same can be said of the first stage of work produced by the Mabou Mines collective, especially the *Animations* sequence prepared by Lee Breuer from 1968 to 1978. During this period Breuer was developing autobiographical material, a sense of the "self as text" as the basis for his performance works. The process of moving away from a theater of social commitment toward one of self was recognized almost immediately by Bonnie Marranca and hailed as "one of the characteristic features of current experimental theater and performance art which in the seventies has been evolving new strategies for dealing with content." In her opinion:

> If theater in the sixties was defined by the collaborative creation of the text, in recent years individual authorship has gained ascendancy; likewise, theater in the sixties (and all offshoots of Happenings, too) was outer-directed whereas now it (and performance art) is inner-directed: perhaps the shift can be said to be from the exploration of environmental space to the exploration of mental space, and from narration to documentation. Following the current interest in America in a highly refined spiritual life and the evolution of new shapes of consciousness, the performing arts are actively redefining their own spirit: in both cases, the emphasis is on the dialogue with the self. (Marranca 1979, 8)

Breuer's work cannot strictly be called antitextual or anti-intellectual, because the *Animations* create a space between the text and visual/aural performance images; each, says Marranca, "suppl[ies] information the other cannot" (1979, 14). Still, Breuer's parodic use of cliched language (Marranca terms his work "Quotation Art"), achronological structures, and mythopoeic elements (by which I mean his use of the mythic past to illuminate and transcend the present moment—Marranca prefers the term "auto-mythopoeic") all link his early work to the formalist and self-conscious art of this second-generation experimental performance.

Paradoxically, perhaps the most intelligent and aggressive assault on the notion of the dramatic text during the period came from the most "literary" figure in performance theater, Richard Foreman. Influenced by Brecht's theories of alienation, but perhaps more profoundly by Gertrude Stein's phenomenological conception of language and perception, Foreman developed a unique performance style for productions of his own works at his Ontological-Hysterical Theater. Generally his plays (covering nearly forty works, including *Angelface* [1968], *Total Recall: Or, Sophia = [Wisdom] Part II* [1970], *Pain[t], and Vertical Mobility: Sophia = [Wisdom] Part IV* [1974], *Birth of the Poet* [with Kathy Acker] [1985]) seek to distance and defamiliarize the spectator from the illusory and empathetic time and space coordinates familiar to traditional drama, and to replace these with objective, painterly tableaux that concentrate the spectator's attention toward his or her own perceptual processes. Foreman's theater ostends and then ironizes traditional modes of spectatorship by awakening people's ability to confront things—words, objects, relationships—on a level of final, physical significance, as diction rather than syntax. His methods of alienating viewers from any sympathetic identification with what takes place on stage include the use of loud buzzers, spotlights focused directly at the spectators, randomly selected words or phrases dangled from the flies, and scripts that reveal neither causality nor characters whom the viewer can invest with Presence.

Such strategies of framing and estranging force the spectator to view objects and events phenomenologically, and to investigate not the fictional world created by a text, but the perceptual processes of one's own consciousness. As Keir Elam notes, "when theatrical semiosis is alienated, made 'strange' rather than automatic, the spectator is encouraged to take note of the semiotic *means,* to become aware of the sign-vehicle and its operations" (Elam 1980, 18–19). Foreman's work usually "performs" the activity of his own artistic and erotic consciousness, and so solipsism is a sophisticated element within his theatrical style. His texts, including his nontheatrical manifestos, are self-referential explorations of how he comes to produce such texts, and they often wittily deconstruct themselves in the very process of their enunciation. Still, Foreman's emphatically apolitical agenda connects him to the other artists of the theater of images, and his essentially formalist approach to theater likewise causes one to question the social function of such performances.

In all of these and other quality works (The Wooster Group's *Sakonnet Point,* some of Meredith Monk's dance-theater work), there are traces of genuine substance and potential indications of an intelligent engagement with the world beyond the self. Still, due in large part to the overt, almost aggressive solipsism that lies at the heart of much of the work, spectators have sometimes been disenchanted with the often empty formalism and ahistoricism of the majority of such performances.

As noted earlier, such work was profoundly influenced by poststructuralist theory (often in a popularized form), and often found itself transfixed by the general premises of deconstruction. Simply to demonstrate logocentrism or to exercise deconstructive power through play and performance can be—in fact must be—a tautologous exercise, especially *in* performance ("Play," remarks Blau, "is dreadful" [1982a,

133]). Further, critics questioned the conservative attitude toward culture that such pieces seemed often to nominate, and wondered if the works' emphases on the deconstructive capacities of performance and a nonsemiotic mise-en-scène were not really simply a mechanism for evading the burdens of consciousness, language, and culture. As a result, a potential shortcoming in experimental theater's vision was being indicated, and a new revisionist perspective slowly emerged within avant-garde discourse. Looking back from the perspectives of the mid-eighties, Bonnie Marranca summarized honestly her own critical re-vision as follows:

> The general shift in tone is from the celebratory mood of discovering new theatrical forms, to more critical understanding of contemporary work in relation to history, to a veritable explosion of discontent and frustration, even bitterness with theater's structural composition and crisis of vision. (Marranca 1985, 27)

The problem, it was suggested, was that much of the work of the seventies had essentially no temporal or thematic relation to history. Carrying on the uniquely American desire of sixties performance theater to find a means to sacramentalize the present and thereby deconstruct representation (and also unify life and art), avant-garde artists of the seventies continued to develop ways of prolonging the dominion of play, the first principle of performance. Creating indeterminate structures of play—rather than the logical or temporal frameworks of a stable narrative—allowed performers and directors to create an immanence of a continuous present, during which the urge to repress experience and sensory input into patterns of determinate, fixed, and (therefore) illusory meaning could be deferred. Instead, unrestricted flows of libidinous energy, of sensory images, and so on, were experienced firsthand, unmediated by any preconditioned schema of meaning. One result, however, was that the liberation from the rational, ordering principles of the mind was tantamount to an abrogation of memory and history. That liberating thought, as it turned out, was as illusory as the notion that such a transcendent moment could be achieved in the theater at all.

Such references to play and deferral show the complicity of early poststructuralist theory with much of the conceptually based theater of the seventies, especially with the work of Wilson and Foreman. Because of its close links to such theory, the work also shared the ahistoricism of that theoretical approach, which was, in its deconstructive or textualist phase, essentially a continuation of formalism. Edward Pechter has traced the reception history of deconstructive theory in America, and by simply substituting "performance" for "text," we can see that his remarks are pertinent to the performance theory and practice of the seventies as well:

> However interesting at the peripheries, it retained the central impulse of formalism to focus on the text in isolation from human will and desire and from the particular social formation within which will and desire are produced, directed, controlled, satisfied, frustrated. (Pechter 1987, 292)

Foreman, for instance, not so interested in the politics of performance or textuality, nevertheless concentrated the mise-en-scène of his Ontological-Hysteric Theater toward the breaking up and estranging of the cultural and subjective accretions that are normally bestowed on objects. The idea, with obvious influences from Brecht, Heidegger, and Merleau-Ponty, was to bypass the ego- and culture-determined consciousness in order to estrange the spectator's natural anthropomorphic urge. Thus a picture frame might be attached by a string to another object to create an alienating compositional scheme, the string both declassifying our expectations regarding the frame (and calling into question the absent representation from within the frame) and keeping it tied down to the here and now, away from the higher, symbolic reality that we associate with objects on the stage. The result is a breaking down of our preconceived notions about the picture frame, the stage, and representation itself.

Foreman's work, in its conceptual sophistication, achieves its aim of focusing on alternative modes or "energies" of perception. Still, despite such a performative demonstration of poststructuralist theory, Foreman's true aim in deconstructing the delusions of drama and representation into ever-widening fields of deferral and play—like Wilson's in his mesmerizing elongations of time and space—is really to achieve a transcendent moment when the mind erupts with a new freedom and throws off the bondage of memory and rational thought. Therefore, Foreman's work, despite its intellectual rigor, suffers from the same illusion of ecstasy that inhabited the experimental theater of the sixties. However, whereas in the sixties this desire was holistic and centrifugal, built around recapturing Presence, in the seventies it was essentially deconstructive, based on the centripetal gesture toward Absence, play, and dispersal.

And so the choice offered by first- and second-generation performance theater seemed to be either to reverse history in a search for the ritual or elemental, or else to bypass history altogether by sacramentalizing and making permanent a present state of becoming. In both cases, however, something akin to the reality principle is lost in the penitence of ritual and the pleasure of play, and with it goes theater's essential commitment to remembrance and history.

Play, itself often hypostatized by popularized poststructuralist discourse, is still an epiphenomenon of mind; what early poststructuralist theory in America failed to emphasize sufficiently was that what "matters" about play is how it is made to function within culture by a perceiving subject. Certainly play can function to perform an indeterminable (and sometimes interminable) series of deconstructions of language, text, and other signifying systems. Often the results elicit a certain fascination—similar to one's first sight of mathematical curiosities like the infinities of the Koch curve or the Sierpinski carpet—but as a growing number of theorists and cultural critics have suggested, there simply isn't much to be accomplished by that function of play.[14] Like the geometric monstrosities mentioned above, these deconstructive exercises usually produce fascinating paradoxes that create a semblance of an infinite and complex surface area, but zero volume: elegant yet empty lattices that give only an illusion of solidity. After all, once the initial recognition is accepted that language is opaque, slippery, and predicated on *différance,* textual deconstructions act only—to use the language of nuclear exchange—to "bounce the rubble." They perform no significant cultural work beyond their particular deconstructive exorcism. Deconstructive practice has significant uses and consequences only when play is made to "intrude," as Huizinga said in *Homo Ludens,* "into the indeterminacy of the cosmos" (1950, 8); for only then does play begin to perform cultural work, and to reveal its inevitable allegiances to hegemonic practices, systems of power relations, and ideologies.[15] As the physicist Joseph Ford once said in response to Einstein's famous question to Niels Bohr, "God *does* play dice with the universe. But they're loaded dice. And the main objective . . . is to find out by what rules were they loaded and how we can use them for our own ends" (Gleick 1987, 314).

The belief that play endlessly defers closure and meaning simply for the consciousness-raising of the subject is a questionable revision of poststructuralist thought, having the same relationship to Derrida's ideas that "moral relativity" has to Einstein's. Meaning does not depend solely on the subjective identity (the theme of most performance theater of the seventies), but on the field of different forces—which certainly includes, but is not limited to, subjectivity and interiority—that produce interpretations. Deconstruction therefore does not define reality or advocate a way of subjective being in the world; it defines a cultural strategy, and like any other strategy its success or failure must be tied not to its approximation to some objective world of which it is a picture, but to its productiveness. For Derrida, deconstruction functions as the means to critique origin and to expose the social forces that create an illusion of origin within pre-existing discourses. *That* kind of intrusive play requires an awareness that the dominion of the ludic performance is neither infinite, nor free of the mind's mediation, nor liberated from culture and ideology (including the politics of play itself).[16] It realizes, in other words, that play is *written,* "amortized," in theater as it is in life, by the estates of time and history:

> What seems to be confirmed by the pursuit of unmediated experience through performance is that there is something in the very nature of performance which, like the repeating spool of the *fort/da* . . . implies *no first time,* no origin, but only recurrence and reproduction, whether improvised or ritualized, rehearsed or aleatoric, whether the performance is meant to give the impression of unviolated naturalness or the dutiful and hieratic obedience to a code. That is why performance seems *written* even if there is no Text, for the writing seems imbedded in the conservatism of the instincts and the linguistic operations of the unconscious. (Blau 1987, 171)

Performance seeks an impossible freedom from textuality, impossible because the latter inscribes, not master narratives *of* history, but a record of the activity of *making* history: textuality writes a history of subjective, but richly political, human activity through the medium of language in the name of human memory. And "history," says Fredric Jameson, "is . . . the experience of Necessity. . . . History is what hurts, it is what refuses desire and sets inexorable limits to individual as well as collective praxis" (Jameson 1981, 102). In the flight from history's refusals and containments in the pursuit of *jouissance,* performances of the seventies were especially apt to ignore the reality of history, to forgo analysis of the manner in which texts deny or repress the contradictions of history, and to concentrate on reducing consciousness of history itself in order to clear the ground for the matrices of new perceptual fields. In doing so, these performance works pursued desire rather than what constrains it, and disregarded culture rather than seeking to understand its power structures. Gone was any awareness of history as struggle or contestation, as the dynamics of the *libido dominandi* were replaced by the play of the libido over pleasures endlessly displaced, deferred, and prolonged. It remained to be discovered that, in Eric Bentley's phrase, "*im*palpability has its dangers" (Bentley 1985, 57).

At their worst, avant-garde pieces of the seventies tended toward such simple evocations of unframed, dispersed perception, while at their best—in performance works by Wilson, Foreman, Mabou Mines, The Wooster Group, Meredith Monk, Lucinda Childs, and others—they achieved a particular order of complexity or genuine substance in which play was not simply gratuitous, but instead emblematic of a profoundly serious engagement with life. But even in the most mature work much was often lost, and there emerged an awareness that such performances needed to reciprocate the heightened perceptions, energies, and transformations of the performing subjects with those of the spectator. As Lily Tomlin once said, "Most actors worry about playing to an empty house. I . . . worry about playing to a full house and leaving the audience empty" (Raven 1988, 210).

Further, the attempts to deconstruct semiosis utterly failed for the same reasons that Dada and other forms of "nonsemiotic" performance have failed: because the continuity, form, context, and meaning of the artwork are provided not so much by the artist as by the spectator. No matter how absurd, random, meaningless, or deconstructive the components of the work are, no matter how huge the gaps in continuity, logic, and sequence, the human mind, if inclined, is instantly capable of filling those gaps and imposing a fabricated version of meaning and even form on the work. As for those artists whose aim it was, as in Wilson's earliest work, to disrupt and destroy discursive language entirely in favor of images and silence, perhaps John Cage's remarks are sufficient: "There is always something to see, something to hear. In fact, try as we may to make a silence, we cannot" (1967, 117). The attempts by second-generation performance theater to circumvent the desire to produce meaning often seem gratuitous, not because they produce nonsense, but because they are unable to create and sustain the activity of making non-sense.[17] While Niels Bohr was devising his principle of complementarity in 1927 he discovered that in the subatomic domain the only way an observer could be uninvolved in the process of creating an interpretation was to observe nothing at all. So too in theater, the *theatron* or seeing-place, where even Beckett's singularly insistent attempts to write interpretation out of his theater and to attain perfect silence have recoiled and doubled him back to language and meaning.

The immediate upshot of the loss of the artist's engagement with language, meaning, and discourse was, in Blau's sober judgment, a "new solipsism, playful and plaintive, open-ended and recessive, still disinherited, apolitical, vain" (Blau 1982b, 257). So much of the best talent in American theater appeared to neglect what Wittgenstein announced powerfully, that "an expression has meaning only in the stream of life." And so, as deconstructionist thought slowly (in America) gave way to a new awareness of historicism—that is, the production of texts and their reception within a network of power relations, and the manner in which certain texts narrate interiority along ideological lines—critical attention turned toward putting the performances back into the context from which they were generated in order to study their relations to culture. Under the same pressures, avant-garde theater began to turn away from the purely deconstructive experiments with space, language, and time that had characterized work throughout the sixties and seventies, and to revive within performance work itself a stronger human and historical reference.

These and other changes in experimental theater after the mid-seventies reflect a more general tendency in contemporary performance theater to rethink the most radical innovations of the previous three decades in light of new theory and historical pressures. This reversion connects, in Bonnie Marranca's view, to "broader cultural implications":

> The earlier experiments with performance space in non-proscenium settings paralleled the loss of perspective on moral and social levels. The return to the proscenium, and with it the growing interest in the text, suggests a more reflective, evaluative attitude on the part of artists. (It may also be related to changing audience taste.) Group theater pieces, previously defined by their lack of a spatially-organized center, and a text comprised of image clusters, sought in their performances to give audiences the experience of an event. Like-

> wise, the audience and critical response then was highly impressionistic: the idea was to give yourself up to the performance, it was wrong to try to analyze or think about it, just let it wash over you. Today we see more frontality—not only in performance but in the new realism plays—which is conducive to a critical approach precisely because of its perspectival centering. Finally, the turn to theoretical criticism in recent years accentuates theater's return to visual and social perspective. (Marranca 1985, 31)

Thus the undeniably beguiling yet sometimes meretricious avant-garde work produced during the seventies diminished in its appeal by the middle of the decade (though much still exists, to be sure). The more significant initiatives of this experimental theater, however, have survived the revision of the avant-garde agenda, and continue to effect reverberations in contemporary mainstream drama. In addition to what the experiments in performance as an autonomous art form gave us—in terms of the new body training, the various uses of technology incorporated into performances, the innovative uses of time and space, and so on, important in themselves—what remains most crucial is the breathing space that performance theater and theory have opened up by their radical critique of representation, of determinate meaning and the structures that give meaning, and of the very barriers (real? imagined?) that have always separated theater and life. The profound questions regarding the true relationship between performance and the dramatic text, immanent in Brecht, Pirandello, Beckett, and other modernist playwrights, found in experimental theater of the sixties and seventies their most explicit and concrete statements. In the early stages of experiment it was perhaps inevitable that certain points of insistence be carried to their nolast term, with something of a disregard for the world that they were trying to ameliorate and for the language they wanted to purify. Eventually, however, at the insistence of that world and that language, such performances were compelled to return to earth.

New Directions

The poststructuralist critique of Presence and the turn toward more culturally contextualized theater have brought textual concerns back into experimental performance theater, as evidenced by a modified use of more conventional narrative strategies found in the work of avant-garde performance groups that had once turned completely away from such structures: Mabou Mines's *Dead End Kids* (1977), The Wooster Group's *L.S.D. (Just the High Points)* (1985), Foreman's *The Birth of the Poet* (1985), and Wilson's *Alcestis* (1986), among others. Often, the narratives are partially determined by the use of texts, as in The Wooster Group's "reading" of Timothy Leary and the Beat poets in *L.S.D.*, and in Foreman's collaboration with writers like Kathy Acker. Similarly, Wilson seems less inclined lately to work solely within the parameters of the essentially nonverbal "theater of images" with which he was associated for many years. In his most recent productions (*Hamletmachine, Alcestis,* and other collaborations with Heiner Müller, as well as a production of Woolf's *Orlando*), Wilson uses for the first time substantive texts as the basis for his productions, stages his pieces on decidedly "built" sets, and, in the words of critic John Rouse, "has begun to include more recognizable idea and emotional content in his theatrical meditations" (Rouse 1987, 56).

Foreman has directed text-based plays by other playwrights at such bastions of relative orthodoxy as the Guthrie Theater and the New York Shakespeare Festival. His own work, too, appears to be moving toward more historical awareness and context. A recent performance work, *The Birth of the Poet,* stages three parallel moments of trauma in world history that give rise to the need for the poet. And although Kathy Acker's pre-script is, like Foreman's own writing, fractured and playfully engaged with notions of self-consciousness, solipsism, and artistic subjectivity, the inclusion of these historical moments outside the domain of the self indicates a new awareness of the relationship of the artist to history and culture. Perhaps most tellingly, Foreman has recently begun to assert the value of his theater as literature, saying "I have confidence . . . that in time people are going to be able to relate to my texts and see that they have the same coherence and density as a lot of twentieth-century poetry" (Foreman 1987, 21).

Lee Breuer, too, in his work away from Mabou Mines, has turned in recent years toward directing more literary works (especially his *Gospel at Colonus* [1985] and *Lear* [1990]) that by their dependency on a controlling text signal a change of artistic direction from the old *Animations* days. And JoAnne Akalaitis, another founder of Mabou Mines, caused a local furor in 1985 when she directed Beckett's *Endgame* at the American Repertory Theater within a historically-specific (or at least suggestive) mise-en-scène. Mabou Mines, as a collective, also shows signs of moving toward a rapprochement with the dramatic text. *Lear,* starring Ruth Malaczech in the title role, shows little evidence of textual elision. Instead, Breuer and Mabou Mines have turned toward investigating, exposing, and overturning centers of power within the existing dramatic text. So, while seeking to supplement the text with new performance strategies, the Mines certainly do not venerate it; like Wilson, Foreman, and a variety of other artists, they have embarked upon a more historicized and culturally situated deconstruction of literary drama, which, instead of simply parodying the text or reducing it to rubble to be bounced, seeks its collusions and collisions with other texts and with the society that produces the entire apparatus of representation.

The significant point here is that none of these artists or collectives are simply becoming avatars of the cultural establishment. All retain a great many avant-garde performance concepts and strategies in their work, and all remain staunchly opposed to traditional literary structure and function. But in their performances and those of other artists, a general trend toward reinvesting in—and reinvestigating—traditional dramatic elements (usually drastically modified and radicalized by previous experiment) like discursive language, plot, narrative, and so on, is apparent and signals a new and significant direction for contemporary theater as a whole.

This revival of text and narrative and their power to frame and enhance performance is complemented by a new awareness of the framing powers of the stage itself. There is still, to be sure, important performance work being done in various nontraditional environments and built spaces. But more and more, artists who had for a time sworn never to step onto a proscenium stage are returning to box sets and discovering the peculiar power of such perspectival centering. Foreman's Ontological-Hysteric Theater work proved long ago that the proscenium need not limit or make less ironic and provocative the performances staged within its arch. More recent pieces by auteurs like Wilson, performance artists like Ping Chong and Laurie Anderson, and collectives like Chicago's Impossible Theater suggest that the notion that the proscenium stage is limited to presenting a monological, enclosed, or unified point of view for the audience reveals an oversimplified understanding of theatrical communication and the reading strategies of spectators.

Due also in part to Derrida's critique of Presence, the avant-garde's resistance to referential language has also waned. Though experiments with alternative forms and functions of language continue to produce provocative theater, current work reveals an attempt to mark and resist the political power inherent in existing modes of discourse, rather than repeating the earlier efforts to raise consciousness by subverting language altogether. "Breakdown of language equals breakdown of values, of modes of insight, of the sick rationale," wrote Julian Beck, expressing the attitude of first-generation alternative theater: "Breakdown of language means invention of fresh forms of communication" (Beck [1972] 1986, 35). With its rational emphasis, its power to structure and constrain experience, and its comfortable coexistence with the propagandizing power structure, language was the natural foe of early performance theater. Avant-garde artists reacted to this debased use of language the same way they reacted to the text, to traditional staging, and to naturalistic acting: they either parodied it mercilessly or threw it out as being intellectually and theatrically corrupt. They then tried to replace the rejected tongue with alternative versions of language that would disempower writing and return speech to its proper elemental level in order to reclaim the community of the tribe.

Thus there were (and continue to be) performances, built on the earlier critique of language initiated by the surrealists and absurdists, that exposed the clichés and misstatements of mass culture (during the sixties, it was Van Itallie's *Interview* and Megan Terry's *The Gloaming Oh My Darling;* in the seventies there was Wilson). Experiments in the use of remote languages were also conducted, as is still the case with the Yoshi and Suzuki companies of Japan, which perform in an ancient Japanese dialect that even native Japanese speakers barely recognize. These languages function, as had Peter Brooks's use of Greek, Sanskrit, and the "Orghast language" concocted by Ted Hughes, to develop Andrei Serban's (1986) notions of nonreferential speech as the "life in sound." In addition, under the influence of theories of ethnopoesis, there are continued attempts, especially by Brook and Eugenio Barba, to activate some kind of transcultural *communitas* by performing in polyglot or dead languages that will act as a universal tongue that speaks directly to desire and the instincts rather than to the mind. These functions of language are all, of course, related to Artaud's desire for a gestural theater and to experimental theater's privileging of physical aspects of performance over the rational elements of literary drama.

Such experiments with nontraditional uses of language and sounding were closely allied with the avant-garde's dream of the collective and with the sincere desire for wholeness and therapy. The foundations for the desire, however, were the same as those that motivated the valorization of Presence, and shared the same suspect biases regarding the precedence of spontaneous speech over controlled, "written" discourse. The desire was still for the sounded enactment of an authentic moment, an uninterrupted, hypostatized, and ritualized present; but, as Derrida argues, such moments cannot escape the "arche-writing" that stains each present with the trace. In addition, the failure to create that illusory present left the performances, again, with an ahistorical quality that disturbed a practitioner/critic like Blau, who still felt that "if we are to continue in the *making* of history—that is, exercising through the theater some measure of control of our presence in it—our work must include a critique of the illusion of an uninterrupted present, keeping it in mind" (Blau 1982a, 75). For Blau, whose dual roles as director of a widely respected performance collective (KRAKEN) and more recently as an articulate theorist lend his views some weight, "language is having the last word" (1982a, 83). Commenting on his own work with KRAKEN, he admits that "our work was highly charged in the body, ideographic, but every time we came back, we ran into language, and the ubiquitous tangle of words—whether we worked with a classic text or not" (1982a, 79). Having discovered the encompassing power of language and its determined hold over consciousness, Blau also realized its connections to history, culture, and memory:

> All said and done, not only do words count, they count all the more when *we* are exhausted. When we try to drop out of social reality, they keep us anchored. Fallen into the world (if the myths are true), they are historical accretions and keep us attached to history, in history. When we turn from words to things to block off history, we do it with words in mind. . . . [W]ords demarcate an order of being arisen from long usage. They memorize us. Without them, we literally forget who we are. Among the delusions of the period not entirely past was the idea that such forgetfulness might be desirable. It was the idiocy of the Identity Crisis. So the titillations and exacerbations of quick apocalypse and ecstasy. But such transcendencies (as opposed to those of language) are short-lived, and when we come back to earth, the only one we know whether or not we know ourselves, we descend like fallen angels with words upon our tongues. (1982a, 86)

Few directors and performers shared Blau's reflective capacities and his grudging acknowledgment of the amortized lifespan of the life in sound, and so the experiments with language continued throughout the sixties and into the second generation of avant-garde artists in the seventies and eighties. And in each period the troubling thought remained that in rejecting rational language, theater was essentially neglecting history and refusing to contemplate its own ambiguous place in culture. Blau, again, having the last word:

> What was lost in the abuses of language during this period—both by those who continued lying in it and those who thought they would stop the lying by forgetting how to use it—was the continuity of a tradition which sees the exactitude of language as the sustenance of integrity. The falling away from language was to begin with misguided; at its extreme, it was ethically irresponsible, as if language can be exempt, literally, out of this world; or as if you can be in this world, significantly, literate without language. (1982a, 87)

The "new" art of performance theater emerging from the experiments of the last three decades is often more literate, more "ethical" in Blau's sense. The use of modernist texts in performances by The Wooster Group (Eliot's poetry and plays, Wilder's *Our Town*) is neither gratuitous nor simply parodic, but indicative of an impulse to understand and critique modernist discourse and its ideologies. JoAnne Akalaitis's recuperation of the writings of Colette in the Mabou Mines production of *Dressed Like an Egg* acts as the privileged mechanism by which the group examines the creative processes of writing. The attempt is to use performance not to get beyond what has been written, but to enact the activity of writing as a way to "investigate romantic form *through* acting, movement, and theatrical conventions" (1984, 193; emphasis added). In such work, language is not devalued; but neither is it given the privileged status it had formerly enjoyed in literary drama. The oedipal *logos* is now understood as pre-existent discourse that needs to be re-marked and contextualized so that an understanding of its affiliations to culture and to various acculturating agencies can be exposed.

The altered state of language in the most recent wave of experimental performance reveals a growing curiosity about the connections between theater and other discourses in contemporary culture. More and more, playwrights and performance groups are investigating the political nature of theater itself, as well as theater's complex relations to other discourses that are empowered to create and reproduce meaning. Rather than trying to move past traditional text-centered theater—whether by performance-as-ritual, or by performance-as-play/deferral—contemporary artists are more inclined to critique theater's bases of reproduction from within its own theatrical, dramatic, and performative matrices. Thus contemporary theater continues the avant-garde's insistence on a re-vision of orthodox theater, but a revision that includes the presence of traditional elements within it. In a typically postmodern strategy, the very elements that make up theater must be recuperated in order to be exposed and juxtaposed in new ways that will deconstruct their foundations and reveal their relationships to prevailing ideologies. By destructuring the orders of representation in order to critique and re-inscribe them, avant-garde theater eventually rediscovers its social context and becomes, once again, an art directly related to the polis.[18]

The change parallels events in contemporary visual arts, where the values and conceptual power of abstract art are still acknowledged, even as its absolute claims are being rejected. The referential, mediating, even "moral" function of art—its age-old purpose—is being appealed to once again. The importance of content and meaning is being reaffirmed, and traditional subject matter is being re-introduced into new contexts. One thinks of the apocryphal tale of David Parks gathering up his abstract expressionist canvases in 1949 and driving to a Berkeley city dump to destroy them. He wanted, he is to have said, to stop producing "paintings" and start painting "pictures," a notion that led to a flourishing of more representational work in the Bay Area for the next two decades.

Perhaps feeling that abstraction and artistic self-consciousness have become doctrinaire and have reached their limits, many artists search for fresh inspiration among the objects, events, and emotions of their time or their past, not to repeat the experiments of their predecessors, but to investigate the ways that artistic meaning is created and acculturated. One result, in a painter like Anselm Kiefer, for instance, is a provocative style in which abstract art is combined with referential subject matter to create a hybrid form that questions the nature of opposing modes of perception, and opposing strategies for narrating history and interiority. In somewhat the same fashion, the abstract and formal performances of the seventies (the "paintings") might have represented the tentative beginnings of a "postmodern" theater, while the more dynamic and culturally situated forms currently evolving from them (the "pictures") herald a more mature stage of development.

While experimental performance theater has been changing and incorporating radicalized elements of more orthodox drama within it, a reflex action has also occurred within text-oriented drama. Among a variety of significant conventional playwrights—Sam Shepard, Megan Terry, David Mamet, Tina Howe, and David Rabe, among others in America, and Samuel Beckett, Tom Stoppard, Caryl Churchill, Edward Bond, and Pam Gems among British writers—certain avant-garde performance techniques, strategies, and theatrical functions have been appropriated and put to new uses within orthodox dramatic texts.[19] For instance, new emphases on the physical presence and discipline of the actor are utilized throughout Beckett's work and in selected plays by Shepard and Rabe, as well as in Stoppard's *Jumpers* and in Churchill's recent play, *Serious Money*. Experiments in making language more physical and privileging it over plot and character occur in Mamet, Shepard, and Stoppard, while Churchill has developed a variety of theatrical strategies designed to deconstruct integrative relationships between characters, chronology, and plot. Megan Terry, once among the most prominent literary voices in the performance-oriented Open Theater, is one of many playwrights whose use of transformational acting exercises, a staple in performance theater, gives her recent plays (*Mollie Bailey's Traveling Family Circus* comes to mind) an atmosphere of Heraclitean flux, which stands as testament to her belief in the capacity for people to redefine and reshape social and gender roles. In these playwrights and a host of others, the decentering and deconstruction of plot, character, and narrative through the exercise of performance serve to open up textuality and its dependency on coherent character psychology and development, its tendency toward narrative closure, and its advocacy of a monological vision or "worldview" that we can ascribe to the author. New interests arise in exploring the nature of representation itself, in locating the sources of the spectator's pleasure and desire within a social structure or web of hegemonic structures, and in critiquing the act of interpretation that lies at the heart of theater.

Here, too, we do not have a case of an omophagic response by a devouring orthodoxy that simply recuperates avant-garde initiatives to be chic (an image sometimes conjured up by avant-garde artists and critics). If theater history of the last three decades has taught us anything, it is that tradition need not enervate what it recuperates, and indeed that it can re-energize what it subsumes even as the tradition itself finds new life by the accumulation of new, sometimes conflicting idioms within its capacious margins. Especially in the contemporary period, with its penchant for eclecticism and art-historical consciousness, the probability exists that artistic idioms will supplement and not supplant one another, and that interactive forms of performance and drama will emerge and become increasingly important in the dramatic canon.[20] We are seeing today the initial development of such complementary interaction between seemingly unrelated, even antagonistic, theatrical forms; and so, despite the ontological and conceptual differences between traditional literary drama and performance theater, tracing the sources and energies of contemporary theater means tracing the dynamic between the two in order to determine the important points of contact out of which the two mutually deconstruct, interanimate, and redefine one another.

Whether or not these new hybrids will survive or provide artists with sufficient cultural address is of course impossible to determine. Still, the works under scrutiny here seem more compelling and intriguing than anything else that is being done in either mainstream literary drama or avant-garde performance art. They maintain the search for new and vital modes of theatrical expression characteristic of experimental theater, while avoiding the avant-garde's sometimes self-conscious aestheticism and its self-indulgent and naive ahistoricism. In addition, as Elin Diamond has remarked in another context, these hybrids "avail themselves of realism's referential power without succumbing to its ideological conservatism" (Diamond 1989, 68). As a result, we see a reinvestment in the human reference that has traditionally characterized theater and a return to theater's social perspective. At the same time, these works revivify traditional textuality by incorporating avant-garde idioms and performance strategies as a language within the dramatic text, an idiom appropriate to the theatricalized and transformational sensibilities of the present day. Finally, these strategies also help to unmask the ideologies that have for centuries empowered drama and placed it in the privileged cultural context in which we find it today.

Such uncomfortable combinations of performance and drama often produce the antitheses to what have long been considered well-made plays. The very confusion and lack of resolution arising out of the quantum babble of dramatic and performative languages, in fact, constitute one of the hybrid's greatest strengths; this indeterminate dialectic is the language that best exemplifies contemporary culture and its need for an art that, in Jean-François Lyotard's phrase, unsentimentally—and often unaesthetically—"puts forward the unpresentable in presentation itself; that which denies itself the solace of good forms, the consensus of a taste that would make it possible to share collectively the nostalgia for the unattainable; that which searches for new presentations, not in order to enjoy them but in order to impart a stronger sense of the unpresentable" (Lyotard 1984, 81). Thus denied the solace of "pure" forms and "total" art—in either the text or in performance—artists and audiences alike must look to dynamic and unstable forms that combine the high humanistic velocity of great literary drama with the heightened expressiveness and deconstructive edge of performance theater to produce the kind of "pied beauty" that characterizes current aesthetics. By thus turning away from what we have always considered theater to be, we still stand a chance of reinvigorating it, not "as a whole," but as the site of dynamic difference it has become.

Chapter 2

"The sad tale a last time told": Closing Performance and Liberating the Text in the Plays of Samuel Beckett

As described in the last chapter, the past three decades of American theater are characterized by radical experiments in the use of various forms of performance as the privileged mechanism for displacing and deconstructing the dramatic text and for positing the flow of unchained signifiers as the primary power of theater. The seams or margins inherent in performance itself, however, have compelled a number of recent artists to question whether performance can function as a strictly autonomous form of theater. Many have consequently begun to seek a less confrontational, more fruitful relationship between performance and the dramatic text. These artists recognize that drama and performance share an asymptotic freedom, an attitude that describes the bearing of those subatomic particles which have the beautiful property of moving freely when in proximity to one another, but which are reined in by increasingly powerful nuclear forces when they begin to drift too far apart. Since experiments in separating performance from drama and the text failed to achieve the desired spiritual transcendence or free-floating deconstructions artists sought, a new strategy has been emerging, one that positions text and performance in a kind of complementarity—a relationship that is undeniably contradictory, yet necessary to sustain the most complete possible description of nature. ("Dissonance," wrote William Carlos Williams, "(if you are interested) / leads to discovery.") In the ensuing interface, performance, as well as the text itself, has been radically changed.

The nature of these reconfigurations, as might be expected, varies quite widely. So before moving on in later chapters to investigate specific new relationships between text and performance in both contemporary alternative theater and mainstream textual drama, it is useful first to posit a paradigm in order to provide a reference point for what follows. The paradigm should first be descriptive, in the sense that it will elucidate a general model of the dynamic interaction between performance and drama that can be applied to other examples in contemporary theater. But the model can also be prescriptive, by which I mean it ought to aspire toward something more ambitious: to posit an ideal relationship between theater's dynamic modes of expression, an alliance out of which a viable new form of drama can emerge. Finally, the paradigm should also record the process of its own formation, so as to indicate what lies behind its making and perhaps suggest what lies before it in the future.

Many playwrights, directors, and performers span the decades I am considering. While a smaller number of those (artists like Kaprow, Cage, and so on) might provide a descriptive model of the text/performance dynamic, fewer have achieved a sufficient level of self-conscious mastery over the shifting relations between text and performance, and over the theoretical consequences that follow, to function as an accurate paradigm. Fewer still have exhibited sufficient artistic integrity to acknowledge the ontological limits imposed on both text and performance and to confront without sentimentality or guile the irremediable spectacle of representation as it fails to speak itself wholly.

Ultimately, only Samuel Beckett's canon exemplifies the range and probity of vision necessary to furnish an ideal model; for it is in Beckett's search for a paradoxical "authorial impotence" that we first find in the theater a consistent, theorized desire to displace authorial control through performance. More significantly, Beckett's willingness to accede to his eventual failure in this quest, and to confess to both the failure to write textuality completely out of his plays and to his own profound and contradictory desires for textual order and control in his work, eventually makes it possible for him to move beyond nominating either power or powerlessness, text or performance, as the single privileged form of expression. Instead, Beckett's latest work reveals an attempt to seek new, double-coded and self-contradictory relationships between the omnipotence of the text and the impotence of performance.

Beckett's plays and narratives acutely disclose the ill-defined perturbations that initiate the movement away from the modernist cultural orbit toward the postmodern. Beyond that, his last works indicate new alternatives to the postmodern, and map out what likely will displace that which had already become insipid and chic in postmodernism. That is to say, Beckett is a transitional figure whose contradictory agenda straddles the modern and what follows upon it, occupying a relative position both behind contemporary theater artists (as a brooding modernist influence upon them) and somehow before them (as an explorer of what they are currently discovering). As Herbert Blau positions him, Beckett both reflects and engenders significant shifts in contemporary culture and consciousness:

> Outside ideology, and a marginal figure in the evolution of the modern (to the master of the Wake, an attendant lord), Beckett surfaced in the fifties when the modern seemed to be running out of desire. . . . If he became, nevertheless, a talismanic force during the sixties for releasing an awakened negativity into a culture biding its time, he was a touchstone after the sixties, with the Movement disillusioned and its projects incomplete, for releasing into the postmodern the flow-producing aporias of unfinishable forms. (Blau 1987, xviii–xix)

Such remarks, of course, have more to do with the process of Beckett's critical reception than with the playwright's own agenda. His plays have been awakening negativity and producing aporias since he first began writing them ("L'art adore les sauts," he notes in the *Disjecta*), and his relationship to aporias and unfinishable forms of play is always tempered by the closure inscribed by that very expression of negativity. In fact, Blau's assessment itself stops short by neglecting to indicate how Beckett continued to expose new boundaries by enacting in his late plays what lies beyond the poststructuralist horizon in contemporary theater. Beyond the aporias lie Beckett's acknowledgment of the margins ingrained in a "flow-producing" dramaturgy and the latent discovery of a complementary relationship between the expressive power of the text and the deconstructive strategies of performance. Amanuensis to the master of the Wake, Beckett early on had his head peopled with Shems and Shauns, sundry Gripses and Mookses, Ondts and Gracehoppers, Butts and Taffs, and other "doubleparalleled twixtytwins" who come together in HCE to form the dynamic synthesis between those "overlorded by fate and interlarded with accidence"—which is to say, those occupying the space between the values associated with the closure and determinism of textuality and the indeterminacies of performance. "I am working out a quantum theory about it for it is really a most tantumising state of affairs," wrote Joyce in *Finnegans Wake*. Within the theater, Beckett continues a similar search for a standard model of complementarity between the text and performance.

Blau's remarks do accurately reflect the extent to which critics and playwrights alike have turned to Beckett as an exemplary barometer of changing literary culture over the past four decades. This has moved numerous critics to document Beckett's influence on several generations of mainstream literary playwrights, often with the intent of discussing what the theater looks like "after Beckett."[1] Interestingly, though, given Beckett's penchant for minimalizing traditional theatrical elements nearly out of existence and for deconstructing our conventional notions of drama, fewer critics have thought to trace his significant presence within avant-garde performance theater, even though such an alternative to traditional drama seems a logical place to look for parallels to Beckett's own insurgencies against the dramatic text.

The reticence is understandable, as it seems odd to align Beckett's irredeemably dark world with the holy theater ecstasies of first-generation experimental theater practitioners and performance theorists like The Living Theater, Jerzy Grotowski, and Richard Schechner's Performance Group. "Not for me these Grotowskis and Methods," Beckett once reported: "The best possible play is one in which there are no actors, only the text. I'm trying to find a way to write one" (Bair 1978, 722). Beckett is perhaps in less-strange company when his work is compared to that of later performance-oriented director/auteurs like Richard Foreman and Robert Wilson and of performance collectives like Mabou Mines and The Wooster Group. Still, as Jonathan Kalb argues, the time has arrived to consider carefully the question of Beckett's fuller context, and to open up new perspectives on his work and its relation to more radical theater: "One would think from these pieces," comments Kalb on a recent Beckett festschrift that overlooks the playwright's influence on alternative theater, "that the critics in question had never heard of Mabou Mines or been to La Mama" (Kalb 1986, 34). Had they gone there, they would have found Beckett present in spirit well before them.

There have been, of course, attempts to connect various surface qualities of Beckett's plays with similar elements found in alternative theater work. The sometimes brilliant productions by Mabou Mines of Beckett's short plays and his prose fiction have influenced the stagecraft of that group's own collective performances. Witness, for instance, the thin beams of inquisitorial light that rove over scenes in *Dressed Like an Egg* and, in the Mines's production of Beckett's prose piece *The Lost Ones,* the representation of a stage narrator whose character constantly shifts and threatens to disappear, a performance strategy that has become a staple in the group's own work. Foreman's trademark spotlights, shining into the faces of audiences at Ontological-Hysteric productions, seem a witty reversal of the painful beams that harass the actors in *Play*. Wilson's carefully coordinated stage movements parallel the emphasis on precise lines and gestures in Beckett's plays, especially in the latter's works for mime—the *Quadrats,* for example. Similar borrowings of such stark stage images by contemporary artists continue to remind us of Beckett's radical innovations within his dwindling mise-en-scènes: California visual theater virtuoso Paul Dreschler's merciless spotlights in *Slow Fire,* the obsessive pacing of Robert Wilson's somnambulant performers in *Deafman Glance* (recalling May's rhythmic tread in *Footfalls*), the fragmented and objectified body parts that eerily inhabit the stages of Wilson, Foreman, and others, and the use of video equipment—Krapp dragged into the video generation—to evoke disjunctive psychological, chronological, and linguistic structures in pieces by Laurie Anderson, Meredith Monk, and a host of other performance artists.

Despite such tenuous connections, however, there is a sense that Beckett's crucial relationship to avant-garde performance theater has been, until very recently, largely overlooked. For if we remember the most essential experiments that have taken place with performance—that is, performance as a mechanism for dislocating the power of the dramatic text—over the last thirty years, we find that most are either anticipated or paralleled by Beckett's own innovations. Beckett, for instance, building upon tentative initiatives of Pirandello and Brecht, is among the first playwrights to produce a radical deprivileging of the orthodox dramatic text and, by extension, of the author's position in the theatrical hierarchy. This in turn leads to Beckett's well-known experiments with new functions of the mise-en-scène, with dramatic language, and with the use (or abuse) of the actor—all concerns in experimental theater as well. These theatrical elements, tightly constrained and formally integrated in conventional literary drama, are often radically disassociated and fragmented by Beckett in order to deconstruct traditional closed structures of meaning and to release meaning and interpretation into the "unfinishable forms" of play. And as Blau's earlier remarks suggest, this establishes important connections between Beckett's work and the valorization of improvisatorial play and performance in experimental theater and recent theory.

Even more important, Beckett also is among the first to discover the margins of such experiments with play and performance and to intuit the closure that inhabits their very structure and amortizes their purchase on play, deferral, and dis-closure. Consequently, Beckett turns in his last works to redeeming both performance and the dramatic text by establishing new relational fields among them. By doing so, he anticipates the contemporary turning away from purely abstract and playful performance techniques on the one hand and tightly causal structures and other conventional textual strategies on the other. His latest contribution to theater may be the fact that he pointed the way toward quantum theater events that unite performance and the text as dynamic and self-effacing complements of one another.

In positing Beckett's plays as a paradigm for the process by which such new theater events come into being, I do not imply a stable pattern of influence between Beckett and experimental theater. Significant differences exist in the way such experiments effect change within particular works, and in the theatrical function they serve. "Beckett," says Kalb, "has done far more than offer modernist technical innovations for clever minds to decode and sensitive writers to inherit; he has changed our very expectations about what is supposed to happen, what can happen, when we enter a theater" (Kalb 1986, 34). We might say of Beckett what Eliot wrote of Yeats, that

> his idiom was too different for there to be any danger of imitation, his opinions too different to flatter and confirm their prejudices. It was good for them to have the spectacle of an unquestionably great living poet, whose style they were not tempted to echo and whose ideas opposed those in vogue among them. You will not see, in their writing, more than passing evidences of the impression he made, but the work, and the man himself as poet, have been of the greatest significance to them all for that. (Eliot 1975, 248–49)

If, then, avant-garde directors, writers, and performers did not benefit directly from Beckett's initiatives, they at least could be assured by his example.

What lies beyond specific ties between Beckett and experimental theater is Beckett's entire dramatic enterprise and his career as an author, which seems to contain always already most of the innovations and experiments that have led to important permutations between "modern" and "postmodern," text and performance, in the theater. These dynamic configurations oscillate within his plays without regard to chronology or flux of fashion, and without seriously altering his bleak vision. And it is in such terms that Beckett's canon provides a paradigm for the dynamic process between text and performance that characterizes so much of our best contemporary theater.

Though Beckett's vision remains relatively stable, recent critical views on Beckett's canon from nontraditional perspectives do insist that the vision has been manifested in ways not sufficiently investigated. We are only beginning to uncover what is truly radical in the work and authorial agenda of this most radical of playwrights. And in indicating the range and depth of his subversions, several of these new approaches have suggested certain links between Beckett and some of the key developments in experimental performance of the past few decades. In fact, it appears that by tracing the curve of Beckett's dramatic career we find a contour not unlike that which describes the crucial movement in experimental theater as a whole, which was outlined in the last chapter.

Beginning in the late fifties, both Beckett and proponents of experimental theater—for quite different reasons—began to work on strategies for displacing the author's traditional function in theater and to undermine the very notions of the orthodox dramatic text and its power to order reality and create a charismatic Presence within the actor. Interestingly, in both Beckett's plays and later experimental work there is something akin to a "first phase" where an acute awareness of the confines and aesthetic or ideological implications of textuality are initially recognized.[2] After rejecting these textual restraints for various reasons, a number of anti-textual strategies are designed to circumvent what Derrida calls the "preformationist" tendencies of textuality. This means, of course, rejecting entirely bourgeois theater, with its Cartesian psychological frames and quantified sense of time, space, and perspective, as well as its dependence on causality.

The most subversive of these strategies, utilized by both Beckett and avant-garde theater artists, is the intervention of performance against the text, an activity designed to break down the repressive power of the text and its paternal author, thereby disabling the illusion of determinate meaning. What is offered in place of the rational and logocentric text, according to Blau (restating Artaud), is "an idea of performance as multiple, synchronous, and polyscenic, a circuitous torsion of laminated thought, where the masks, costumes, cries, bodies, and the interlacing gestures of limbs and eyes are . . . an intenser form of ratiocination" (Blau 1987, xviii). This conceptual shift toward privileging performance gestures over textual matters is effected by radical changes in traditional dramatic elements and idioms—in the function of the performer, in language, narrative structure, the setting, and so on—that break up the integrative structures and rational bases of the drama that produce the illusory power of the representation and its author.

Such a deconstructive dramaturgy is for Beckett a method for devising plays that express authorial "impotence" instead of "omnipotence" and deflect privileged meanings by undermining referentiality and textual coherence.[3] Lacking organic unity, chronological clarity, and appropriate character development, Beckett's work thus often leads critics to conclude that, in Thomas Whitaker's phrase, it "is, or wants to be, the serious reductio ad absurdum of an age in which the mind has lost its illusions of any divine source, order of values, or sustaining worlds and finds itself trapped in the arbitrary, the incoherent, the meaningless" (Whitaker 1986, 209). In this view, the plays are defined primarily by their absence of a center around which the spectator can engage in a closed form of semiotic exchange and interpretation. And, if this is indeed the case, then Beckett is already (always) a bit ahead of the game, because his agenda clearly resembles a poststructuralist or deconstructionist one. The same agenda might describe the second wave of experimental performance theater, already discussed, where similar developments toward theater events built on deconstructive strategies are found in the work of Foreman, Wilson, and some versions of performance art. Significantly, however, in experimental performance theater there occurs first the interregnum of the holy theater of the sixties, which, we will see, also reveals similarities to Beckett's authorial methods, even though it does not share his particular brooding vision.

But in both Beckett's work and the performance theater of second-generation performance groups, auteurs, and playwrights, such attempts to escape from the culturally coded system of language, to write the author and structures of meaning utterly out of the text, prove only partially successful at best: as Winnie says in *Happy Days,* "Something always remains." Whitaker maintains that we can accept Beckett's art as purely nonreferential "only if we exempt Beckett and ourselves from the condition that we say he is expressing. To write and to interpret his plays requires assumptions about the reliability of perception, the communicability of ideas, and the possibility of informed action that could apply to no condition in which we can connect nothing with nothing" (Whitaker 1986, 209–10). As Beckett and avant-garde theater artists become conscious of a prison house of language that effectively denies powerlessness, they reach a compromise that allows them to produce work utilizing strategies of both textuality and performance or (in Beckett's terms) of omnipotence and impotence.

If we are to understand how Beckett and other artists achieve this complementarity, we must allow them something of the so-called schizoid consciousness that has often been evoked in discussions of postmodern consciousness.[4] Or, we might simply say that their approach to theater recalls what Freud termed the compromise formation, which represents both the gratification of an illicit or impossible desire and the repression or constraint of that desire. For even if, as Whitaker says, the creation of a purely playful, absolutely open and nonreferential theater is impossible, theater history suggests that the desire to create one has been a potent force in various individuals and movements, such as in Dada, some forms of surrealism, and performance art. What we need to investigate, then, is not whether Beckett's work and avant-garde theater "are" referential or not, but why they continually try to *be* nonreferential and why they ultimately fail to achieve this level of impotence.

After all, the failure to appreciate significant similarities between Beckett's development as a playwright and certain tendencies in experimental theater stems mainly from an inability to approach the plays from perspectives that grant contradictory complexes of desire, such as the complementary aspirations for textual power and the breaking down of such power through performance. Early Beckett criticism, for example, to the lasting credit of its many commentators, highlighted so much of the author's omnipotence, his thematic and tropological richness, that it blinded readers to other, more radical possibilities. As Keir Elam notes, "the first duty of interpretive commentary is evidently to save the *sign* at all costs" (Elam 1986, 126). And by consistently emphasizing the metaphorical "meaning" of his plays, we have become—alarmingly, I think—quite comfortable thinking of Beckett as an absurdist, but essentially orthodox, playwright who works within a variable yet fairly local set of semiotic parameters. Early on (according to this view), Beckett realized the need for a new appropriate theatrical grammar, a congruent linguistic form and figuration that could function as the theatrical ideograph of his peculiar vision. Having discovered such a language in an amalgam of dance-hall theatricality, a mordantly cerebral wit, and the theatrical mode we now call minimalism, Beckett ostensibly succeeded in projecting, through a syntax of stripped-down and unexpected—but still conventional, still thoroughly "safe"—theatrical signifiers, an eccentric and ambiguous, yet still verifiable system of signs that, interpreted as a whole, express absurdist or darkly existentialist views of the world. Though discordant and initially a bit disarming (necessarily so, given this semiotic premise), these signs and the view of the world they express are nevertheless susceptible to taxonomy and critical interpretation, and they reveal a relationship between the author and his work and between the work and an external "world" that the work "represents," or "gives shape to," or "interprets." Thus, from this perspective, Beckett's work belongs altogether within an orthodox, relational, and text-centered tradition of drama that presupposes the semantic integrity of the sign and the author's omnipotent ability (and willingness) to render it.

Indeed, Beckett (or at least Beckett criticism) seems quite orthodox, in a relative, modernist sense, in the so-called absurdist plays: *Waiting for Godot, Endgame, Happy Days,* and others that maintain semblances of narrative, dialogue, verifiable characters, and so on. As Patrice Pavis points out, such a theater of the absurd "is a modernist (rather than postmodernist) manifestation, since its nonsense still makes sense and recalls an interpretation of the world" (Pavis 1986, 7).[5] And this means that by casting on such plays an informed hermeneutic gaze we can discover a range of emotional and intellectual affects, an absurdist "vision" or worldview signified metaphorically. "Performance" in these plays, in the sense of activities used to defer privileging determinate classes of interpretation or readings, is certainly evident but relatively limited, and it is ultimately reined in by the text.

However, more recent critics of Beckett's canon, though willing to grant some usefulness to this traditional approach in selected plays, are likely to place his work within the changing cultural milieu, and its altered understanding of the sign, that connects the last gasp of the modern to the first halting breaths of the postmodern. Critics using poststructuralist approaches to writing and language have argued convincingly that, especially in his last works, Beckett increasingly revealed a desire for a nonobjective art and that his method was motivated in part by an intent to *un*do the integrity of the sign.[6] Attempting to describe the manner in which Beckett works toward an art nearly empty of tropological figures and semantic relations, S. E. Gontarski has analyzed the playwright's compositional method in order to offer empirical proof of what has long been known about the plays, that is, that they are often contracted, diffuse, and fragmentary. But, in the same way that Nottebohm's *Beethoveniana* illuminated students about the composer's writing method, Gontarski's study also provides evidence of the processes by which Beckett's work arrives at this fractured state and, by extension, some notion of the aesthetic choices he makes en route. And it is in these choices that the initial similarity to experimental theater and performance can be found.

Gontarski describes Beckett's writing as a process-oriented activity of eliding, from fairly naturalistic (even melodramatic) pre-texts that he has prepared, certain objects, activities, and background information. Beckett's aim here is to "undo the realistic sources of the text, to undo the coherence of character and to undo the author's presence" (Gontarski 1985, 4). His unmaking of texts operates in a manner similar to the revision of the picture plane in Picasso, who once explained that "a picture used to be a sum of additions. In my case a picture is a sum of destructions. I do a picture—then I destroy it. In the end nothing is lost" (Goldwater 1945, 415).

Thus, Beckett's final performance texts, although meticulously crafted and "literary," do not always reveal a signifying system intended to illustrate or confirm coherent relationships between sign and signifiers; in other words, his texts do not always behave like conventional texts should. By creating a plurality of signifieds and by rejecting the traditional hierarchy of sign systems, Beckett refuses to reduce these systems to a fundamental signified, and thus he refuses to interpret. Denied the authoritative voice and rational semiotic arrangement of the text, the appeal of Beckett's work to the spectator must reside in the complex and unending interweaving, displacement, and interplay of signifiers—achieved in part through the transformational power of performance—rather than in their decoding. Firmly secure in his distaste for what he once called "the vulgarity of a plausible concatenation," Beckett designs strategies to subvert causality and cathexis when possible so as to defer and deconstruct an exact rendering of a determinate meaning or anticipated emotional response. For Beckett, the contours of words and other signifiers, the means of transforming narrative and other relationships in a play of shifting referents, and the "shape" as opposed to the referentiality of ideas are of primary interest.

Beckett's authorial and theatrical methods here—if not his dramatic intention—suggest resemblances to the work of early practitioners and theorists of experimental performance like Grotowski, Eugenio Barba, Richard Schechner, Peter Brook, Joseph Chaikin, and others. Like Beckett, these first-generation performance theater directors and the performance groups they collaborated with began to agitate against the orthodox dramatic text as the sacred and inseminating source of meaning and power toward which they must show absolute fidelity. And, like Beckett, these performers, groups, and directors were not beyond revising, eliding, and scissoring texts that had been constructed on that assumption of authorial omnipotence, though unlike Beckett they were usually eliding the work of other authors. In both cases, however, the result of such elision is the undermining of orthodox functions of plot, character development, linguistic referentiality, and so on, and the production of theater events that are not so much dramas as structures of play, rhythms of ritual emotion, or improvisational performances of unchained signifiers. This reveals that both Beckett and performance practitioners share a similar desire to deconstruct the orthodox dramatic text and the author's privileged status within the theater in order to discover some new power (for holy theater adepts) or powerlessness (for Beckett) within a new kind of performance text.

Thus, Beckett's "intent of undoing" in the early drafts of his own plays initially uncovers some unexpected connections to, say, the productions of Brook, Grotowski, and Schechner, who regularly revised and elided the determinate structures of certain classical texts (*A Midsummer Night's Dream, Macbeth,* Wyspianski's *Akropolis,* Marlowe's *Dr. Faustus, The Bacchae*) in order to neutralize their naturalistic bases and organic structures. For example, Brook and Schechner regularly cut scenes from existing texts, and rearranged others, in order to develop specific "rhythms of performance" that they chose to emphasize over the linear plot and integrated narrative of the original text. And when Grotowski began preparations for *Akropolis* he rearranged parts of Wyspianski's text so that by displacing the plot of the text he could create "the reality of the extermination camp . . . poetically, from allusions, short-cuts, and metaphors" (Osinski 1986, 67). Grotowski also, through obsessive repetition, "hammered out the phrases 'our Akropolis' and 'cemetery of the tribes,' which turned into catch words governing the organization of the production," another practice often used also by Schechner (Osinski 1986, 67). Grotowski's and Schechner's intent was to ascribe a quality of ritual to the performance and to imbue the language with the power of incantation.

These effects, derived from the (virtual) deconstruction of existing texts, define some of the most recognizable and unique mechanics of a typical Beckett play. For instance, Beckett's skeletal narrative structures usually hang together not by a causal, logical skein or through-line of action, but by ritual repetitions, essential spatial metaphors connoted through the mise-en-scène, Beckett's incantatory poetic language, and open-ended, allusive references. These spatial and linguistic elements merge but do not combine organically to form a stable dramatic action that conveys a determinate subtext to the spectator. Instead, like the performance directors above, Beckett creates a kind of "environmental space" that seeks an open-ended transaction with the spectator, who is invited to make connections, fill in the narrative gaps of the *troué* script, and otherwise actively engage Beckett's "undone" texts and their imposing pauses.[7]

Beckett also uses repetitive language and recursive plot structures to create a ritualized sense of language, time, space, and reality. The function of such transformed elements is of course for Beckett quite removed from that of holy theater, which sought to create a real sense of ritual time and sacred space within the context of performative acts. Beckett, on the other hand, in early plays like *Waiting for Godot* and *Endgame,* had broken up linear plot progression and blended it into recursive structures built on verbal and gestural repetitions mainly as a means to enact dramatically the entropy that burdens his characters as they devolve toward muteness. This tendency is exaggerated in later plays and the works for mime, until causal plotting and a sense of linear narrative momentum nearly disappear in the more austere and decentered formal structures that dominate pieces like the *Quadrats.* Increasingly, Beckett's recursions were directed toward enacting the game structures that he posits as a means of resisting stasis, for unchaining conventional signifieds, and for demythicizing the sustaining narratives of Western culture.[8]

Perhaps Beckett's work that most closely recalls the kind of elision and formal restructuring common to early holy theater is *Not I,* where the poetic quadrilateral ordering of the play by repetition of key phrases and ritualized gestures ("what? . . . who? . . . no! . . . she! . . . *pause and movement*") suggests significant resemblances between the nonnarrative structural principles used by Beckett and artists like Grotowski.[9] Even Grotowski's suggestion of an entropic rhythm in *Akropolis* (by virtue of the steadily completed crematorium) rather than an eternally recursive progression of the "plot" is present in Beckett's diminuendo of the Auditor's gesture: "It lessens with each recurrence till scarcely perceptible at third" (215).

In addition to breaking down remnants of naturalistic causality that might remain in the original texts and replacing them with ritual rhythms or cyclical structures, experimental theater artists of the sixties also tended to treat the mise-en-scène ahistorically and flexibly. Theatrical space was seldom used to invoke a specific place or time that would contribute to the illusion created within the text (here Grotowski's work is sometimes an exception), but would function instead as a performance environment capable of affecting audience interaction as well as the textures of light, sound, and movement within the performance itself. Little regard was paid to locating the performances within a space that foregrounded or complemented the specific chronological or spatial location of the "world" being represented in the text. Schechner, for one, regularly created his environments in the Performance Garage with the actor-spectator relationship uppermost in mind. In *Dionysus in 69*, for example, the terraced scaffolding, the drapery, and the light fixtures were designed not to invoke a specific locale or chronological frame, but to induce different spatial relationships between the actors and the spectators from one performance to the next. The emphasis here is not on reproducing or supplementing the mise-en-scène of the text, but rather on finding new interactive possibilities between actor and spectator during each performance.[10] And even though Grotowski often placed his works in somewhat more specific historical and spatial sites, he never allowed his pre-text to determine the nature of the mise-en-scène. The "rhythm" of *Akropolis,* in fact, is achieved just by the actual enactment of the building of the crematorium into which the performers eventually descend. In this case, the activity of the performers themselves creates the scene, and the process of performing that task determines the rhythm and experience—the "meaning"—of the performance.

Beckett's development of his trademark minimalist mise-en-scène reveals similarities to the stage designs of these first-generation performance directors. Like them, Beckett almost never situates his plays in an identifiable context of time and place. His severe response to JoAnne Akalaitis's 1984 production of *Endgame,* set in a bombed-out subway tunnel, indicates that for Beckett this atemporality of the setting is essential. To hazard references to time and place is to assume authorial power and interpretive omnipotence over a solid, given reality; further, it might distract spectators from the essential transformations of shapes, textures, and rhythm that are created by language, light, shadow, subtle gesture, and the movements or activities—however restrained, however minimal—of the performers within their urns, or rocking chairs, or mounds of dirt.

Numerous other parallels exist between Beckett's deconstructions of the text by performance and those initiated in early alternative theater. Beckett's use of dramatic language, that weird negative rhetoric of anaphoric and synecdochical enunciation that sometimes seems to obliterate and recreate the function of the sign entirely, has certain connections to alternative theater's attempts to create pseudo-languages that would operate, in Artaud's words, "half way between gesture and thought." Avant-garde performance theorists and directors of the sixties tried to follow the recommendation made in *The Theater and Its Double* "to make language express what it does not ordinarily express . . . to reveal its possibilities for producing physical shock . . . to deal in intonations in an absolutely concrete manner, restoring their power to shatter as well as really to manifest something; to turn against language and its basely utilitarian, one could say alimentary, sources" (Artaud 1958, 46).[11] Many experimental productions were based on this search for a new performance language absolved of its affiliation to referential speech and the pathological rationale of the power structures that controlled it. There are as examples Andre Serban's attempts to discover a "life in sound" by staging *Medea* in a mixture of Latin and Greek, or the eponymic Orghast-tongue invented for Peter Brooks's performance, as well as the exaltation of primal emotions enunciated by the chants and howls of The Living Theater.

All of these verbal experiments have been approximated at some point in Beckett's work, from the physical shock of mere suspiration in *Breath,* to the tessellated and overlapping speeches in *Play,* to the "three very different sounds" that echo in *Come and Go*. In addition, though heroic attempts have been made, no avant-garde director or performer has surpassed Beckett's ability to dramatize the refusal of the gesture of language itself. The performance collectives and directors of the sixties based their rejection of discursive language on extrinsic sources—a political agenda, a psychological or sociological theory, a desire for transcendence. Freedom from language meant freedom from a power (political and/or psychological) they abhorred, and one that they had never themselves exercised: and so there was little evidence that they could acknowledge what was sacrificed for an ecstasy and liberation simply proclaimed by fiat. Beckett, on the other hand, was by his denial of language disempowering the very activity that rendered his theater substantial. As Kalb points out, "You have to be quite a writer before your refusal to write can be received as a statement in itself" (Kalb 1989, 160).

Grotowski, perhaps understanding most sympathetically, along with Beckett, Artaud's pleas for a gestural language, responded to this challenge to generate a nonrational language by creating in his productions a form of *Sprechstimme* or incantation built on what Jan Kott describes as "a trans-accentuation foreign to Polish metrics, and the splitting of words into segments in order to restore 'metaphysical' shocks by sound alone" (Kott 1980, 29). In somewhat the same way Beckett will often create similarly unnatural cadences and broken speech patterns to impose what Elam calls "quasi-musical structure[s]" that "*materialize* the speech continuum and thus . . . foreground the *phōne* itself as stage 'presence'" (Elam 1986, 139–40).[12] In these examples, language is rendered as a pure phenomenological gesture that virtually enacts the loss of a syntactical expression of a dismembered reality, and as the penitent act of gathering fragments to shore against the ruins.

These and other practices, sometimes pioneered by Beckett and in other instances shared between his work and experimental theater, are apparent throughout Beckett's canon. The use of ritual structures and repetitive performance rhythms is discovered in early works—the slow unwrapping of Hamm in *Endgame* (distended to a full fifteen minutes in the famous Herbert Blau production), May's haunting tread in *Footfalls,* and the agonizingly precise verbal overlaps of the sharply lit figures in *Play*. More aleatoric structures, similar to those advocated by John Cage and avant-garde performance directors like Michael Kirby, can be found in Beckett's prose work *Lessness* (adapted for performance on the BBC), which in the permutations of its events and dialogue offers literally hundreds of possible performance combinations. In addition, the presentation of disorienting repetitions and distentions of space and time to promote the sensation of duration and to make the theatrical moment "presently present" (to crib Gertrude Stein's phrase), soon to be popular in works by Wilson and Foreman, is anticipated by the collapsing of time in *Breath* and its doubling up, by way of the tape recorder, in *Krapp's Last Tape*.

Finally, the incredible discipline and physical presence required of the actors in *That Time, Play,* and especially *Not I* set a standard for the "affective athleticism" that Artaud prescribes and which eventually becomes a mainstay in the acting theories and performances of Grotowski, Schechner, and a host of other directors and performers.[13] This increased emphasis on the body (or, in Beckett, its *disjecta membra*), and on the *via negativa* of its repression or constraint as an expressive medium to invent new repertories of physical expression, is designed by both Beckett and avant-garde artists to give testimony to what one otherwise might not find a way to transmit. In addition, as Kalb points out, Beckett's habit is to "make the actor's denuding a part of his subject matter" (Kalb 1989, 146), a sometimes agonizing strategy that, when stripped of the spiritualism inherent in Grotowski's formulation, echoes the Polish director's process of "self-penetration" upon which his own acting theory is built.

Still, this is not to say that the works produced by Beckett and early, first-generation performance collaboratives were altogether similar. Important distinctions must be drawn regarding the function of such practices in the actual theatrical event. The use of these kinds of performance strategies in alternative theater, for instance, served a variety of purposes, but a common denominator among them is their function as the kind of psychospiritual therapy characteristic of much avant-garde theater of the sixties. For advocates of holy theater, the intent to undo the closure of textuality satisfies a social and often a utopian thrust, a yearning for the breakdown of rational structures of thought and feeling and for the revelation of new worlds or transcendent signs based on holistic relationships discovered in the act of performance itself, where a true, "total" act takes place in the body. Such views are predicated on beliefs in absolutes or transcendental signifieds that, once discovered, can reveal new languages and organic systems to be realized within the individual, and which might even be projected into the world to promote positive changes in consciousness, politics, faith, intercultural exchange, and so on (hence this period's flirtation with theater therapy, guerilla theater, holy theater, and ethnopoesis).

For Beckett, to whom the world discloses itself as a purgatory in which "the only Absolute is the absolute absence of the Absolute," no such belief in the capacity to rediscover such lost origins and sources exists: the trail to his Limbo crosses over Lethe. But this does not negate the similar attempts in his work to overcome the closure of textuality. Beckett shares with these experimental theater artists a belief that violating the constraints of the orthodox dramatic text by using various performance strategies will allow him the freedom to express something that cannot be expressed through the structures offered by traditional textuality. His rejection of absolutes and his search for a true artistic "impotence" suggest, however, that Beckett's reasons for deconstructing textuality represent a desire quite unlike that of, say, Grotowski, and are closer in spirit to those inscribed within poststructuralist theory. For instead of deconstructing the authorially empowered text simply to recreate Presence from the enlightened perspective of the director or collective, and thereby enable it as a spiritual catalyst, Beckett desires to escape the process of empowerment completely.

We must remember, of course, that such an agenda does not appear to be Beckett's focus in all his plays; despite what seems to be a remarkable integrity of style and content throughout his work, Beckett has altered slightly, if not the vision itself, at least the vision's relation to the external world. In the fifties, as I have suggested, Beckett and other absurdist playwrights radicalized certain elements of the dramatic text, like referential language, consistent character psychology and development, causal narrative structure, and so on. However, the absurdists did so not to undermine the text but to recreate it in order to present the experience of what Derrida calls, in his essay "Structure, Sign, and Play in the Human Sciences," the "structuralist thematic of broken immediacy" and its vision of retrospection, despair, and guilt (Derrida 1978, 292). As Esslin described the agenda, "the Theater of the Absurd has renounced arguing *about* the absurdity of the human condition; it merely *presents* it in being—that is, in terms of concrete stage images" (Esslin [1961] 1969, 6). That expression of absurdity was still presumably the potent expression of an interpretation of the world. The fact that the perception was predicated on disorienting premises did little to deconstruct its theatrical evocation and interpretation of a world existing outside the text.

But how does one approach Beckett's postabsurdist plays—especially the later austere "dramaticules"—in which semantic disintegration is nearly complete and the expressive investment in the sign all but empty; plays, that is, that emphasize not Beckett's interpretation of the world, but his impotence and unwillingness or inability to interpret at all? Such plays reveal many of the most crucial differences between modernist and contemporary theater, for what lies at the heart of the matter is what Blau (elucidating Derrida) refers to as "the irreducible differences" between the structuralist thematic and "'the *seminal* adventure of the trace,' in which Beckett is engaged, but 'which is no longer turned toward the origin' as it maintains the notion of 'full presence, the reassuring foundation, the origin, and the end of play'" (Blau 1987, 69). Beckett's engagement with the poststructuralist adventure therefore anticipates movements in second-generation experimental theater away from the holy-theater alternatives of the sixties and early seventies and toward the nonobjective and deconstructive spectacles of Robert Wilson, Richard Foreman, John Jesurun, The Wooster Group, Michael Kirby, and a variety of other directors and performance artists. And once again, Beckett's work is both paradigmatic of the shift and instructive of its implications.

Both Beckett's later work and deconstructive theory are characterized by an acknowledgment of and a search for powerlessness. As Frank Lentricchia (1983, 51) puts it—explicating the postmodern in Beckett's own words—"deconstruction . . . teaches the many ways to say that there is nothing to be done." Beckett implied this early on with his comments on finding an artistic impotence—as opposed to Joycean "omnipotence"—in the face of his material. The kinds of textual deconstructions already mentioned form his initial response to the problem, but do not produce a sufficiently powerless and deconstructive art. As Beckett continues to explore new ground, he moves away from the early absurdist works and toward increasingly abstract and rigidly formalized spectacles. His intent to undo the sign and textuality assumes greater importance, and as a result the plays become less relational, less directed toward textual omnipotence, and more oriented toward deconstructive performance and its consequent powerlessness.

In order to accommodate the critical mess that Beckett creates through these works, recent criticism has turned to poststructuralist theories of language and textuality. From these perspectives, we discover that Beckett's plays—even plays already analyzed by the sign-bound interpretive community—reveal desires for a "nonrelational art" (Dearlove 1982), for an "intent of undoing" (Gontarski 1985), for a dramaturgy built around negative rhetorical figures of synecdoche and litotes rather than the more generative tropes of metaphor (Elam 1986), and, finally, for a deconstructive dramaturgy so corrosive that it subverts even the poststructuralist panaceas of play and performance (Blau 1987). In other words, there is a growing consensus that Beckett's plays may be "about" the very process of not being about anything. As James Knowlson says in the conclusion to his analysis of the manuscript notes for Beckett's own production of *Geister Trio,* "if I have understood [the play] correctly, the 'meaning' is itself the undefinable, the absent center" (Knowlson 1986, 205). The absence of a fixed locus of relations and meanings forces the spectator to find relative perspectives among the formal elements of the performance and their arrangements in the work. To find meaning, the spectator must exercise not the kind of hermeneutic gaze we usually direct toward a conventional text, but literally the Berkleyean/Beckettian *esse est percepi* that we authorize when we experience a performance.

This relativistic, multiperspectival dramaturgy inhabits all of Beckett's postabsurdist work, but only becomes a force in experimental theater in the later seventies. For advocates of performance during the sixties, as I have mentioned, the liberation from the text promised an escape from a sense of "broken immediacy" and the sadness and guilt it evokes. In this early stage of experimental theater, a return to the ritual and primitive sources of theater is desired. This, in turn, would lead to the rediscovery of a method for healing the painful breaches—revealed most vividly by the absurdists—between spirit and flesh, word and object, art and life. But such a strictly utopian function of play in performance theater is mainly restricted to the sixties and early seventies, before political agendas took a conservative turn and a growing critical revision of experimental theater placed the pretensions of performance under close scrutiny for the first time. These and other pressures caused an important shift in the direction of performance theater for the next decade, a shift already assimilated in Beckett's work.

These second-generation performance works of the seventies, informed by the failure of earlier attempts to effect the kinds of changes in society and individual/communal consciousness its practitioners had envisioned, and influenced somewhat more directly by currents in poststructuralist literary theory, are characterized by a more sophisticated conceptual grounding and the loss of any recognizable political agenda. Such experimental theater usually takes the form of a cool formalism that, for all its conceptual polish, lacks the raw social commitment of earlier work. In fact, the new emphasis on conceptual sophistication and formal complexity is likely related to the consequent political lassitude, for these works—early pieces by Wilson, Foreman, Mabou Mines and The Wooster Group, Meredith Monk, Laurie Anderson, and others—are denied much social or political commitment by their adherence to an essentially ahistorical and apolitical poststructuralist thematic. As Philip Auslander notes, "the deconstructive modality of much current experimental theater is inherently antithetical to meaningful political praxis. Deconstruction and apoliticality are often linked . . . [and] deconstruction is seen as a characteristically postmodern aesthetic strategy, apoliticality as either a cause or a symptom of the deconstructive aesthetic" (Auslander 1987, 22).

This deconstructionist conceptual framework differs from the predicates of earlier performance theory in that it is resigned to poststructuralist linguistic skepticism and to the consequent dissolution of that "structuralist immediacy" of which Derrida speaks, which is diffused into the disseminated indeterminacies of the trace. Thus, instead of functioning to reflect the sense of guilt at the loss of origins and meaning (as in late modernist playwrights like the absurdists), or to regain such sources (as in experimental theater of the sixties: *Paradise, Now!*), performance theater in the seventies tends toward an affirmation of play and deferral. In a world created by a language that itself exists without origin or immediacy and is always reconstituted, deconstructive play displaces the text and substitutes its dispersal of signs for the determinacies of the text.

Experimental theater events of the period approach this new concept of play in different ways, but they share to an extent a dramaturgy that, unlike Beckett's, confirms performance and play as the standard response to the pluralism inherent in the "postmodern condition." Richard Foreman's works for his Ontological-Hysteric Theater, for instance, move toward creating what he terms a "totally polyphonic theater," in which "all elements work to fragment each other so that the spectator is relatively free from empathy and identification and instead may savor the full 'playfulness' of theatrical elements . . . [M]y goal has always been to transcend very 'painful' material with the dance of manic theatricality" (Foreman 1985, 112). Robert Wilson's image-operas are equally fragmentary and disjunct, based as they are at times on the thought patterns and arrangement of space/time continua and images suggested by an autistic actor in his company. The repetitions of music, speech, gesture, and imagery in these pieces lead the spectator to forfeit any verbal, intellectual, or discursive analysis and to concentrate instead on the rhythms of the performance itself and the phenomenological processes of perceiving it. As Stefan Brecht describes it, the works

> can not be construed as the making of a statement: there is, for the maker, no question of truth or plausibility; . . . there is, for the maker, no question of meaning. The maker's intent is not to induce pity, terror, or hilarity . . . nor to induce [the spectator] to change society or to give him (or her) information useful to this, but to impart the vision and a sense of its importance and significance. (Brecht 1978, 9)

In the work of these and other artists (and this includes, with some important reservations, Beckett), play replaces the old *dynamis* of textual determinacy, and acts instead to foster impotence, powerlessness, a refusal of authorial power and its release toward the spectator. At its best, such theater offers tantalizing visions of new gestalten and perceptual modes; but even here the nagging suspicion remains that the perceptions might, like New Age synthesized music, only induce atmosphere without substance, an unchanging and utterly passive ether in which the spectatorial subject floats freely. When this is the case, the theatrical event becomes literally (and nothing more than) diverting. Similar states can be evoked by Beckett's plays as well (as anyone who has tried to sit through a triple bill can attest), when the recursive torsions of verbal play can become, virtually, interminable.

But in the extremely abstract experimental theater of the period, these gratuitous elongations of verbal, gestural, and imagistic play (virtually enacted in Wilson's monstrously lengthy works) are intended not, as in Beckett, to attest to an agonizing logorrhea, but to create a seemingly perpetual present. And this suggests a certain connection to performance practices and theory of the previous generation, in that such a notion of play carries on the desire of early performance theater to find a means to sacramentalize the present and thereby negate representation entirely. Play generates recursive structures in which images and activities recur but do not *reoccur,* where nothing is repeated and everything is therefore presented, not re-presented. Such structures promise an end to reproduction altogether, which means that all time is hypostatized and made presently present. Play thus motivates an unrestricted flow of desire unmediated by any closure or restraint, and this flow presumably acts to relieve the burdens of self-consciousness by breaking the circle of representation and reflection. All too often, however, this occurs in the performer but not the spectator; and when the work of lesser artists cannot attain even that self-reflexive and transcendent state, it too often devolves simply into a didactic enactment of deconstructionist theory. Too, in the dazzling but essentially dehumanizing torrent of disorienting images and deconstructions that follow, there lurks the danger of an abrogation of history. Because the tendency is toward the momentary rather than the momentous, it creates an aptitude, says Blau, "for what's happening now, rather than in a time-bound, causal remembrance of experience, with a plotted afterlife" (Blau 1982b, 260). The fear is that, neglecting to plot the afterlife of the felt or perceived moment, we liberate ourselves not only from the burdens of history and consciousness, but also from the very construction of history through the *activity* of consciousness.

Even though Beckett is fond of using game structures and strategies of play in his narratives and dramatic texts, their function is radically different from that of performance theater's. He never falls prey to the lure of performance and play as therapy or as the appropriate response to the burdens of postmodern consciousness. Instead, Beckett utilizes performance to undermine play's attributes, to expose its own margins. His plays subvert the postmodern panaceas of choice by exposing play and deferral as a naive, impossible, and eventually agonizing praxis: As Hamm says, "Use your head, can't you, use your head, you're on earth, there's no cure for that!" In every painful play of language, for instance, Beckett dramatizes both the openness and the impedance of words, creating a voice that constantly revises itself and seeks a re-vision of the world around it. According to Bert O. States, this voice is "helplessly haunted by its images but it cannot help refining them, as they occur, as if it were seeking some entelechial form in which they might all come to rest" (States 1988, 459). That such quests for entelechial expression through language are always already doomed to fail might for others release the libidinal ecstasy of indeterminacy, but in Beckett's case the repetitions and revisions only endow the voice with a heavily lyric or elegiac tone.

Similarly, on a larger formal level, Beckett's game structures and strategies of playful recursiveness do not produce the kinds of aporia that lead to feelings of open-ended pleasure. Instead they testify to the margins of play by returning over and over to the play within the play, "which," Blau soberly states, "causes us to remember that play, agitated and multicolored by the phenomena of *its* hours, is inevitably deadly," or amortized (Blau 1987, 70). Even as we playfully curve back upon previous words, actions, objects, and gestures, even as we "repeat play," Beckett forces us to reflect upon and feel the tremendous energy lost entropically in the ordeal. Thus what for a postmodernist might be liberating in play is for Beckett the painful exercise of power and work.

Yet it is important to remember that such leakage of energy in Beckett's plays need not—possibly cannot—end in absolute powerlessness and despair, a playful but downward slide toward disorganization. "I know now, all that was just . . . play," intones M, but the pun interrogates the premise of play, asking if it does not contain in its own processes its own justification.[14] Play, Beckett suggests, ultimately functions as a "just" refusal of powerlessness and chaos because, despite its painful exertions, it remains a source of momentum. "The universe is randomness and dissipation, yes" says James Gleick. "But randomness with direction can produce surprising complexity. . . . [D]issipation is an agent of order" (Gleick 1987, 314). In the so-called Brussels school of thermodynamics, Ilya Prigogine and others have detected fluctuation in even the most closed systems, and have located moments of "bifurcation" or singularity that anticipate a revolutionary change in a given system toward either chaos or higher levels of order in dissipative structures (that is, structures that require more energy to sustain them). Since it is inherently impossible to determine in advance which path the system will take, observers must be content to let chance prevail, to let momentum be steered in an uncertain course, and to be satisfied that disorder is only one possible result. Order may lead to chaos, but chaos might just as well determine a new shape of order. In this sense, chaos is generative of new order and an essential aspect of nature itself. Similarly, in human consciousness the attenuation of the drive for entelechial forms need not necessarily signal entropy and decline: as Cage remarked in *Silence* (1961, 195), the mind's greatest capacity "is that it can turn its own tables and see meaninglessness as ultimate meaning."

Beckett's plays posit, like such quantum relations, a world in which humans—as subjects, rather than observers, of the indeterminate dynamics—do not control their direction, but are responsible for providing the energy for their own momentum. The search for Presence (truth, a sense of self) confirms the only "just" exercise of power in a world inherently unstable and indeterminate. The quest is doomed to fail, of course, but to cultivate a will to powerlessness is seemingly as impossible as it is impracticable. For Beckett, life and consciousness are determined by both the desire for indeterminacy, play, and deferral of absolute meaning on the one hand, and the exercise of power, the seeking of closure and the absolutes, on the other. Each necessitates the existence of the other, and it is only in the unending, dynamic interaction between the irreconcilable desires that life is fully lived. Beckett's plays enact a process by which the self enjoins existence as a play of contradictions that, as Nietzsche maintains in the myth of eternal recurrence, exists as "a becoming that knows no satiety, no disgust, no weariness."

This dynamic extends beyond the plight of Beckett's actors, implicating the spectator as well. Since the world we construct, rather than perceive, is fabricated in the playful interaction between subject and object, then a theater that recreates that complementary epistemology reconstitutes the nature of spectatorship. We are seldom allowed, in Beckett's theater, to feel comfortable exercising solely our desires for closure and interpretation *or* our preferences for play and deferral. When we exert the former, we find ourselves implicated in the characters' search for authenticity and self-affirmed being, and face their interrogation of that premise: "Am I as much as . . . being seen?" asks M in *Play*, interrogating both the spectator and the conventional *theatron* itself, the identity of both of which is staked on a stable view of self and world (157). Should we rather attempt to lose ourselves in the play of interpretation and the dance of signifiers, however, we confront and are chastised by the spectacle of these same characters as they enact the penitent gestures that define their only attempt at grace: "*W1*: 'Is it that I do not tell the truth, is that it, that some day somehow I may tell the truth at last and then no more light at last, for the truth?'" (153) Beckett demands that the spectator's reading strategies and emotions partake of the same interactive dynamic between text and performance, power and powerlessness, that determines the content of the plays.

In Beckett's work, then, even the negative exertion of impotence, powerlessness, and play finally generates sufficient kinesis to ensure an exercise of power. Any expenditure of work, of course, is bound by the second law of thermodynamics to result in entropy, a leaching of energy into dissipation. But in Beckett's theater, the dissipation can itself be the herald of new order, a moment of eventual bifurcation and possible transformation. Ultimately, then, absolute powerlessness is as illusory as absolute power, and, it seems, equally corrupting.

So at the point where play and performance reach their margins, their writing degree zero, Beckett's attempt to reach for powerlessness falls back to earth. Although his search for a completely nonauthoritarian, nonreferential art appears to be a sincere and devoted one, Beckett discovers that even utilizing the free structures of performance and play as a means of deferring determinate reference and meaning is never wholly successful. His strategies of textual undoing are, says Gontarski, "multiple, varied, even contradictory, and finally unsuccessful" (Gontarski 1985, 21). Beckett is trapped not only by linguistic conventions of referentiality and the spectator's natural urge for order and interpretation, but also by culture coded forms of literature and their reading strategies as well; he is "unable to slough off his literary past . . . as easily as he would like. As much as Beckett might resist the notion, he finds himself already written into the text of Western literature" (1985, xiv). The attempt to subvert authorial power utterly, then, is fruitless, as even "the erasure of authorial presence creates an authorial presence erasing" (1985, 17).

We see here the paradox in Beckett's work, one that is shared by performance theater artists whose agendas include similar attempts to escape entirely from textuality. While the intent is to transgress and undo the text in order to move toward the pure, unmediated and unmediating expression of play, of "performance," there is a countercurrent to this refusal of power: the artist's struggle to accommodate the mess by imposing order upon it. The struggle is thus between gratifying the desire for pure play and powerlessness, and the suppression of that desire by the imposition of order and authorial omnipotence. This rage for order was nowhere more in evidence than in Beckett's other roles as director and copyright-protected executor of his works, where he consistently showed a tendency to control as much as possible all elements of production and text dispersal. Gerald Rabkin has shown how the Beckett-Brustein brouhaha over the American Repertory Theater's production of *Endgame* brought the paradox out of Beckett's psychic closet and into the courts.[15]

Even here, in Beckett's contradictory pattern of conflicting desires, his response stands as something of a reflection of the process by which performance theater attempts to free itself from the text and then is pulled ineluctably back toward it. Beckett's is, Gontarski concludes, an "aesthetics of compromise," and this again suggests connections to the Freudian compromise formation, as well as to the complementary double-coding between text and performance that we will discover in other examples of contemporary theater.

The working out of this formation achieves, in Beckett's later work, a kind of ambivalent response to the conflict between authorial control and performative openness, power and powerlessness. Instead of trying to create a completely nonrelational, nontextual art, Beckett is satisfied to commingle elements of traditional textuality with more subversive performance strategies; and the result is an ironic and complementary, rather than dominant or hierarchical, relationship between the two. His strategy here looks less like a modernist attempt to transgress textuality than it does a poststructuralist desire to resist the text's closure by deconstructing it in order to reinscribe representation as a critique of its own practices. (A disorienting, but hardly new, strategy for a cricket aficionado whose ability to bowl "googlies" [that is, balls bowled to swerve one way but break the other] once caught the appreciative eye of Harold Hobson.) The result of the strategy, as Dearlove notes, is that Beckett can "accept both the impossibility of a nonrelational art and the improbability of a relational one, and in doing so he finds yet another shape for the ambiguity, fluidity, and uncertainty of the human condition" (Dearlove 1982, 14).

For Beckett, the compromise is realized first not in his plays but in the narratives, where as early as *Enough* (1966) he appears to move toward a more comfortable acceptance of objects and speech, and the possibility of hazarding a more emotional, referential, and human-centered prose. These changes emerge more slowly and diffusely in the dramas, though in a play like *Rockaby* (1981) there is heard a voice that speaks, as States says, in "the language one speaks in the Beckett world in order to make such sense as there is" (States 1988, 459). But without trying to put too specific a location on what is surely a subtle and shifting change, it seems that in *Ohio Impromptu* (1981), where the very language expressing the loss of a text at a point when "nothing is left to tell" articulates the fullness of human presence, Beckett has clearly realized a reconciliation between relational and nonrelational elements, between power and powerlessness. In plays such as these, Beckett appears to be more comfortable again expressing an interpretation of reality, of exercising authorial judgment on the world—even if only to suggest that to "fuck life," or to announce that "the sad tale [is] a last time told," is to exert some power over existence and language. Skeptical of the early postmodernist urge to escape into the endless dispersals of performance, Beckett is satisfied to create work that, as the poet Robert Hass writes, is "curiously shaped," yet unable to avoid imposing its own strange form and order upon "every / thing touched casually. . . . all things lustered / by the steady thoughtlessness / of human use" ("Songs to Survive in the Summer").

We must, however, be wary of assigning any specific chronology to such changes in Beckett's approach. Certainly we find no fixed point at which Beckett "turns away" from his search for a decentered universe and returns to a comfortably relational world. *Quad,* surely one of Beckett's most abstract and unchained theatrical maneuvers, was first transmitted in 1982 (pub. 1984), suggesting that the incapacity to assume a stable center was still very much on his mind and in his work. Evidence indicates, however, that Beckett was becoming increasingly self-conscious about his own double-coding of abstract performance and historically contextualized drama in his last works. *Catastrophe* (1982), dedicated to the then-imprisoned Czech playwright Vaclav Havel, develops a seriocomic irony between a Director who attempts to create a theater-of-images stage tableau (to be called "catastrophe") by objectifying and disciplining the body of his Protagonist, and the Protagonist himself, whose last baleful gaze at the audience mortifies the storm of applause that follows his abstract "performance." The Assistant's suggestions for some relational context between the politically charged theme of catastrophe and the absolutely apolitical mise-en-scène ("[*Timidly.*] What about a little . . . a little . . . gag?") enrage the Beckett-like Director, who obviously prefers the indeterminacy and suspension of logocentric interpretation to such transparent symbolic closure ("For God's sake! This craze for explicitation! Every i dotted to death! Little gag! For God's sake!").[16] Beckett's own relationship to abstract, open-ended, and otherworldly performance is thus questioned, indicating his acutely conscious awareness for the necessity of textuality and its commitment to the fields of human presence, memory, history, and culture.

Beckett's response to the terminus created by the contradictions between the closure and artificiality of the text and the dispersed, deconstructive nature of performance provides a useful analogy to the initial development of experimental performance theater, its discovery of the ultimate margins of play, and new alternative directions for such avant-garde art. Just as Beckett struggles with contradictory desires for both kinds of expression, so too directors and performance groups have split from orthodox, text-centered drama in order to give free play to what that drama traditionally suppresses, that is, play and performance. And, just as Beckett discovers a pentimento of desire for control and clarity beneath an antithetical desire for powerlessness and opacity, so too many practitioners of avant-garde performance have recently turned to layering both textual and performative strategies within their work. Grown wary of the unchallenged acceptance of play and performance as the single privileged conceptual approach to the problems of postmodern consciousness, these artists have begun to bring theater back into a more recognizably human context by reviving a radicalized text. And again, when they arrived at this juncture there was Beckett, already behind, yet always before them.

The Wooster Group, *Nayatt School.*
Directed by Elizabeth LeCompte, Performance Garage, 1978.

Chapter 3

The Fractal Dimensions of a Fractious Culture: The Wooster Group and the Politics of Performance

Our feeling for beauty is inspired by the harmonious arrangement of order and disorder as it occurs in natural objects—in clouds, trees, mountain ranges, or snow crystals. The shape of all these are dynamical processes jelled into physical forms, and particular combinations of order and disorder are typical for them.

—Gert Eilenberger, superconductivity physicist

Is it possible that mathematical pathology, i.e. chaos, is health? And that mathematical health, which is the predictability and differentiability of this kind of structure, is disease?

—Arnold Mandel, psychiatrist and dynamicist

"You must paint them to tame them," said Paul Cézanne, explaining why he had moved away from earlier, purely impressionist styles toward the more solid and classical work of his postimpressionist period. Elizabeth LeCompte, current director of The Wooster Group, is fond of drawing parallels between her own work and that of the painter, remarking once that "he doesn't finish a line. He leaves the canvas showing here and there. It gives a space and an air; it doesn't solidify it into a form that's not breakable. I can't stand it when something becomes perfect, enclosed. I like to leave the system open" (Aronson 1985, 352). The aesthetic reflects an acute awareness of the shape of reality as it is currently being reconfigured by artists and scientists, where recognition of the disorderliness, indeterminacy, and processual nature of the universe has become common knowledge.

Still, for all its emphasis on openness, LeCompte's aesthetic is in its way as double-coded as Beckett's. Even as she evolves pieces that exhibit a space and air that do not "solidify" into fixed dramatic form, her work shows an increasing awareness of the need or desire to impose some lines and to fill in her stage canvases. Like Cézanne, LeCompte reveals a poignant awareness that the old tonal coherence of traditional art has been irretrievably lost. She would agree with the playwright Heiner Müller that "fragments have a special value today, because all the coherent stories we used to tell ourselves to make sense of life have collapsed" (Holmberg 1990, 60). Instead of simply paying nostalgic tribute to the old dreams of literary drama and its theological stage, however, and rather than abandoning it and representation entirely, The Group has embarked on a quest to find new and viable forms. "We must do Poussin over again, this time according to nature," announced Cézanne: we might say that LeCompte stands in the same relationship to her own literary progenitors, O'Neill, Miller, and (especially) Wilder.

In doing over the essential shape of American drama according to the nature of its subject, The Wooster Group also reshapes our notions of performance and textuality. LeCompte explores an aesthetic based upon a rejection of Euclidean order and measurement of the type we see in the classic text—and by extension of that world over which humans exerted control as both absolute measure and measurer—and instead investigates qualities of dimension and texture. She follows in the line of several contemporary artists, including Beckett, but her real allegiance seems rather to contemporary science and its mind-numbingly conceptual explanations of reality. Sometimes attempts to expose these similarities are reductive: the initial reaction to her work by many spectators and critics is simply to equate it with the notions of relativity and indeterminacy that are the staple of much twentieth-century art. The Group's work, it is often remarked, has "no fixed meaning," no "privileged discourses" or single principle for ordering thematic material. True enough, but to see The Group's performances from only these perspectives is to deny the real complexity of its work.

LeCompte, like Cézanne, is a geometer of reality, but she represents a new breed of that science. Classical, Euclidean geometry builds itself around certain abstractions of reality—triangles, spheres, various polyhedra—that are endowed with a great deal of intrinsic value by an *épistémè* stressing harmony, balance, and proportion. Such shapes have been naturalized in Western culture to the extent that they are often accepted as Plato's "essential Forms of Goodness." Yet contemporary scientists studying dynamic systems that reveal disequilibrium and disorder—in everything ranging from mathematical intervals like those found in the Cantor dust to economic distribution, the movement of the Great Red Spot of Jupiter, noise-bursts in telecommunication, the dynamics of population biology—have discovered that Euclidean geometry is the wrong kind of abstraction for understanding complex and nonlinear systems. Until very recently, however, no alternative existed. An entirely new geometry was needed, one that could, according to one scientist, "mirror a universe that is rough, not rounded, scabrous, not smooth. . . . a geometry of the pitted, pocked, and broken up, the twisted, tangled and intertwined" (Gleick 1987, 94).

This pied universe is predicated on a startling assumption, which LeCompte shares with Benoit Mandelbrot, the mathematician who first staked its claim by giving it a visual language: that is, that these odd, irregular shapes may contain the essence of a thing's shape and definition. Recognizing that Euclidean geometry failed to measure accurately any irregular shape, or to render mathematically the peculiar quality of that shape, Mandelbrot devised in 1975 a new tool for gauging objects and qualities that have no regular or periodic definition. Called "fractal geometry," the new calculations made it possible to claim that discontinuity in nature remains constant over different scales; that is, that irregularity can itself be periodic, regular. The often absurd, playful shapes generated by Mandelbrot's geometry—sponges, curds, gaskets, sheets—can open up new pictures of complexity and irregularity, and reveal startling new methods for looking at the hidden orders contained in even the most scabrous physical systems. Mandelbrot's fractal shapes destroy the single sense of scale inherent in conventional geometric solids, and replace it with an appreciation for multidimensional scale and texture. Often they uncover on a very small scale the manner by which large-scale objects are joined or separated, or by which seemingly orderly systems shatter into nonlinear or chaotic forms. Scientists using Mandelbrot's fractal dimensions, in addition to discovering the shapes of chaos, have further suggested that a great deal of the real world seems as likely to be verging on chaos and disequilibrium as it is to be converging on order.

The turbulent mirror held up to reality by such a dynamic geometry reflects the essential qualities of LeCompte's aesthetic, which, like Beckett's and that of other artists to be covered, is constructed within the nonequilibrious, interactive relationship between text and performance.

In LeCompte's fractal theater, systems of order or "solidity"—often conceived as well-shaped, Euclidean texts—transform suddenly into strange fractal shapes that indicate that within such a seemingly orderly system exists an inherent turbulence or nonperiodicity. The reagent of this transformation in LeCompte's work is usually performance, which acts to decenter the dramatic text and to reveal on a microscopic scale its rough edges and internal irregularities.

The exposure of the text's nonlinearity, however, is not simply destructive, but actually fruitful for several reasons. First, the breakdown of order or textuality allows The Group to expose and explore features of history, reading, and culture, and of textuality itself, that might otherwise be naturalized or suppressed by the neatly joined hierarchical discourses of the hegemonic text. In addition, chaotic or nonlinear systems—those rough-edged realities defined and imaged forth by fractal geometry—refuse by their nature the simple, linear equations and closure of Newtonian science. Friction, for instance, cannot be reduced to a linear equation because it depends on speed, which is itself dependent on friction: neither can remain a constant. As John Von Neumann remarked ruefully when confronted with such inconstancy in the Navier-Stokes fluid equation, "The character of the equation . . . changes simultaneously in all relevant respects: Both order and degree change. Hence, bad mathematical difficulties must be expected" (Gleick 1987, 24).

In the same way, The Group's disposition of textuality and performance in its work never follows a linear pattern, and never allows one paradigm to dominate or absorb the other. It is never a matter of thematically privileging performance over drama by displacing the text, or of discovering a neat or stable synthesis between them. Rather, the interanimative fields between the paradigms and their corollaries—different modes of reading, of narrating subjectivity and history, of determining dominant discourses—are left to generate and deconstruct events at an imposing pace, and to reveal by that process the scabrous and mutable shape of contemporary culture. One result is that The Group's performances generate a high degree of ambiguity and spectator interaction, as the works virtually perform the kind of quantum subject-object blends that much modern art simply imposes as an intellectual donnée.

Contrary to Von Neumann's anxiety, however, for LeCompte and the performers the subsequent "difficulties" are the site of a rich field of difference to be explored and exploited. For, as we have seen in Beckett's work, the acceptance of certain kinds of chaos need not necessarily lead to disorder, meaninglessness, and despair. On the contrary, LeCompte's work seems virtually to enact the paradoxical process by which chaos, entropy, disequilibrium, and disorganization "evolve" into a new kind of order—transient and unstable to be sure, but for the moment retaining its own order of equilibrium. "It turns out," says Douglas Hofstadter, "that an eerie type of chaos can lurk behind a facade of order—and yet, deep inside the chaos lurks an even eerier type of order" ([1979] 1989, 211). Like ancient cultures that originally looked at chaos as something immensely creative, The Wooster Group has learned to cultivate a certain degree of disorder so that it can generate new ways of making sense. As James Gleick notes, "Nonlinearity means that the act of the playing the game has a way of changing the rules" (Gleick 1987, 24).

Perhaps that transformative relationship to the "rules" of traditional drama and theater describes more accurately The Group's aesthetic than does the title (*Breaking the Rules*) of a fine critical study of its work.[1] David Savran's analysis of The Wooster Group is unique in that he "lived in" with the performers during a brief period and observed their work habits, an important point of vantage for anyone wishing to understand how The Group's work emerges from the processes of its productions. Savran suggests that there are certain recurring techniques and conceptual approaches (the two are often inextricably bound together) that help to characterize most of the performances. First, in a strategy that recalls Beckett, The Group's working method itself disrupts the most essential element of conventional scripted drama: the integrity of the sign and an author's ability to manipulate signifiers in order to render a predetermined meaning or theme external to the work. "Ideas and themes which emerge from the pieces," Savran posits, "do so only in retrospect, as a residue of the textualizing process. . . . And for all the pieces, the reagent is the spectator" (Savran 1986b, 54). As in much twentieth-century visual and literary art, the movement is away from a single-point or Newtonian perspective toward a relativistic multiplication of spacetime "events" and possibilities. Thus in The Group's performances, the shapes that evolve from this process are bound to be less formalized and solid than those of the conventional text, more polysemous, multiple, and shifting.

In the case of The Wooster Group, this explosion of possible perspectives is a necessary consequence of the performers' inclination to devise scripts, literally, as they rehearse them. Working from a variety of found objects, improvisational rehearsal exercises, the performers' confrontations with one another, taped images and events, and even (sometimes) with existing literary texts, The Group's pieces truly evolve (and are often presented in workshops) as works in progress. Though that process is not truly aleatoric (LeCompte has come increasingly to be responsible for structuring the use of these elements within each production), it certainly involves a great deal of chance procedure. Especially in the rehearsal stages, each work reaches its own moment of singularity, and that moment will result in a breakdown of order as often as it does in an imposition of higher order.

A consequent common denominator in The Group's various works is, then, the disruption and dislocation of cause-and-effect connections between events within the performance. Instead, qualitative or associative links sustain emotional and intellectual arcs that rise and fall throughout the performances, acting as residue for the spectator to engage, sometimes from one work to the next. Connections are made not so often between thematic or character relations as between the initial impulses for the performances, the evolution of the mise-en-scènes, and the transformation of leftover dialogue or conceptual schema from previous rehearsals. Such a performance strategy obviously undermines almost entirely any attempt to render an integrated story or philosophical perspective, and instead concentrates the bulk of performative energy on the breakup of master narratives and on a better appreciation of processes.

As a further method for undermining determinate meanings and frames of reference, The Group often violently (especially in later work) agitates and explodes a series of texts within a performance. The audience is invited to find meanings, not in a compelling Presence or vision of reality *behind* the text (and catalyzed through the actor), but in the collisions and collusions *between* texts (effected by the intervention of performers who improvise around certain themes). The process emphasizes the constructedness of texts and meaning, and suggests further that these fabricated meanings are shifting and unstable. In practices that resemble post-quantum theory experiments in particle physics, the "reality" or vision to come out of a piece is more likely to result from what is gleaned during the breakup of the accelerated fragments of texts thrown together with amazing performative force. And—to continue the quantum analogy—what is observed and taken for signs or "meaning" is transient, uncertain, and best understood probabilistically.

In the earlier work, such "texts" came almost exclusively out of the rehearsal process and the performers' vocal and gestural improvisations with one another, with "found" objects and props, and with video- and audio-taped material. In certain performances (as with the "text" of recorded interviews that one of the performers, Spalding Gray, brought to *Rumstick Road*) one text dominates the others, though most often all are arranged in a kind of bricolage by LeCompte and the performers, a structure that both combines the elements and at the same time places them disjunctively in ironic opposition to one another.[2] As The Group begins to recognize the need to move outside the domain of strictly personal and group relations and interactions, however, the works begin to engage conventional texts more representative of, and contextualized by, American culture.

These various techniques foreground a conceptual approach to performance that partakes of the more general agenda in avant-garde art of the late sixties and early seventies, that is, toward the use of performance to deconstruct and sometimes to replace the logocentric center of the oedipal text. The approach, it has been noted, has obvious connections to French deconstructionist theory, yet even here it is important to make careful distinctions between the thought of Foucault and Derrida and the practices of The Group. When Arnold Aronson (1985, 345) says that The Group's work after *Nayatt School* "provides virtually the only example of deconstructionist ideas put into practice in the American theater," he overstates LeCompte's dependence on Derridean theory (which, as Aronson admits, LeCompte maintains she is aware of but has not read) and neglects the process of reception and coalescence that this theory has undergone, especially in America.[3]

As already argued, in the early "Yale school" of poststructuralism, American deconstructionist theory and practice tended to restore and venerate the text at the expense of larger social questions.[4] Recent advocates of new historicism argue that early poststructuralist criticism was essentially formalist, and that a more mature deconstructionist strategy can evolve only if critics begin to focus on the text not as an isolated literary structure, but as a product of human will, desire, and social needs.

In the earliest phase of transcribing Derridean theory in America, textual contradictions and aporias often became mere occasions for arguing the ecstasy of liberation through the medium of deconstructed language, or else for expressing the despair of servitude *to* an opaque language. Since this manifestation of deconstruction abrogates history and often fails to acknowledge the interaction of culture upon the making and unmaking of texts (as well as the making of history), it dulls and even negates a desire for significant content within criticism and art influenced by such a rendering of Derridean theory.[5]

A corresponding phase of performance theater follows such critical practices in several revealing ways. In its early stages (and continuing in later work, especially in most performance art), performance theater tends toward an uncritical deconstruction of texts, of language, and of representation. What arises from such performances is simply a strong sense (even a message) that the deconstructive agenda—the displacement of referentiality, the endless dissemination of possible meaning in a galaxy of traces, the active, "performative" function of the decentered reader/spectator—provides either the liberating ecstasy of play, for canny readers, or the darker threat of an end to discourse altogether, for those unable or unwilling to join in the dance of unchained signifiers. As Lentricchia (1983, 43) has written of Paul de Man's use of deconstruction, it "will deny lucidity to the intellect and guarantee in the end that no mind knows what it is doing—no mind, apparently, except de Man's, which lucidly knows that no lucidity is possible." Similar to the situation in English studies and theory, the problem in many of these performances is that a depoliticized version of analysis becomes a transcendent moral value, with the result in most cases that the connections between textuality and the culture that produces, re-presents, and receives texts are minimized and even lost.[6]

The Wooster Group, like other artists, critics, and theorists, has moved through such a phase of deconstructionist activity, where the work is primarily self-referential, self-contained, playful, and indeterminate, and thus essentially apolitical and outside history. Although it would be useful to find a fixed point in The Group's history at which such activity subsides and a new, more "political" art emerges, such a referent does not exist.[7] The Group's work has never, even after the shift in relations initiated within it by departing members, totally lost its autobiographical sources, nor turned away from its metatheatrical investigations. What does occur after the initial pieces (especially *Sakonnet Point*) is that these forays into performance increasingly have come to subject the texts used, the nature of the representation, and the dynamics of The Group itself to close scrutiny in order to map out their relations to existing cultural paradigms and power relations. The agenda (such as one exists) is turned more and more away from the simple deconstruction of textuality by the intervention of performance, toward an undermining of drama and performance, and the culture they inhabit and re-present, from within. Thus, the increasing use of dynamic and shifting combinations of orthodox dramatic texts and more open-ended performance strategies in The Group's work is really a natural activity, since one of the works' functions is to implicate the paradigms of textuality and performance in a general critique of contemporary society. This corroding process comes eventually to taint even The Group's own performances, to reveal such mis-representations as another site of the schism and brutality engrailed in the culture out of which they come and in which they take place.[8]

The Group's initial work is, owing in part to its affinities to the disorienting practices of a completely open-ended deconstructive aesthetic, perhaps its most forbidding. *Sakonnet Point* (1975), like some of the later work, did not arise from any central thematic or structural imperative. Instead, Spalding Gray suggested that his dance work with Robert Wilson's Byrd Hoffman School of Byrds be used to initiate sets of improvisations within the Performing Garage space, and from these open-ended "rehearsals" emerged a series of activities (mainly dancing) and interactions with found props that would eventually inhabit the performing space. The autobiographical elements implicit in the title, and later enhanced by the use of recorded tapes of Gray's memories of family life, were "projections" layered onto the work during rehearsals and in response to initial audience responses.

The process suggests a great deal of chance procedure, of bringing objects, movements, and ideas together randomly to fill up the space of a performance. Indeed, LeCompte insists that the work is "not an intention, really, other than to get things together in a space" (Savran 1986b, 58). This emphasis on the making of a piece, on the process over the product, is a staple of The Wooster Group and performance theater in general. Its most significant effect is to unchain causality and other signifiers, an alienating activity that transforms the spectator from a passive consumer of a stable narrative or a naturalized sequence of signifiers into an active (perhaps unwilling) participant in the phenomenological events of the performance and in the creation of a work's multilayered meaning. All that is required is that the spectator avail himself of the opportunity to enter into a dialogue with the work and absorb the performative experience itself.

Significant in terms of The Group's later direction, *Sakonnet Point* does not evolve from an existing literary text or set of texts. As in other early work by avant-garde artists of the period (especially Robert Wilson) there is a studied insistence on the part of The Group to avoid being confined by literary structures. Gray says that the work was a "radical departure from the way we had worked with Richard [Schechner], following a story line" (Savran 1986b, 59), even though Schechner's own plot lines were themselves only the elided vestiges of a deconstructed text. LeCompte considers the work "more dance than theater," and suggests that the piece is analogous to a still life by Cézanne in the way it imposes a rigid formal structure upon a group of seemingly unrelated objects and movements (Savran 1986b, 59). The dominance of visual images and abstract dance movements in the work does evoke for many spectators the theme of a preverbal world of childlike innocence or an unmediated dream state, which emerge in the form of what Gray refers to (in a telling phrase) as "images without thought" (Gray 1979, 35). These images are almost always derived from movement, gesture, and lighting; and while these are contained and scrutinized within their own semiotic space, there is no attempt to engage the language or thought ingrained in written texts. In addition, images and gestures are not brought together in an integrated form (as in most textual drama, especially realist drama), but are arranged asynchronously so that one dislocates another: music, for instance, is played out of rhythm with movements, various media collide and overlap, and all the image and movement "texts" rupture one another. One effect, which becomes an important staple in LeCompte's development of a fractal theater, is to expose the disjunct nature of representation itself, to foreground the obscured breach that exists between experiential "found" material and theatricalized material. Instead of trying to bridge that art/life gap, as, say, Schechner was trying to do with The Performance Group, or instead of trying to cover up or occlude the process, as is the case with realist drama, Gray and LeCompte disclose the schisms through the medium of performance. Rejecting the smooth shape of reality offered by the first two forms of theater, The Group opts to focus the spectator's vision on the rough texture and unstable jointure of both the performance and the reality it purposes to represent.

Such a process of course calls into question the very nature of representation, which is always trying and failing to look like "actual" reality and human experience. *Sakonnet Point* reveals that representation is always necessarily a simulacrum that mediates and transforms reality.

Consciousness itself is conceived, in terms familiar from German romantic epistemology (and revamped within performance theories of the sixties), not as a wholeness existing in some primal state of unity with reality, but as always in arrears. Because consciousness results from a split between being and thought, a split that individuates the "I" from the "not-I" or Other, we are left only with immortal intimations (akin to Blau's "ghost") of unmediated being. Existing thus, consciousness apprehends the world only as its own re-presentation of it, and one suggestion of the performance is simply that, as a constituent activity of being, we "perform" ourselves.[9]

Despite such interpretive possibilities, as Gray himself admits, "The Trilogy isn't really about memory. . . . [T]hey're art pieces, they're not referential" (Savran 1986b, 70). LeCompte agrees, and maintains that much rearranging and restructuring was done, Beckett-like, to elide and deconstruct patterns of reference in plot, the mise-en-scène, and the psychological development of characters.

Due to the lack of specific themes, rational language and action, and psychological continuity, then, the piece comes across as extremely abstract, especially in relation to the two works and epilogue that follow in *The Rhode Island Trilogy*. The latter pieces bring out more clearly the connection between Gray's reminiscences and certain elements of the performance, while in *Sakonnet Point,* where the associations are personal and random, these transitions are utterly ambiguous (since the spectator cannot share the original context in which they arise). That work denies by its structure and its dependence on self-reflexive gestural, kinesic, and scenic languages any common chain of signifiers to be shared by performer and spectator. In so doing, it shows affinities to other avant-garde performances, especially (we shall see) to Wilson's productions during his "theater of visions" phase.

While suggesting a subtle critique of the way that representation deforms and inauthentically objectifies human beings, emotions, and actual events, *Sakonnet Point* remains essentially a self-referential meta-commentary on the individual "performative" psyche of Spalding Gray and on the abstract theme of loss. The only real connection the work makes to an external world is an incomplete one, where the barriers of solipsism and the margins of theatrical representation prohibit the piece from actually presenting Gray's "reality" in its essence to a spectator whose empathy can be actively engaged. Because the structure of this reality would necessarily be disfigured by a cause-and-effect narrative, a more random and associative sequence is substituted. And, even though thus formalized the structure defers closure and avoids the constraints of textuality and mimesis, it nevertheless fails to capture Gray's Presence wholly. As a by-product of this failure, the prevalence of performance in our lives and its margins within theater are suggested.

A problem arises, however, that will haunt later performances by The Group as well. Because *Sakonnet Point* never sufficiently foregrounds or investigates this ontological uncertainty, what prevails in the piece is a sense that performance, as a way of being in the world and representing it, is superior to the rigidity and closure of textuality. The piece appears to "argue," by its rejection of a controlling text and the rational order of textuality, that Gray's self-conscious and transformative performance style captures an essence of self and reality denied within textual representation. As in other performance-oriented work of the period, no complementarity exists between text and performance: the latter is simply privileged as the proper alternative to the closure of textuality and the power of the author. Yet we have seen that in Beckett such a performative strategy eventually revealed itself as fruitless, as simply an illusion of powerlessness. In *Sakonnet Point,* The Group retains the avant-garde urge to displace the text with performance without questioning the validity of the latter term.

When, for instance, Savran describes Gray's performance strategies in the piece as "a physical impulse . . . [that] is never conceived as a manifestation of hidden desires or psychological obscurities," he assumes that such unmediated, spontaneous, and "unwritten" physical-abstract movement is possible (Savran 1986b, 65). But neither Savran nor The Group interrogates this premise, which, as with many of the notions regarding Presence discussed already in relation to sixties performance theory, has been problematized by poststructuralist views on language and gesture.[10] The assumption that it lies within a performer's capacity to enter such a state, to become entirely present to himself or to an audience, has been powerfully challenged. The challenge, however, is never taken up in *Sakonnet Point,* and the result of the neglect is that the piece is not sufficiently self-reflexive to scrutinize its own complicity with the illusion-making apparatus of theater. As Jonathan Kalb says, "theater is not mendacious when it avoids explicit contact with social issues; it is rather mendacious and manipulative when it fails to proclaim its own duplicity" (Kalb 1989, 147). At this point in The Group's history, the work shows signs of such manipulation, and the structure of reality portrayed—or the lack of it—is irregular but still Euclidean, still smooth and undeformed by difference or contradiction.

After the initial work with *Sakonnet Point* had been completed, Gray and LeCompte traveled with the still-existing Performance Group to India to perform *Mother Courage*. Gray had been recording conversations with his grandmothers about their lives and their recollections of Margaret (Bette) Gray, Spalding's mother, who had been diagnosed as paranoid before committing suicide in 1967. While in India, he decided to use *Sakonnet Point* as the first part of a trilogy. When he returned, he began the second piece by adding more taped material, including painful conversations with his father and a secretly recorded telephone call to the psychiatrist who had treated his mother. Gray says that the conversations were not formal interviews, or intended to concentrate on the subject of his mother's death; rather, they were more similar to the kinds of "action-reaction" improvisations he had worked through with members of LeCompte's company in preparation for *Sakonnet Point* (Gray 1979, 38–39).

In rehearsal, members of the company listened to Gray's tapes and performed structured improvisations around them. The process, though similar to the kinds of preparation and stage-rewriting common to any number of playwrights and actors, is significantly different in that it produced no single "text" accruing from the improvisations, but a series of texts that exist in a variety of relationships to one another. For instance, Gray remembers one such "text" in the piece coming mainly out of group associations built around the facts of his own experience, but which eventually included additional material from all the performers. This sort of preparation signals an important shift in The Group's creative process, because in this instance the open-ended improvisational performance and Gray's abstract self-expressiveness are not allowed wholly to carry the day. Instead, LeCompte structures *Rumstick Road* so that Gray's subjective approach is resisted by its more objective complement, textuality. This does not necessarily imply, however, that an established dramatic text must be used. More inclined to think in terms of structure, mise-en-scène, and controlling imagery, LeCompte said that although the material (Gray's tapes) "indicated the approach," it was a spatial image that defined her conceptual attitude toward the work's structure:

> I began working with two things. One was a lecture demonstration set-up from renaissance teaching, which has the instructor sitting

> high on a balcony over a table and the demonstrators . . . in the middle. The doctor is above, and on either side, facing him, are the students. That and the triptichs . . . with the Godhead rising and the hell down below, and on either side the domestic scenes, the Madonna on one side and a scene from the previous life on the other. Everything comes together in the center and goes out. (Champagne 1981, 22)

We see here a potential ambiguity in the piece, as Gray develops an open, performance-oriented approach to his material while LeCompte literally "sets the stage" for a perspectival, lecture-demonstration that suggests objectivity, impressive professorial interpretation, and textual closure.[11] In the set for *Rumstick Road,* LeCompte's textualist themes are realized as three contiguous vertical spaces, the middle one a protruding control booth from which the Operator plays tapes and records and directs the lighting. The forced perspective of the rooms suggests the kind of spatial arrangements common to Renaissance painting, which draws the spectator's eye toward the compositional center. This also is reminiscent of the subject-object relationship in the classic text. Significantly, the seating arrangement for the audience echoes this, so that another vanishing point is located at the apex directly in front of the control booth. Between them stands an examination table, suggesting the anatomical lecture-demonstration that LeCompte uses as a frame for the action.

The two approaches, Gray's performative, subjective, and autobiographical one and LeCompte's textualist, objective and authorial version, thus co-inhabit the theatrical space. The "anatomical" setting relates to Gray's notion of the piece as autobiographical and representative of his interiority; as Schechner says, it suggests a horizontal section of a human head (Schechner 1982, 84). But, as Schechner goes on to ask, what is the perspective of the audience: inside looking out, or vice versa? For Gray, primarily interested in expressing his own inner being, the former seems more likely as an appropriate space for "performing the body," as performance theorists refer to such activity. For LeCompte, however, the notion of the outside, of a perspectival, empirical observation point, seems paramount. Thus to Gray the mise-en-scène and the "text" of the performance constitute a kind of avant-garde psychodrama (or psychoperformance), while for LeCompte the scene becomes a microscopic "cross-section" and the performance "text" a perceptual ex-

The Wooster Group, *Rumstick Road.*
Libby Howes, Bruce Porter, Spalding Gray. Directed by Elizabeth LeCompte, Performance Garage, 1977. Photo by Ken Kobland.

periment under the direction of the "Operator" who controls—like an author—the mise-en-scène from the outside, within the booth. Neither metaphor dominates or effaces the other, and the scene sustains both as the piece enacts the movement toward a point at which the two "texts" will collide, a moment of singularity at which it will either explode into chaos and disorganization or else achieve a higher structure.

Throughout the piece, both conceptions exist simultaneously in a field relationship in which they are allowed to interact and to redefine one another. As Xerxes Mehta has remarked, the setting is "both stark and lush, hospitable to fact, memory, and dream" (Mehta 1979, 6). It is also hospitable to both performance and textuality, as Gray's desire to perform a "dream"-like, open-ended, and nonreferential accretion of personal and interactive improvisations is linked to LeCompte's inclination to devise a structure that suggests (however ironically) an objective and empirical point of observation from which "fact, memory," and interpretation are empowered.

An example of how the two conceptual approaches, the decentered/performative and the empirical/textual, collaborate to form actions used in the performance is described by Gray:

> We would do our regular physical warm-ups while the tapes played and then we would try to explore through structured improvisations, some of the situations recorded on tape. An example of this is the mention of my mother's visitation from Christ and her subsequent healing. We worked on the situation of [Ron] Vawter [the Man] being a Christ figure and [Libby] Howes [the Woman] the mother figure. We read from *Acts* in the Bible and one image, the image of Christ healing a sick person by spitting in his ear, captured our imaginations. This led to Vawter becoming more directly physical with Howes and expressing a desire to tickle her stomach. Vawter slowly dropped out of the role of Christ and began to improvise a kind of mad Esalen-type of doctor-healer who both healed and tickled his patient to the point of very real and uncontrolled laughter on the part of Howes, the mother-patient. (Gray 1978, 90)

In the interplay of the improvisation, Gray's autobiography and the interaction of the performers motivate, and are in part transformed into, the kind of clinical empirical observation (that of the abusive doctor).

that LeCompte wants to investigate. Again, as we have already seen in Beckett and as will later appear in the work of Wilson and Shepard, such ironic double-coding of the functions between performance and textuality is an integral part of the theatrical experience. It is the mechanism by which a new mutualist space is carved out, a space that can bear meanings perhaps unbearable or unspeakable within a dominant hierarchy that privileges text *or* performance.

But while providing an interesting interaction between the deconstructive displacements of performance and the interpretive closure of textuality, the results sometimes raise disturbing questions. In the improvisation described above, for instance, what is originally an exploration of an important event in Bette Gray's life—presumably the core of Gray's autobiographical "narrative"—is soon reduced to an abstract, dancelike performance gesture that seems to empty the scene of any significant content. As Schechner notes:

> These sequences nudge me away from identification with Gray toward accepting the story as a set of (abstract) moves, as a dance: Brecht's theater without politics, the distance without the urge to action outside and/or after the theater. It's the oldest road in Western theater travelled in the opposite direction from usual. Critics from Aristotle onwards have told us that theater should be used to approach truth: to find out what is. But Gray and LeCompte . . . use Gray's life (= truth) as a way of approaching beauty.
>
> It's life for art's sake. (Schechner 1982, 85)

Schechner's critique seems accurate if only this element—essentially Gray's abstract performance "text" within the piece—is considered. Gray has consistently admitted that his contributions to all of The Wooster Group's work in which he has taken part are motivated by solipsistic and narcissistic impulses, and by an urge to transform his private experience into the kind of "personal-abstract movement" that he had learned from Robert Wilson.[12] It is therefore in the interest of his performance style that Gray transforms his personal experience into abstract metaphors expressing his own consciousness. But Gray also realized what Schechner apparently does not, that *Rumstick Road* was truly collaborative, "field work" in the sense that it explores the interactive space or field between text and performance. Gray in fact knew that his individual vision of what the performance should "be" would naturally change in the very process of colliding other views and texts with his personal recollections and performative desires. "I think we *used* my self-consciousness and narcissism in the pieces, and, in doing so, avoided self-indulgence" (Gray 1979, 36).

What keeps *Rumstick Road,* then, from remaining merely solipsistic, unengaged formalism or performance art—life for art's sake—is the ironic, deconstructive space opened up by LeCompte's empirical, or textual, structure. Her concept for the piece requires the presence of an abstract, autobiographical, and intensely personal counterstructure that rubs against the empirical lecture-demonstration model she delineates through the mise-en-scène and elsewhere. And what better to act as counterpoise to such empirical and documentary activities than solipsistic reveries and abstract movement, the meaning of which is comprehended only by the performer and not the spectator? Thus in the long run the piece is both "about" (i.e., refers to) Gray's performance of an inside (his family history and his personal experience) and, simultaneously and contiguously, "about" an outside, that is, how we empirically observe and interpret a work that attempts to reproduce through text and documentation Gray's (or anyone else's) history and interiority. Since neither Gray nor LeCompte is looking for a smoothly surfaced synthesis between inside and outside, the work takes on the fractal shape of nonlinear structures. That is, it reveals the rough junctures at which inside and outside join, and makes their jagged, unfinished texture the source of their power and their delight. As an added feature, such fractal structures—like the tissues of the lungs and the weird shapes of the Koch curve—have the paradoxical quality of containing a tremendous surface capacity within a bounded area. LeCompte thus finds herself able to condense a great deal of material into this densely layered dialogic structure.

LeCompte's real subject here, as it was marginally in *Sakonnet Point* and will be more forcefully in later work, is the paradoxical nature of representation itself. Her investigation in *Rumstick Road,* however, includes what was left out in *Sakonnet Point,* that is, the scrutiny and deconstruction of Gray's own theory of performance, which rejects the Stanislavskian observation of the "Other" as a source for expressive material. Gray relates the way he came upon his performance-oriented notion of acting by describing how "somewhere . . . I came to realize that I could only guess at knowing this 'other,' I could only pretend"

(Gray 1979, 35). Since the subjectivity of the observed Other always remained an opacity, trying to fix it in order to play it "froze and congealed any fluid essence." Gray turned therefore to exploring himself as Other, "the constant witness, the constant consciousness of self"; and this highly reflexive and self-conscious style produced "a play of moods, energies, aspects of self. It became the many-in-the-one that had its source in the archetype of the performer, not in the text" (1979, 35). This view of the performative self is thus predicated on a ground of difference, slippage, a series of masks. Instead of providing the theatrical Presence of the character "as a whole" (derived from a transparent text), we discover instead the self already performing itself. As Gray says, "Look at me, I am one who sees himself seeing himself" (1979, 35): and this self-reflexiveness creates representation, in Savran's phrase, "to, of and by self" (Savran 1986b, 64). Gray's change in method is thus from an acting style suitable for mimetic textual drama to one appropriate for a highly subjective style of performance art.

Yet a closer examination of Gray's acting method reveals that it shares the same solipsistic and apolitical attitudes that characterize performance theater of the seventies. Gray uses his method to allow for a free play of "energies" and selves to emerge during performance, and assumes that such flows are interactive with the energies and desires of the audience. He relies on LeCompte and the improvisations among other members of The Group to impose a form upon the actions he takes into a performance: "I was free to do what I wanted, be who I was, and trust that the text would give this freedom a structure" (Gray 1979, 33). Gray is not overly concerned with the effects of form on his own performance because his transformations of energies are destined to undermine such structures anyway. He seeks another form of theater-as-therapy (Gray himself suggests this), different from that of Schechner and other experimental groups of the sixties primarily in that it discovers this healing process in the postmodern panacea of deconstructing Presence, power, and wholeness in order to foreground multiplicity, deferral, and powerlessness.

As in early stages of literary deconstruction, the emphasis here is on the process of decentering the text (or fixed subject) for the sake of a liberation from the text/subject. Little in the way of relating the effects of deconstructive activity to larger questions about the text/self, or to the culture that produces and controls the representation of it, is offered; and herein lies the essentially conservative, quietistic quality of Gray's ontology of acting. For playing a multiplicity of roles and performing them is never politically innocent. The manner in which people, in and outside theater, choose to represent their various "selves," and the way that empowered discourses represent themselves and their relations to marginalized ones, are central concerns of contemporary political thought. In his transformations of the many-in-the-one, Gray, like any performance artist, risks (I would say, desires) creating not Absence and powerlessness, but a new power or Presence—or else risks allowing the spectator to construct one—that will limit his open-ended and ludic diffractions of self and consequently engender a new charismatic power, even as he undermines the old. As a character in Jane Wagner's *The Search for Signs of Intelligent Life in the Universe* responds to such an aesthetic, "Your acting like you've transcended your own ego is the biggest ego trip of all!" But, like Beckett's self-effacing texts, Gray may be powerless to effect/affect impotence; and like Beckett's plays, Gray's acting ontology reveals an underlying desire for control over meaning and the spectator, that is, for power. In essence, the charismatic Presence of the performer is effected by his very ability to connote himself as the privileged product of postmodernist theorized chic—decentered, multifaceted, free of the oedipal dominance of the ego.

Then, too, Gray never considers how this performative consciousness is allied to the image-making power of the modern media, nor how the transformational exercise of the "many-in-the-one" can become merely the refractions of desire determined by the mass market, an ingredient of the administered society. In his narcissistic pursuit of himself as Other, Gray assumes that his performances will transform him, and that these transformations will be in some way spiritually enlightening. Certainly the act of performing as Gray describes it has the capacity to transform: Grotowski's work revealed this on a profound level. But as Blau observes acutely, such potential for transcendence is intimately embedded in the culture in which the performance takes place. And, in our late capitalist culture of the spectacle,

> at the level of community, whatever the powers of performance were, they no longer are. . . . [T]he performative instinct has been so distributed in art and thought and everyday life that we find it harder to discern the special value of performance *as* transformation, when transformation seems, moreover, in a culture of signs—with

the supersaturation of images in the media—a universal way of life. (Blau 1987, 185)

Performance, like any form of revolt, requires an "agency of repression." In contemporary life that agency has become so diffused as to be invisible, so powerful as to be capable of fabricating and engineering one's own interiority, even to the extent of shaping one's desire to revolt against or transcend the oppressive agency. We might well question, then, whether Gray's later version of the holy theater's archetypal actor in pursuit of "visible impulses" (now projected as a syncopated array of spontaneous improvisations) reflects even a pure solipsism. With the splitting, unfixing, and death of the subject preached first in Warholism and later proclaimed in poststructuralist theory, Gray's activity might just as reasonably be described as reflecting the fetishization of the multiple and transformed image that has motivated MTV, the many "faces" of pop icons like David Bowie, Madonna, and Prince, and television's need for "composite characters."[13]

Fortunately, in an important step for The Group's art, in *Rumstick Road* the representation of the subjective self as performative, fragmented, and multiplicative is "examined" by the manners of inquiry to which we traditionally ascribe the greatest degree of veracity, that is, empirical observation and objective documentation. This empirical examination takes place at the same time that psychological states and emotional flows are being improvised and performed by Gray within the space of their purest representation, the theater. In effect, the two simultaneous modes of theater mutually undermine one another, for even while Gray's abstract and self-referential performance is being documented, interpreted, and textualized by the spectator (whose perspective, we remember, is that of the Renaissance anatomy chamber), documents and texts are themselves being trans-/performed on the stage, as taped conversations between Gray and his mother's doctor are heard and documents relating to Bette Gray's life are read into the performance.

Instead of trying to nominate performance as a privileged discourse, or even attempting to create a synthesis between objective and subjective representation, between outside and inside, and between the acting discourses of "drama" and "performance," LeCompte deconstructs both as privileged master narratives that fail equally to capture or defer Presence. *Rumstick Road* does not, like a dramatic text, attempt to represent

Bette Gray as an absent source for whom the text "stands in"; but neither does it privilege Gray's performance by granting him an unmediated flow of "moods, energies, aspects of the self," because his transformations are not free-floating, but dependent on the media—the documents and texts—he has gathered. Rather, the piece interrogates the notion that any representation, textual or performative, can successfully recapture the reality of Bette Gray's insanity or Gray's performative personalities. Instead of affirming drama or performance, *Rumstick Road* enacts and indicts the interpretive and voyeuristic gaze of both by paralleling them to the clinical perception of the Psychologist, and to the gaze of the spectator as well.

Gray's subjective expression of his personal memories re-presents his mother's own subjective state, and thereby violates her to the same degree that the clinical gaze of the doctors (and the spectators) dehumanizes her. Neither "gaze" is innocent, as in both theater and the anatomy lecture-demonstration hall, a lifeless subject is held up for close scrutiny so that active, but detached, observers can analyze the subject and explain its pathologies. The subject is dissected and objectified while the lecturer (or "Operator," playwright, authentic performer) discourses from on high and tries to "re-animate" and explain or capture its being. The student/spectator's gaze is also directed downward as he examines and judges what is being shown. The point of the entire demonstration is clinical, and for that reason a high degree of detachment is necessary.

The nature of this gaze, in both its clinical and its theatrical form, is investigated throughout *Rumstick Road* in a number of ways. In "The First Examination," Ron Vawter facetiously explains his clinical exercise in massage therapy, then proceeds to run his mouth and tongue over the exposed torso of the first passive, then convulsive, Woman (Libby Howes). The deceptively detached and diagnostic language screens the process by which the clinician turns the Woman into an object requiring therapy, and by which such objectification (as seems to have been the case with Bette Gray) can eventually become, despite even good motives, part of an illness.

Later, when the Operator plays the tape of Gray's phone call (recorded without permission) with the psychiatrist who had been treating his mother, the unwitting brutality of the clinical gaze is again evoked.[14] The doctor explains to Gray why his mother received electric shock treatment, covers more recent techniques for treating depression and schizophrenia, and concludes by telling Gray not to be frightened by a "hereditary predisposition": "Don't equate it with manic depressiveness and a depressive episode just because something goes wrong, you hear?"[15] He ends by saying to Gray, in a touchingly ambiguous phrase, "I have to let you go now." Despite the doctor's essentially sympathetic representation, Gray and the spectator are left with a terrifying sense of the brutality that follows unconsciously from a clinical perspective that reduces humans to objects to be jazzed with electricity, rendered toxic by drugs, and left to the whims of DNA.

Still, the piece never remains merely a condemnation of medical science and its objective gaze; LeCompte recognizes that theater itself, whether strictly mimetic and textual or performance-oriented, partakes of the same chain of brutalizing representation that characterizes the lecture-demonstration. Like clinical analysis, theater turns actions and characters into objects to be probed, studied, and analyzed. Gray's personal life and the events of his mother's life are transformed in the very act of being documented. First, memory itself transforms the subject, violates its authenticity, and re-presents it from the perspective of the witnesses. In the next stage, these memories are further tainted as they are made into public acts that ask the spectator to make connections, associations, and even judgments regarding them. The result is not so much that Gray's personal being(s) and experiences are thereby realized accurately or fully on stage, as it is that the subjective spaces of the mise-en-scène itself and of the spectator effectively rewrite the material in their own image. The subject is violated and objectified in order to transform it into an aesthetic artifact, as Schechner suggests. And Gray, as fetishized performer and fetishizing subject, is implicated in the process.

But LeCompte seems aware of the duplicity of the theatrical event, something that Schechner never realized fully in his work with The Performance Group.[16] LeCompte insistently implicates the theatrical apparatus of which she is an important part by subjecting its elements to the same kind of gaze that is turned toward Gray's past experiences. In *Rumstick Road,* the use of the actual taped conversations in performance, rather than the use of transcribed lines filtered through an actor, reveals the way that dialogue is duplicitously appropriated within performance. Also, when Gray plays his taped conversation with the psychiatrist, we feel uneasy because, as Xerxes Mehta notes, "sharp editing has permitted Gray to shape his end of the conversation, presented to us live, whereas his opponent's is frozen forever in time" (Mehta 1979, 7). The theatrical apparatus allows Gray to "shape" the representation of the conversation, and to "play himself" at the expense of the doctor's own subjectivity. LeCompte, however, is able to call attention to the misappropriation by, first, advertising in the program that "Dr. Henry Bradford" is a fictitious name. This suggests that the taped conversation itself is a product of (presumably) Gray's imagination, and possibly a matter of him narrating his own subjectivity. Second, LeCompte has Gray speak his lines "live" against the recording, thereby making the distinction between the "truth" of the conversation more problematic: is it to be found in Absence (mimesis/representation, writing/documentation/recording, objectivity) or Presence (presentation, the aura of the speaking performer, subjectivity)? By making the question of primacy problematic, LeCompte creates a performance that undermines Presence and Absence, thus producing an ambiguous relationship between performer and audience based on a noncharismatic understanding. Since the shape of the theater she describes is uncertain, and its texture scabrous and porous, we should not look for the traditionally seamless bond between the audience and the charismatic performer.

Rumstick Road, then, uses violation as both a subject and a method. In addition to the bugged telephone conversation, the work includes a tape of Gray's grandmother reciting "The Scientific Statement of Being" from the writings of Mary Baker Eddy (Bette Gray had an ambiguous relationship with Christian Science). Before the tape is played, Gray addresses the audience directly, outside the character of "Spalding Gray," and says: "She [Grandma Horton] asked me not to use this tape in the piece. She wanted me to keep it for myself. Something personal" (100). Savran suggests that such violations are the Group's "necessary step toward a radical confrontation of the canons of art and society" (Savran 1986b, 92). Following Roland Barthes's notions of social transgression as a subversive activity that necessarily takes place within the play of structures and writings that inhabit culture, Savran goes on to say that The Group's appropriation of public and personal correspondence is aimed at wrenching such discourse out of the cultural continuum so that "it can be turned against the voice who uttered it" (94).[17]

The idea is illuminating, especially with respect to The Group's later work, but seems not to give due weight to the performers' working methods, which still at this point are directed away from the kind of intentionality implicit in such transgressive activity. It seems more likely, especially given the use of Gray as the supposed psychic "center" for *Rumstick Road,* that such transgressions are effected more as a structural principle for confronting the material "facts" with Gray's subjective rewritings of them. It is another way to investigate the disjunction between the authority of the subject and the author-izing power of the text. In the case of the questionable violation of the psychiatrist and Grandma Horton, the performance works to deconstruct Gray's own Presence as a performer, to undermine his charismatic projection, and to discourage the spectator from endowing either him or "his" representation with absolute authority.

Using a number of extremely provocative performance strategies, then, The Group is able to render problematic the machination of the theatrical enterprise itself. Theater, as a structure existing in a web of power relations to other components of society, is irredeemably caught up in the process of representation that violates and objectifies the subject so that a particular (subjective) vision of reality can be demonstrated. Such a representation will always become (and is sometimes intended to become), despite any claim to objectivity, a misrepresentation, because in it

> a subtle and beautiful phenomenon is distorted beyond all recognition in order that the ephemeral visual clues can be amplified for the benefit of people seated at a distance. . . . [D]emonstrations tend to wrench phenomena from their natural context in order to make a "main point" stand out clearly before the average student. And the most interested and intuitive students must be very uncomfortable when . . . the attention is displaced from the real effect to a substitute or analogue, so that a gross model . . . becomes the means of discussing a basic phenomenon . . . without giving the class a glimpse of the actual case itself. (Quoted in Savran 1986a, 47)

LeCompte told Savran that her initial design for *Rumstick Road* was motivated by Holton's book, which she read "over and over" while putting the work together (Savran 1986b, 47). LeCompte's meditations on the theme reveal not only that demonstrations (scientific or subjective) are simulacra that redefine the phenomena they project, but also that documents, private experience, and memory are equally susceptible to such transformations. The work thus calls into question the verifiability of truth, of anyone's ability to capture and render, through signs, the essence of reality. The Group thus extends Heisenberg's indeterminacy principle to its ontological and semiotic limits, with the added effect of making such uncertainty the matrix for a better understanding of the essentially disorganized nature of reality.

But beyond such an abstract theme lies an acutely political activity: that is, a critique of the power structures that we empower to present things as truth. "Ideas do not succeed in history," writes the sociologist Peter Berger, "by virtue of their truth, but of their relationship to specific social processes" (Berger 1977, 27). Both the lecture-demonstration and the "liberating" activity of the performer and theater are revealed as discourses enabled by, and thus in collusion with, social authority and specific acculturating agencies such as medicine and the media. And both kinds of representation—the objective "drama" of the lecture-demonstration as well as the subjective improvisations of the performer—empower some figure of authority, call it "lecturer/director" or "performer," all of whom are implicated in the process of selectively—and thus inauthentically—representing the illusory as the real.

Still, *Rumstick Road* is hardly a political polemic. Even while it undermines representation and exposes its collusion with other forms of authority, the piece confirms the tremendous appeal of performance as a liberating activity. The performance suggests a joyous affirmation of theater's power, as a special kind of language, to define and image forth the world. One scene in particular is often cited as being highly theatrical in this sense: a slide of Bette Gray's face is projected onto the face of Libby Howes, and for one startling moment it looks as if the performance has succeeded in re-presenting the dead and in bringing Blau's impossible "ghost" into literal being. The illusion, powerful as it is, must of course be ephemeral because as soon as Howes begins to speak she "breaks the picture plane" and disables the illusion. The two realities cannot exist simultaneously, but the spectator is left with a disquieting residue, a mixture of wonder at theater's ability almost to achieve the transcendent through the concrete, on the one hand, and theater's inability really ever to get beyond the concrete on the other.

While the work thus evokes the feelings of loss and pain that are the necessary foundation of consciousness and representation, it also paradoxically affirms the power of such representation. And because it investigates theater's relation to social institutions, *Rumstick Road* shows The Group evolving a different, more culturally contextualized phase of deconstructive dramaturgy. Also significant is the fact that, unlike *Sakonnet Point*, the piece reveals clear connections to orthodox drama: it has dialogue, sequential action, recognizable characters, and so on. And, while all of these elements have been radically modified and reconstituted, their dramatic sources are obvious. This new regard for dramatic convention, however, does not signal a new orthodoxy. Instead, it heralds an important step toward the kind of fractal political art that seems the only viable shape of discourse in a highly pluralistic and destabilized culture, one constructed on relativistic values and a changing sociology of culture. *Rumstick Road* itself, occupying a transitional place in The Group's work, seems to be both partly outside and partly within postmodern culture and theater. Because it foregrounds performance strategies over textual concerns (narrativity, coherent character psychology, and so on), it appears to transgress the domains of orthodox drama. At the same time, these performative elements are not offered as a preferred alternative to textuality. Instead, positioned within theatrical discourse, LeCompte's deconstructions of performance effectively critique the ideologies behind the *épistémè* of performance and expose their processes of production, their materials, and their arrangement in the work.

Granting all this, the emphasis of the work is still restricted to the personal experience and memories of Gray, as well as the other performers' confrontation with these. The critique, too, is aimed primarily at the theatrical enterprise itself, and not at its specific relationships and collusion with other dominant discourses. As a result, the critique cannot be sufficiently self-reflexive; further, to this point, The Group had not sought to confront and deconstruct the most culturally entrenched and transparent element of theater, the dramatic text itself. And, because it does not explicitly investigate textuality and its processes of reproduction, *Rumstick Road* remains somewhat self-enclosed and self-conscious. The modes of representation being undermined are (given the nature of the lecture-demonstration "theater") simply "theatrical."

Perhaps feeling that performance had been sufficiently explored to this point, in The Group's next two pieces in *The Rhode Island Trilogy, Nayatt School* (1978) and the epilogue *Point Judith* (1980), LeCompte begins to examine the nature of the dramatic text and to expose both its beauty and its dangerous power. She reveals an ambivalent attitude toward dramatic texts and toward the question of how to use them in her work. On the one hand, she is obviously committed to deprivileging the text as the locus of absolute power in the theater hierarchy by exposing its collusions—in its use of language, symbols, themes, and structures to convey hegemonic views of reality—with authority. But there remains the fact that LeCompte is attracted to dramatic language and the formal aesthetics that she finds in a variety of plays. In addition, she senses that if The Group is to engage culture as Barthes describes it—as a play of structures and writings that inhabit it—then The Group must contend with writing in order to play with it and resist it.

In *Nayatt School,* the response to this initial confrontation between an orthodox text (Eliot's *The Cocktail Party*) and the more typical collection of other "texts"—performers (adult and children), props, improvisations, records—is, not surprisingly, "an explosion . . . a celebration that is unique among The Wooster Group's work, embodying the thrill of discovery, of coming upon a world alternately sublime and horrific" (Savran 1986b, 102). The play simultaneously celebrates the madness investigated in *Rumstick Road,* delivers a blistering critique of Eliot's sentimental and mystical vision, and exposes victimization as it is produced by males, religion, doctors (again), and the text. The work consists of six sections, each entitled "Examination of the Text," but instead of leading to the kind of closure and smooth geometry of order suggested by the terms "examination," "text," and the "school" of the title, *Nayatt School* exposes the rough shape of each text, explodes them all in turn, and ends in utter chaos. Still, even as order gives way to disorder, there are indications that the hysteria might be the matrix for the creation of a higher order of structure.

The set, foreshadowing the direction of the performance, is designed as a disorienting "anti-gravity room" dropped below floor level, and includes a reverse-perspective house that destroys the fixed perspective used in *Rumstick Road.* There is also a steeply raked auditorium that gives the spectator a dizzying and disorienting perspective on the action.

Into this relativity chamber comes Gray, who performs his first extended monologue—an expressive form he has since made his forte—by relating his experience as an actor in an earlier production of *The Cocktail Party*. He gives a plot summary, plays a record of a performance featuring Alec Guiness, reads his favorite speech from the play, and engages the audience with humorous anecdotes.[18] At this point it appears that Gray has shed his role of performer and that he is addressing the audience as himself. He speaks independently of the text or taped voices of others, and seems free even of the spectator's activity of creating the role of "Spalding." Rather than being objectified and commodified within the performance, then, Gray presents himself as the unviolated subject. He is the auto-performer released from the constraints of any text, free to articulate his own performative subjectivity. Since Gray's monologue appears to derive from neither text nor enacted character, the audience is likely (in the face of Gray's engaging and charismatic delivery) to confer Presence upon him. Thus Gray is free to express his own position in relation to the text and the production of *The Cocktail Party,* which he had once performed, and to articulate the subject's view of the process of being objectified within the space of textual representation.

In the next "Examination," however, we find Gray now *within* the text of Eliot's play, performing the part of the psychiatrist, Reilly. With the version of psychiatry from *Rumstick Road* still resonating in the *Trilogy,* we might expect Gray to provide an especially unsympathetic portrayal of this "very great doctor" through whom Eliot chooses to disseminate his gospel of spiritual salvation. We find instead that Gray, like the other performers in The Group, refuses to "enact" his role and merely stands in for Reilly, going through the necessary motions to suggest his character without attempting to infuse it with any emotional depth—a "dramatic reading" as opposed to an enactment. He sits beside Joan Jonas (playing Celia Copplestone) at a long table, the script of *The Cocktail Party* in plain sight in his hands. As the two read through scenes from the play, they occasionally stop to critique one another's reading: "*Spald:* 'Did you miss that?' *Joan:* 'It's not in my text'" (Savran 1986b, 132). While "Celia" recites in a very mannered delivery her impassioned speech on wanting to transcend the world for a revived feeling of prelapsarian grace, Ron Vawter (also seated at the table) puts soft music on a record player, places glycerine drops in his eyes, and lays his head sideways on the table and "weeps." Gray flips his script over his shoulder and replies with Reilly's speech on choosing the mystical path toward salvation. His delivery here is in the form of a lecture, as he interrupts the scripted speech to clarify certain ambiguities: as LeCompte reported, he acts "simultaneously as Spalding the teacher to the class/audience and Spalding the actor playing Sir Henry" (LeCompte 1978, 84). Meanwhile the music changes to a disco tune. As the music grows increasingly louder, Gray is forced to shout Reilly's final precept: "Go in peace, my daughter. Work out your salvation with diligence."

This "reading" of Eliot's text undermines several elements that empower the author's vision in traditional theater. First, the emotionless and noncontextualized recitation deprives the language of much of its power, reducing Eliot's carefully wrought verse to stilted, childish reading on the one hand, and frenetic gibberish on the other. The physical presence of the scripts, and the discrepancies between them, further destroy the illusion that the text has disappeared behind the performance or that it constitutes a seamless construct of meaning. Music is played that comments neither emotionally nor thematically on the scene. In each case, the process by which in orthodox theater the subjective performer is reduced to an object through which the text flows is marked and resisted. This creates a tension in which the performers try to avert being emptied and re-created as characters within the text; since, however, they are directed to enact the scenes, they are forced to be both subjects and objects, both themselves and a part of Eliot's text. As Savran suggests, this exposes the "femininity" of the performers (and all nonlinguistic symbolic apparatuses within the performance), the fact that, "in order to mean, they will have to be emptied, violated, transgressed" by Eliot's text (Savran 1986b, 115).

Part 3 provides three vignettes taken from an Arch Oboler comedy album (*Drop Dead*) and a scene written by Jim Strahs. In enacting the Oboler "horror stories" ("A Day at the Dentist" and "The Chicken Heart"), LeCompte provides associations with the earlier examples of objectification and femininity of the subject by recalling the doctor-patient relationship prominent in *Rumstick Road,* and by using the red tent that had been used as a haven for female figures in the first two pieces of the *Trilogy*. This time, the tent appears not as a breast-symbol connoting nurturance and safety, but as a "monster" that pursues, chews up, and swallows the Woman, as well as the children who have appeared on stage. The scene written by Strahs, "The Breast Examination," is accompanied by a Folkways instructional recording, "The Understanding and Self-Examination of Breast Cancer." The transgressive gaze and cruel insensitivity of the doctor (played, significantly, by Gray) and his transvestite nurse, and their violation of the patient's subjectivity and her body—LeCompte wanted the scene to look "very close to pornography," and throughout the scene the Patient's breasts are taped and brutally handled—recall Reilly's cavalier objectification of other characters in *The Cocktail Party,* especially his attempts to de-eroticize Celia. In addition, as opposed to the cathartic impulses of Eliot's text, structured on a psychoanalytic model, *Nayatt School* introduces images that suggest a kind of spiritual and social cancer that is beyond therapy or purgation. While the breast cancer record plays, films showing the development of lung cancer are projected on the back wall. Cancer cells are depicted in a state of fantastic replication and growth. At the same time, fragments from the recording comment objectively on the phenomenon: "Some medical scientists feel that cancer cells appear to represent anarchy. They seem to go berserk or run wild in the body. . . . Here science is in trouble" (Savran 1986b, 125).

The prevailing sense is that reality is not governed by laws of stability and order, nor by simple reconcilable oppositions like sick/cured, patient/doctor, performance/text. Instead, the sovereign force is an unreflexive and chaotic growth that eventually replicates itself beyond what the body can endure before destroying its host. But can we assign a negative point of view even to this picture of chaotic growth? If chaotic systems—including the pathological replication of cancer cells—are one source of newer, highly structured order, then might not the spread of the disease be the harbinger of the higher life that waits behind "death's twilight kingdom," the site of the salvation promised by Reilly? Such a chaotic pathology applies to the text as well, for in the next two "Examinations," Eliot's text is first eroded from within and then virtually ripped apart and demolished in the closing action of the play. Here again, the emphasis is placed not on textual deconstruction for its own sake, but on the re-inscription of textuality into a new image of order, that is, from the Euclidean order of *The Cocktail Party* to the fractal order of *Nayatt School*.

In part 5, the third act of *The Cocktail Party* is represented by a mixture of the performers from The Group and a band of children. These performers act out segments of Eliot's text around a series of increasingly frenzied improvisations, until all of the children "die" within specified "dead circles" painted on the floor. As a series of fragmented recordings (sections from the Berlioz "Requiem," the breast cancer and disco recordings, etc.) thunders in the background, the children are martyred, like Celia Copplestone, by representatives of the adult world of order and wellness. The essence of Eliot's text, with its message of sacrifice, denial, and penitence, overwhelms the representatives of innocence and freedom and murders them.

The adults' "victory" is only short-lived, though, as they turn and begin to destroy the records themselves. Using knives, crayons, scissors, and sometimes an electric drill, the now half-naked performers defile and assault the records while "A Mighty Fortress is Our God" blasts from the speakers. Like those pertaining to Bette Gray kept by the authority-figure psychiatrist from *Rumstick Road,* these "records" will not be kept;

whatever subjectivity and pseudo-objective information they have inscribed upon them is ephemeral. The destruction of the text(s) is accomplished by an onslaught of furious energy, which might look like simple turbulence. Yet out of that chaos a new system of order arises, based on interactive energies between the oppositions built up within the performance. In essence, the destruction of the text has evolved into a more complex dissipative system—the performance of *Nayatt School* itself.

The frenzied release of performative energy against the text accomplishes its goal. After the unrestrained destruction is finished, the Man and Woman streak (literally) across a narrow plank suspended precariously thirty feet above the playing area, while Spalding remains in the house below, listening to the soothing strains of a Bach partita.

The image is a powerful one, suggesting a galaxy of meanings. On the one hand, the fleeing performers evoke a picture of Adam and Eve fleeing Eden (Ron Vawter, as the Man, even mentions feeling like a figure from Masaccio's rendering of the subject). Perhaps from this perspective the mutual deconstruction of performance (the spontaneous, innocent children) and the text (the fixed Eliot text and the records) will create new theatrical possibilities and effect a renewed beginning for the evicted pair ("The world was all before them, where to choose / Their place of rest, and Providence their guide: / They hand in hand with wand'ring steps and slow, / Through Eden took their solitary way"). On another level, the performers are escaping the chaos that remains below, and since the two are often associated with Gray's mother and father throughout the *Trilogy,* this may evoke an image of the now-isolated Gray achieving adulthood and individual identity. But again, the image might just as well suggest that while others escape into the ecstasy of chaos and disorder, Gray is captive-ated by another form of artistic order and control, Bach's music, which will doubtless—after the disco music and the noise of the drills—captivate some spectators as well. These and other possibilities form a dense constellation of images and interpretations, none of which, in light of the devastating critique of ontological certainty that has been offered, can be foregrounded as the overarching or "correct" reading.

The performance, then, uses the text of *The Cocktail Party* to produce a temporary feeling of centeredness and security in the cathartic possibilities of drama, religious faith, and medicine. Once this smooth surface is evoked, The Group explores its implications and the ideologies it derives from and perpetuates. Instead of naturalizing these discourses, as in realist drama, The Group exposes them to the scrutiny of the spectator and reveals their rough and corrosive edges. LeCompte's fractal shaping of Western culture reveals its microscopic dimensions, and perhaps those false centers exposed are the self-repeating capillary connections that circulate power and construct matrices of control in our culture. The result is not unlike Brecht's alienation effect, except that The Group does not—indeed, given their predicates, cannot—imply another coherent system that can be offered as an alternative to existing culture and society.[19] Instead the cancer cells, replicating randomly and without restraint or order, evoke a world of chaos. Those figures who would impose order and authority and thereby invoke a center are exposed as cruel charlatans and victimizers. Eliot's mystical path is revealed as a patriarchal and self-serving philosophy, while the text that produces it is exposed as, itself, a fractal system—corrupt, internally fragmented, and seemingly disorganized. Doctors and dentists are arrogant and inhumane, while science is depicted as at the mercy of cancer. And finally, the empathic performer who introduced the performance—Gray, appearing as unreconstituted subject, "speaker," and the spectator's charismatic source of understanding and feeling—is an *ignis fatuus,* another "ruse," as Savran explains:

> Spalding Gray's engagement of the spectator in the opening monologue is the beginning of a process that leads to the speaker's fragmentation and the audience's estrangement, as "Spalding" is gradually subsumed by a host of other parts. By the end of the piece, after he has played an assortment of pathological roles, it becomes clear that his charm and charisma have been used to make him a pretext, a false center. *Nayatt School* suggests that rather than being a fixed point of reference, a stable personality, Gray's appearance as "Spalding" is only one role among many. . . . It may well be that he is simply the collection of the roles he plays: Sir Henry, teacher, mad scientist, dentist, doctor, son. (1986b, 113)

Again, however, these metaphysical probings into the nature of character also include a political critique, though Savran neglects this element of the work. For the piece explores and reveals the political implications of the type of performance-oriented acting ontology that Gray himself uses. We see the darker side of what Gray had described (in regard to his acting in *Sakonnet Point*) as "the many-in-the-one" and the notion of performance-as-praxis. Like Schechner and many other first-generation directors and performers, Gray feels that "pure," uninhibited performance is a therapeutic or liberating activity, for himself and perhaps for the audience. Such views on acting reveal a lack of awareness regarding the collusion between structures of authority and Presence. History, and especially recent history, shows conclusively that theatrical manipulations of Presence have been assimilated into politics and the mediatized spectacle it now represents. Simply put, in the political arena performance is used to manipulate Presence (as in the concept of political charisma), in order to acculturate certain values and perceptions that make up public "opinion." The disquieting theatricality (i.e., the use of "scenarios," the changing of masks and roles, the glib transformations of opinion and policy) that permeated political discourse and the media during the Vietnam War, Watergate, and our more recent scandals reveals the other side to Gray's ontology of performance. Within the structure of *Nayatt School,* his demise from engaging interlocutor to paternalistic psychiatrist, and from there to mad scientist, suggests a Nixonesque fragmentation of the "many-in-the-one," a devolution of empowered selves that reveals the connections between the authoritative Presence of the "public performer" and other centers of power. And thus it seems natural that, when we last "see" Gray working with The Group (in *Route 1 & 9*), we actually only hear his taped voice assuming the role of the Director who oversees the "blind building" of a house: behind the scenes, absent and supposedly fallen from power, yet (like a fallen president) still exercising a disembodied authority as a voice of expertise and authority, a kind of false center.

Such implications of Gray's position as performer within The Group's work are explored further in *Point Judith,* the epilogue to *The Rhode Island Trilogy* and Gray's final "live" appearance as a member of The Group.[20] The work suggests certain possible impulses within the trilogy that are completed in the epilogue (even the title is a final handoff from *Sakonnet Point*), a movement toward equilibrium, formal balance, and drama, and away from chaos, disjunct structure, and performance.[21] Regarding Gray himself, the piece reveals a journey from performer to actor, as he takes on three essentially nonautobiographical roles: Stew in Jim Strah's play "Rig," Stew as Tyrone in a wild version of *Long Day's Journey into Night,* and the nun "Mother Elizabeth" in the film by Ken Kobland that ends the piece, *By the Sea.*

The piece, however, is not an affirmation of drama over performance, or classical over contemporary aesthetics. LeCompte again introduces centrality and balance only as a means to investigate their implications. She calls *Point Judith* a "big transition" for her because in it she finally begins to move Gray out of the center—as "the pretext, the storyteller"—and to assert more of her own personality (Savran 1986b, 150). That personality is both more overtly political and more female than Gray's, and such imperatives signal subtle changes in The Group's methods and performances. For, as Jill Dolan (1989b, 69) has argued:

> Feminist postmodernism does not play indulgently with meaninglessness or plurality, charges that might be leveled against some postmodern performance auteurs. Feminist postmodernism is committed to meaning, to sifting through the referents of material reality and drawing blueprints of their construction that can be historically revised and changed.

Generally, this shift follows the transition from what Philip Auslander calls a "*transgressive* to *resistant* political art" (1987, 21). Auslander describes culture in terms that parallel LeCompte's representations of it in her work, as chaotic, nonlinear, and fractious, "a conjuncture of adversarial practices and discourses" (33). He argues that The Group's work inhabits postmodern culture and works its deconstructions from within it. From that position, The Group uses its performances to provide "cognitive maps," which encourage "a mode of perception that will enable the spectator to make sense of the dislocating postmodern sensorium" (33). The resulting maps are necessarily fractal in nature, unsuitable for measuring neatly a culture's linear progress or decline or for drawing its regular shape, but still the perfect abstract shape to gauge accurately the scabrous edges of a pluralistic and contentious society. LeCompte's oddly shaped outline of culture is derived from performance strategies that deconstruct the equilibristic text and other institutions of control. The resulting fractals lay bare American culture's attempts to eradicate difference, revealing the replicating, self-similar patterns of hegemonic discourses that give that culture its shape of order. But The Group's performances go farther still, to expose the intractable, ragged edges of that culture, the obscure traces of disorder that are embedded within even the most hegemonic discourses. Their work reflects an attempt to project an accurate map of American society that charts the available paths for marginalized, nonhegemonic discourses, marking dangerous routes through the centers of cultural power.

Since, however, to substitute any one nonhegemonic discourse for the hegemonic simply creates a new dominant discourse—the pitfall of much modernist art and theory—The Group never simply transgresses or transcends the old order. Instead, its work projects an image of culture as fractious and contentious, an arena where texts and other loci of control deconstruct one another and reveal a society based not on transcendent, universal values shared by all, but on difference. The Group's work effects this change of image by adjusting the viewer's sense of scale or perspective, revealing not the smooth, untroubled surface of American life as it is perceived "from afar" through the media and other hegemonic forms of representation, but by exposing instead the microscopic detail and fascinating complexity of its varied and disjunct textures. As Richard Foreman (a frequent collaborator with The Group) has written, the audience needs to learn to "see small" because to do so means to engage the quantum level of reality, where contradictions are anchored (Foreman 1976, 145).

LeCompte's work, I have tried to suggest, has been both transgressive and resistant from the beginning, but with the break from the *Rhode Island* plays the shift toward a resistant political theater becomes more pronounced. The works that follow—*Route 1 & 9 (The Last Act)* (1981), *L.S.D (Just the High Points)* (1984), and *Frank Dell's The Temptation of Saint Anthony* (1987)—reveal a maturing sense of vision and function in The Group's work.[22] While continuing to create an alternative theater language and to redefine the orthodox dramatic elements of narrative, character, theme, and so on, The Group comes increasingly to recognize that performance and a deconstructive dramaturgy themselves do not offer a final solution to the burdens of contemporary American culture. Instead, the works infiltrate that culture by subjecting its institutions—especially those autonomized by forms of writing—to a critique that marks and subverts sources of power. Eventually, they develop an ironic and deconstructive edge so corrosive that it subsumes the ideologies behind the works' own enactments, and exposes The Group as ambivalent performers in a cultural spectacle that consistently obscures difference and promotes images of the dominant discourses.

Route 1 & 9 takes perhaps the American theater's most emphatic statement of universal human nature, Wilder's *Our Town,* and investigates both the power of that statement and its implications. In breaking up Wilder's poignant fantasy of American culture, The Group again flirts with parody, especially in the first act where Ron Vawter delivers a facetious video "lecture" on Wilder's play, based on a 1965 Encyclopedia Britannica teaching film starring Clifton Fadiman. The Lecturer, here as in previous work, is the "center" and voice of authority who masters the complexities of Wilder's dramatic text and then "objectively" renders that knowledge and presents it transparently to the spectator. Vawter wonderfully mimics the Lecturer's unsubtle illustrative gestures and ponderous phrases ("the play helps us to understand and so accept our existence on earth"), but despite the pretention and the Lecturer's obvious attempt to dilute individual resistance to prevailing metaphysical and social discourses, the speeches possess an attractive quality.[23] LeCompte herself told Savran that she liked the original Britannica film, "but was bothered about liking it. It touched nostalgic chords of comfort for me that made me angry. It pressed two buttons in me simultaneously. And I found myself unable to accept either in comfort. I couldn't destroy it, and I couldn't go with it and be satisfied" (Savran 1986b, 17).

Here, in what the Lecturer might call "the condensed line or word," lies the heart of the process behind *Route 1 & 9*. Opposing discourses are double-coded into the performance, and cause ambiguous responses that cannot be reconciled. However, instead of falsifying the antinomies by bringing them together in a synthesis, or of foregrounding one over the other, The Group investigates the implications of both and refuses to reconcile them, to derive an interpretation of the world from them. To do so would simply repeat the approach of the Lecturer, and would possibly instill in the spectator a similar sense of interpretive power and control. By leaving the issues dynamic and ambiguous within a quantum field of interactive energies, The Group makes possible a truly nondominant relationship between the performance and the spectator. It creates the subject-object blends that allow for the "necessary fuzziness" of reality that Heisenberg announced in the indeterminacy principle, and through which LeCompte shapes The Group's vision of American culture.

Like the illusory, engaging monologist Gray had created in the first section of *Rumstick Road,* the parody of "The Lecture" is, first, a ruse; it creates in the audience feelings of superiority and group affinity that are subsequently destroyed and exposed in the following acts. This, too, is evidence of The Group's attempts to politicize its work, because it re-

The Wooster Group, *Route 1 & 9 (The Last Act).*
Ron Vawter. Directed by Elizabeth LeCompte, Performance Garage, 1981. Photo by Nancy Campbell.

veals how performance itself (rather than the authorially empowered text) can be (ab)used to create forms of privileged discourse. Almost all the charismatic attraction of the lecture comes not from the language but from the gestures, forced playfulness and mock seriousness conveyed by Vawter, which come together to constitute the Lecturer as a false center of majority and dominance. Like Gray's performance as "Spalding," the interlocutor of *Nayatt School,* Vawter's performance strategies, more than what he says, create a Presence, though at this stage in The Group's work that Presence is always an ironic one. The Lecturer's "extremely white analysis" (as LeCompte calls it) of Wilder's play also implicates the audience itself as a possible center, as invariably they are predominantly whites who have seen and probably felt the power of Wilder's play.[24]

"The Lecture," and the remainder of *Route 1 & 9* as well, is never allowed to remain simply a parody. The performance is also a tribute to Wilder, whom LeCompte refers to as her "predecessor."[25] Both director-playwrights react against naturalism by creating performance spaces as opposed to realistic settings (yielding the fruits of previous work by Reinhardt, Meyerhold, and Vakhtangov), and both share to a large extent what Wilder called the "four fundamental conditions of the drama: The theater is an art which reposes upon the work of many collaborators; It is addressed to the group mind; It is based upon a pretense and its very nature calls out a multiplication of pretenses; Its action takes place in a perpetual present time" (Wilder 1974, 891). LeCompte's sincerest homage to Wilder—who always demanded that the drama indict as well as delight the spectator—is that she has radicalized each of these notions to the point where they can be turned upon Wilder's own somber (and white middle-class) view of "the group mind."

LeCompte deconstructs Wilder's vision of Grover's Corners by eradicating its predicate of a universal and transcendent human nature. Wilder's play is built upon connections revealed between Jane Crofut, the Crofut farm, Grover's Corners, and so on, up to and including the Universe and the Mind of God. The physical and the metaphysical are united to form a picture of "the days and deaths," in Brooks Atkinson's famous phrase, "of the brotherhood of man." But that picture is a simulacrum that distorts and obliterates difference—even Simon Stimson is eventually brought within the fold of the town's (and Wilder's) capacious humanity. The "sentimentality" that LeCompte is drawn to in *Our Town* derives from this evocation of communality, which itself comes partly from the beautifully rendered language shared by all the figures in the play. And whatever troubling ethnic or material differences that exist do so outside Grover's Corners proper: "Polish Town's across the tracks and some Canuck families." The presentational mode of Wilder's play, too, breaks down the performance/spectator barriers integral to realistic drama, but only to bring the action of the play and the spectator into closer communion. As Wilder said, the presentational effect "raises the action from the specific to the general," a strategy designed to promote homogeneity among the spectators (1974, 892). Although *Our Town* contains a subtext that reveals Wilder's keen awareness of what is painful to human existence—Grover's Corners has a jail, promising youths like Joe Crowell perish in foreign wars, artists drink and commit suicide—American audiences have historically viewed the play as an homage to an ideal period in their history. Perceived by many as a Disneyland "imagineer," Wilder is thought to have largely weeded out what hurts in American culture and recreated a generalized portrait of what "Main Street U.S.A." *should* look like. *Our Town* is therefore generally accepted as America limned in Euclidean terms, while *Route 1 & 9* reveals the fractal shapes beneath it, the ragged edges—as well as the potentially deadly harmonious patterns—that underlie its smooth surfaces.[26]

In order to subvert Wilder's universalizing and to reclaim the specific, LeCompte and The Group found it necessary to commit their most significant "transgression" to date: the use of performers in blackface to enact a scatological vaudeville routine ("The Party") by Pigmeat Markham. After the video monitors darken following "The Lecture," we hear bustling figures on the stage and a taped improvisation left over from *Point Judith* (including the voice of the absent Spalding Gray) playing over the speakers. As the lights come up, the spectator is greeted with the sight of two men in blackface wearing "blind man" sunglasses in the act of constructing a skeletal house. The builders "feel" a floor plan while the taped voices discuss the great demand for wall-less houses with no heating. The buildings are especially attractive to families in Jersey (along which U.S. Routes 1 and 9 run), where, the taped voices report, there are "Cold people . . . Indifferent people . . . all over" (7). As the men mime the blind building, "Ann" and "Willie" appear and make phone calls to one another and to various actual New York fast food chains to order food for Willie's birthday party. They speak in vaudeville black jive, and are sometimes successful at enticing a delivery to Wooster Street. They end by calling the builders, now called Kenny and Pigmeat, and telling them to bring liquor to the party. After meeting and dancing wildly, the four come together within the skeletal house, where Pigmeat lets on that he has inadvertently stolen castor oil instead of rye. After they drink, joke, and dance some more, they announce one by one that they have to leave to "send a telegram." Finally, Pigmeat stops the music and is asked if he must send the telegram, to which he replies, "No, no, I done sent mine." The lights go down, school bells ring, Charles Ives's "Three Places in New England" comes on, and four monitors are cranked from the ceiling until they are each seven feet above the stage. The screens light up, and Emily Gibbs says "hello."

The details of the ensuing scandal that erupted over the blackface routine have been sufficiently documented elsewhere.[27] The adverse reaction, though nearly devastating for The Group's existence, nevertheless vividly revealed, first, that the provocative performances were indeed "pressing two buttons at once" and, second, that The Group's aggressive techniques in the piece still had not been contextualized within the audiences of alternative theater. There is nothing "racist" (in the usual sense of the term) in the work if it is analyzed, as Bonnie Marranca insists it should be,

> within the Group's history and development of techniques and themes that define its style: distortion, exploration of character types, juxtaposition of several art forms, masking, identity crises, demystifying social and family traditions of white America, satiric and ironic modes of performance, play-within-play structures, deconstruction of space. (Marranca 1984, 125)

Critics of the work did not comprehend that blackface itself is a form of self-irony and effacement. As Savran (1986b, 30–33) explains, for black performers like Markham, the application of blackface was liberating because it was originally devised for white performers. By using it on themselves, black performers did not create "real" black characters, but rather portrayed laughable stereotypes previously created and naturalized by the white community. Such stereotypes, though they will be perceived as real and racist by liberal whites, can be turned against the racial majority by using laughter to expose the cultural ideas behind the stereotypes. LeCompte recognizes that, unable to "speak" the Other in performance, she could nevertheless avoid simply opaquely speaking herself (a white female) through blacks by performing an easily recognized form of cultural appropriation, that is, blackface vaudeville.

In addition, as LeCompte told Tish Dace, "The blackface is not sociological. It's a theatrical metaphor" (Dace 1982, 5–6). Like Wilder's Stage Manager, the blackface is deployed by LeCompte to break up the integrated illusion of realist drama in order to present not a slice of life, but a distanced view of it: epic theater, not dramatic realism. However, though influenced by Brecht's theories and Wilder's precedents, this contemporary epic theater does not foreground a privileged political or ethical position. Instead, the blackface opens up an ambiguous space in the performance and pushes two buttons at once. It is first, as LeCompte says, a "painful" representation of racial difference, and a dangerous strategy as well, because it asks us to find humor in a racial stereotype that has already been a source of cruel humor for hundreds of years. But it is also a wildly liberating representation, especially coming in between the dry lecture and "underacted" scenes from *Our Town* that follow. The blackface performers provide the first vitality in the piece, and the only act that duplicates this energy is, significantly, the Ghoul Dance at the end of part 3. The racial difference thus appears to represent a polarity of the inhibited but elegant text of Wilder and the vitally energetic yet disturbing performance routines of Markham.

Still, what seems to have especially disturbed audiences was LeCompte's deconstruction of the sense of a universal community inscribed in Wilder's play, and its world of a capacious humanity that glosses over difference and the fractal shapes of culture that underlie its apparently smooth contours. Without that *communitas,* there is no center, no point of reference by which to guide moral, ethical, and political choice. But LeCompte posits difference as the center, as white people in blackface enact stereotypes that blacks themselves see as representative of white thinking and oppression. She breaks down oppositional categories (white/black, repressed/liberated, mind/body) so that she can, in Savran's estimation, "implicate the spectator in the performance as both black and white, free and enslaved. It offers no ideological haven from which the action may be watched with impunity" (Savran 1986b, 31). And, when the excerpts from Wilder's play begin on the videos, the blackface performers try to remain still and unobtrusive: but the masks of black paint begin to drip off with the exertion of the dancing, and for a moment the performers are revealed as black *and* white, not black or white.

Above the continuing (but now muted) party arrive the video monitors on which the last act of *Our Town* is played, the two scenes commenting ironically on one another. On the one level Wilder's romantic vision of love, birth, and death is played out in a beautifully expressive language that captivates the spectator; below it, the party persists as quiet laughter, the clinking of glasses, and the sound of spilling booze are heard. Above, everything is unimpassioned and detached from life, and the only scene of passion (George Webb's arrival at the cemetery) is an affront: "Goodness. That ain't no way to behave!" The comment is directed not only at George, but at the social and dramatic affront of Pigmeat's defecation and the entire party scene below. While the performers offer real life, the videos capture what is artificial. Still, since LeCompte insists on pressing the two buttons simultaneously, the spectator's response is ambivalent, disoriented. Even though the video speeches are artificial, they contain the most moving language to be heard in the entire performance. As Bonnie Marranca describes her own experience of the work, "the highly charged expressive language that Wilder's characters speak overwhelms video technology. I found myself watching a monitor furthest from where I was sitting because the dialogue was too powerful . . . for a film medium. What's more, I realize how much I regret the absence of inflected, unself-conscious stage speech" (Marranca 1984, 124). Even spatially the spectator's view is pulled in opposite directions: vertically and upward toward the closely framed and enclosed nostalgic view of life and death that Wilder describes, and also downward and horizontally toward the performers who, unframed and unrestrained, have so vividly evoked the physical. Like Claudius at prayer—himself both murderer/king, uncle/father, adulterer/husband, sinner/penitent—the spectator is "to double business bound," and can find no relish of salvation while words fly up and thoughts remain below.

The last acted portion of *Route 1 & 9* is the Ghoul Dance that follows the reading of *Our Town*. After the self-restraint and denial of Wilder's characters (framed within the video monitors) and the muted revelers (framed by the open-walled skeletal house), this unframed frenetic *danse macabre* introduces another vision of life and death. Shaking wildly in front of the audience, drooling stage blood and exposing themselves, the performers unleash a furious and libidinous energy that virtually overwhelms the measured cadences of Wilder's language, and the repressed sexuality of his characters. Like Markham's defecation, the dance sends a message: in addition to reaffirming the difference between videotaped drama and live performance, the dance exposes what Wilder, and American culture in general, tries to cover up—sex, the body, sexual difference, and so on.

The final affront in the performance is a porn film that plays silently on a stage television while above, on the color monitors, a movie is shown. In the upper film a driver (LeCompte) winds her way through New York and out onto the freeway, driving toward New Jersey and U.S. Routes 1 and 9. She picks up two hitchhikers, who are also the performers in the porn film. The images recall but do not reconcile the major antitheses between text and performance that frame the piece: the control of driving and the sense of having a destination, as opposed to the lack of control implicit in the act of giving strangers a ride; the movement out of the theater and into the "real" world of Routes 1 and 9, as opposed to the theatricalized vision of what those roads lead to within the performance space (and the monitors) itself; and finally, visions of life and death, or life in death, as LeCompte drives through a glimmering sunset toward the "Cold . . . Indifferent" people that inhabit the stretch of highway, while the two porn stars engage in an oddly sterile procreative act—again framed within the space of a television box—which in its last shudder makes for a final quietus.

LeCompte's treatment of the dramatic text in *Route 1 & 9* parallels her treatment of American culture and The Group's position as avant-garde artists within it. There is no longer a drive toward simply transcending, parodying, or deconstructing completely the text under scrutiny. Instead of facetiously rejecting or attempting to transgress textuality, The Group simultaneously occupies and resists the structure of the logocentric text. The Group's occupation of Wilder's play reveals its own affiliations to the experimental ideas of a predecessor, and also discloses the beauty and power of such representations. However, painful as it might be, The Group then resists these institutionalized forms of erotics and power by subjecting them to complex ironies that expose their sentimental bases and insidious relations to dominant discourses. Finally, in the most radical irony of all, The Group reveals how its own theatrical appropriation of material perverts and corrupts certain natural and traditional activities, beliefs, and icons—from defecation, to racial stereotypes, to sex, and to language. In the wake of such a performance little is left to grasp and believe in, as previously held notions of community, universal values, and transcendence are replaced by a sometimes frightening vision of difference, strife, and irreconcilable oppositions. Still, by directing the deconstructive performance toward such radical exposures there is the hope that some of the most deeply ingrained American cultural habits—the eradication of racial difference, the suppression of marginal discourses, the mostly misguided urge for transcendence and stable, self-authenticating oppositions—have been marked and exposed. And there may be further hope that these revelations can enable individuals to discern more accurately their position within the complex pattern of affinities and relations that makes up America's disorienting fractal culture.

In the second piece of the trilogy, *L.S.D. (Just the High Points),* The Group extends its investigations into a more specific historical domain. Like earlier work, the piece is a "memory play," but significant in terms of The Group's evolution toward more political activity is the fact that cultural, rather than personal, memory is now being scrutinized. Savran rightly calls it The Group's most "historiographic" work (1986b, 6), yet the emphasis is very much on the state of contemporary America, and the view of history presented is anything but stable or determinate. Instead, the historiography is similar to the genealogies of Michel Foucault, which concentrate on local, discontinuous, illegitimized forms of knowledge and history. As in Foucault, the genealogy drawn by The Group in *L.S.D.* functions as a critique of traditional methods of writing history, and exposes such writing to be ideological, contingent, and in the end an extremely fragile vehicle for humanity's record.

The pre-texts are Arthur Miller's *The Crucible* and the writings of Timothy Leary and the Beat poets of the fifties and sixties, both interacting within the performance in a complex historical relationship. Miller's play historicizes the seventeenth-century Salem witch trials by commenting overtly on the political climate in America during the fifties, while *L.S.D.* historicizes Miller's play by subjecting it to a postmodern political critique that itself evokes the Beat writers of the fifties. Each text in some way undermines the others, with the result that no one method of verifying history, of re-presenting it, is privileged. Once again, the performance itself is interrogated and revealed as a distortion, a hallucination. In the process of that revelation, however, The Group again exposes the method by which such political and cultural representations work to suppress difference, to manipulate Presence and its authority, and to restrain any kind of marginal or subversive activity.

Indeed, more so than in any of the previous works, the production itself mirrored the very aspects of cultural contestation that underlie *L.S.D.* Owing at least partly to the reaction and economic suppression imposed on *Route 1 & 9*, LeCompte began planning a "season" of plays in repertory for the summer of 1983. With the theme of persecution no doubt in mind, the first "readings" were built around *The Crucible*. After building additional material around the reading in rehearsal, The Group staged the piece as a work in progress. Then The Group invited Miller to view a performance of the work, to which Miller reacted ambivalently: while admitting he was intrigued and pleased by this version of the work, Miller expressed some trepidation over the speed at which his play's lines were delivered, fearing perhaps that the audience would see The Group's frenzied performance as a parody of *The Crucible,* a work he still believed might someday be revived in New York. As The Group continued to work on the piece, adding the readings from Leary and the Beats, as well as the Leary–G. Gordon Liddy debates, Miller apparently had reservations about the appropriation of his play and began to exert legal pressure through his attorney. The Group altered the performance several times to accommodate copyright restrictions, but, having failed to appease Miller, the production was finally forced to close in January 1985.[28]

The very process by which American culture empowers certain kinds of hegemonic representations, while simultaneously marginalizing and suppressing others, is thus rendered in the piece both internally, as a theme, and externally, as the subversive activity of the performance itself. Notions of how histories are inscribed within culture as re-presentations of actual events are investigated and revealed to be not "historical fact" but "texts," and specifically texts that have been deconstructed by performance. The Group enacts Barthes's view of the text as "a multidimensional space in which a variety of writings, none of them original, blend and clash. The text is a tissue of quotations drawn from the innumerable centers of culture" (Barthes 1977a, 46). What LeCompte adds by way of the performance is a suggestion that such "centers of culture" are inevitably those of empowered discourses, which go on to create their own hegemonic representations of reality at the expense of others. History, then, is not an immanent "fact," but the text of power relations that inscribes the narrative of the victors.

As the foundations for American culture come more and more to be understood by LeCompte as depending on writing and textuality, The Group finds its own relationship to texts changing. Whereas earlier work tends to deconstruct textuality partly to discredit it in hopes of escaping from its constraints, The Group's more mature pieces recognize that it is the text and its language that keep theater anchored to culture and to history. Indeed, LeCompte acknowledges that, given the insubstantial nature of history, texts are inscriptions of the activity of making history, an activity with important political consequences. The new awareness of the text's political position instigates new approaches to the activity of reading, and to an interrogation of how that activity is institutionalized in American culture. This in turn leads The Group to ground its work more emphatically in cultural texts and thus to complicate its relationships to them. Working from within such texts, the performances both occupy and resist them. The effect opens up but also limits The Group's work, as it allows the performers simultaneously, in Auslander's phrase, to expose the "processes of cultural control and emphasize the traces of nonhegemonic discourses within the dominant without claiming to transcend its terms" (Auslander 1987, 23). The formulation resembles Derrida's desire to find "an exit and a deconstruction without changing terrain, by repeating what is implicit in the founding concepts and the original problematic, by using against the edifice the instruments or stones available in the house" (Derrida 1982, 135).[29]

The first section of *L.S.D.* (entitled "Newton's Center") virtually stages the activity of reading, but problematizes it by dispersing the activity among a variety of reading modes. Several male performers sit at a lectern-table and read mostly random selections from the "great books" of Timothy Leary and other writers associated with the Beats (William Burroughs, Jack Kerouac, Arthur Koestler, Alan Watts, and others). The performers never enact the roles of the authors they read, but instead introduce themselves by their real names and then comment on one another's selections and reading style. They consciously separate themselves from the ideas and "voices" of the authors, thereby distinguishing their activity as reading and not "dramatic reading." Meanwhile, Nancy Reilly (the Babysitter) sits at the end of the table wearing headphones. She listens to taped interviews with Ann Rower, a former babysitter for Leary's children, who after seeing an early version of *L.S.D.* had offered her memories as material. Reilly interrupts the readings occasionally by repeating, in an exaggerated "telephone-operator" nasal tone, selected portions of the interview. Rower's memoir, unlike the written records of the times being read by the men, is rambling, filled with gaps, hiatuses, and solecisms. Meanwhile, the last reader sits in a

The Wooster Group, *L.S.D. (Just the High Points)*.
Ron Vawter, Kate Valk, Willem Dafoe. Directed by Elizabeth LeCompte, Performance Garage, 1984. Photo by Nancy Campbell.

trough in front of the table, quoting from interviews with Jackie Leary, Timothy's son.

Two "records" of the period are thus evoked, one written and inscribed within a text, the other oral and performed. The written texts, though read randomly, evoke an unusually cogent description of the form and pressure of the fifties and sixties. The several writers are universally optimistic, even effusive, in their belief that recent experiments with drugs and counterculture lifestyles are heralding a new age of higher consciousness. And, as Ron Vawter points out, their words recreate the beliefs and ideals of The Performance Group, forcing the performers in its contemporary avatar The Wooster Group to confront their new post–holy theater position and ideals (Savran 1986b, 183). Reactions are ambivalent, as the naïveté of some of the earlier work and the unquestioning loyalty to the former guru-director Richard Schechner are balanced against the recent accusations of apoliticality and irresponsibility made against *Route 1 & 9*. The spectator, like the performers, is left to weigh these written memoirs from a disturbing period in American history, and to ponder what was lost in the haste to escape it by a return to orthodoxy and political quiescence.

Such a view is quarrelled over in the interview material from Rower and Jackie Leary. The oral memoirs are also ambivalent, but there is an edge of bitterness and mocking irony in them. Rower describes Leary in anything but romantic terms, as a liar and a sexually repressed man who never recovered from the suicide of his first wife. Jackie Leary goes so far as to suggest that his father probably sold out members of the Weathermen and S.D.S. in return for amnesty on his drug charges. This further complicates the reading of history, as written and oral accounts appear to differ markedly, creating an ambivalent text. No one mode of writing or reading history is foregrounded as absolute, and neither seems to capture wholly the "truth" of the period.

Since the view proposed by the writers gives the appearance of being more systematic, however, there is a tendency to grant that record a measure of authority and Presence. LeCompte, however, still suspicious of texts even while inhabiting them in performance, ends part 1 with a "reenactment" of an incident at Leary's house. As Reilly enacts the reading of Rower's recollection of the event, the men casually act out a scene where Koestler, high on acid, stumbles across Alan Ginsberg and Peter Orlovsky in bed making love. Koestler "screams . . . freaks out," and runs from the house (Savran 1986b, 187). Since Koestler was a well-known proponent of and polemicist for uninhibited sexual practices, the audience is left wondering which history provides the "true" portrait of Koestler. In addition, one wonders why the written accounts were granted such privileged status in the first place.

In addition to creating ambiguities regarding historical verifiability, part 1 also introduces the concepts of paranoia and schizophrenia as factors in the creating of history. The passages from Leary and the others reveal the sense of foreboding these individuals felt—a consciousness that, as marginal figures, subversives, they were being watched and "staked out" for eventual suppression. Leary's manifestation of this paranoia was an increasing belief in his own importance and "aura." As the government placed more and more pressure on him, his instinctive but repugnant response was to inflate his own position within the revolution. The sad result, seen so often in counterculture movements, was simply that Leary began to affect the role of guru, a "sage-mythic male" whose potency (often described in sexual terms) is the reagent for revolutionary ideas and movements. But such a conception simply co-opts established sources of power and authority in Western culture, translating them into personal aggrandizement. The guru ends up not creating a new and freer society but simply appropriating acceptable forms of cultural control and restating them to empower his own agenda.

Leary's self-confirming gestures alarmingly recall attitudes expressed by holy-theater directors and performers of the same period, whose displacement of authorial control was often simply a pretext for assuming the same kind of Presence usually conferred on the text. LeCompte, like Beckett and other contemporary theater artists, remains unwilling to grant uncritically the power of performance—itself characterized by the schizoid consciousness of the "many-in-the-one"—to transform the individual into a more privileged or transcendent state of being. Instead, amortized by the limits of desire and the unconscious, performance is just as likely to create the illusion of power and potency as is the dramatic text. In LeCompte's deconstructions of Presence, neither term is allowed to absorb or invalidate the other, and both are challenged.

Performance thus indicted, LeCompte turns toward textuality. Part 1 of *L.S.D.* calls up history only to confuse it and to reveal that it is unstable, shifting, and culturally controlled. Written texts, the privileged sources of historical information, are deconstructed by what is usually excluded from historical accounts, that is, oral records, subtle implications, casual remarks or occurrences, and so on. The relationship between text and history problematized, The Group then brings on in part 2 a fictionalized historical document, Arthur Miller's play *The Crucible*. Like *L.S.D.*, that play contradicts history, because in it Miller takes one series of historical events and alters it in order to comment on another, specifically the proceedings of the House Un-American Affairs Committee during the fifties.

The reading of *The Crucible* continues the process of disintegrating the activity of reading that was begun in part 1. In theater, as elsewhere, reading is usually considered the necessary pre-text to internalizing the transparent "meaning" of a text. The reader/actor's task is to translate this meaning through his or her character and the character's relation to the larger structure of action. Traditionally, the actor's Presence is created largely by his ability to render this meaning (which is empowered by the text) while keeping the text hidden. In realist theater, though the intrusion of an actor's or director's "interpretation" is always recognized, it is also minimized. But in *L.S.D.* this process of reading is deconstructed simply by exaggerating and reducing the use of the text as guide. First, texts are always in sight of the spectator, whether the performers are simply reading them (as in part 1) or "acting" them (part 2). The acting strategies themselves also confuse the relationship between text and reader/performer. When Willem Dafoe (Proctor) reads his scenes, no attempt is made to invest the material with an acted personality; it is simply read. When highly charged emotion is needed, little "real" emotion is forthcoming, as it would be from a Method actor. Instead, Dafoe plays Proctor's breakdown in wildly histrionic gestures (which the text calls for), and again uses a bottle of glycerin drops to stand in for tears. Vawter (Reverend Parris), on the other hand, plays gestures and facial expressions in good Method style, seemingly the result of having internalized the text. Yet when he delivers his lines, he does so at a frenzied pace, sometimes even substituting gibberish for the written dialogue. Auslander concludes that "while Dafoe adhered to the text, he created its externalizations artificially; Vawter, who seemed to produce emotion from within himself, garbled the text" (1987, 29).

Instead of staging reading as an activity leading to transparent meaning and knowledge, then, the performance of *The Crucible* emphasizes the discontinuities inherent in reading: between the temporalities of the writer and those of the reader, the intentions of the writer and the reader's interpretation, and so on. Reading is staged not as a passive activity but as the writing or the inscription of a text, as an act of interpretation, an exercise of power—things read are things *as* read, to paraphrase Wallace Stevens. Further, since part 1 suggests that history itself is a tissue of writings and readings, then the record of history necessarily shares these temporal and interpretive dislocations and becomes essentially a misreading of the past, a fiction created in a confusion of cross-purposes, and a nightmare from which it seems impossible to awake. Such historiography seems to destroy the idea of history, and to restate the desire of a deconstructionist theorist like de Man to paralyze the gesture *toward* history. The crucial difference is that while de Man posits his view as a transcendent fact of language, LeCompte and The Group use this idea of history as the starting point for an investigation of how a culture creates its history through language and texts. Ultimately The Group's view of history is rhetorical, similar to the historiography of someone like Kenneth Burke, who (here interpreted through Frank Lentricchia) sees that "history . . . is a kind of conversation . . . whose discourse is rhetorical and without foundation and whose ends are never assured because rhetorical process, unlike teleological process, is free. It assumes that people do things not because they must but because they are persuaded to do them" (Lentricchia 1983, 13). And this free discussion of how we are persuaded to accept some versions of history at the neglect and expense of others is the central concern of *L.S.D.*

The Group interrogates Miller's text by foregrounding the author's own persuasive methods. First, by transgressing accepted norms of propriety and legal bases of ownership, The Group appropriated Miller's text in order to interpret it. This raised questions regarding the nature of the text itself, and of its ownership. Miller's response was unequivocal: "I don't want the play mangled that way. Period" (Shewey 1984, 123). The fact that Miller was able to force the closing of *L.S.D.* confirmed, as Savran notes, "the suggestion that the sphere of interpretation is not a pure, aesthetic realm but the world of political power. In this world, Miller's own reading of the play is distinguished from all others not because it is more correct but because it is empowered by the force of law" (Savran 1986b, 219). The Group's reading thus becomes, like Leary's use of drugs, marginalized and threatened, denied the status of cultural acceptance.

The conflict also naturally calls up questions regarding artistic responsibility and integrity. For The Group, however, the criticisms of its work that focus narrowly on these concerns simply reflect the same power structures that govern aesthetic taste. LeCompte suggests that "responsible" art is traditionally "work that illustrates a theme toward which you already have a clear-cut 'moral' attitude." The problem, she admits, is that "that's not the way we work" (Savran 1986b, 206). In its process-oriented performances, The Group produces a kind of ambivalent text that has been marginalized by the artistic and cultural establishment. It refuses linearity by beginning and ending without "a clear-cut 'moral' attitude," and by insistently pushing more than one button at a time. Such work is usually criticized as "opaque," "willfully obscure," and "apolitical." In truth the performances are primarily political, but their politics happens not to coincide with empowered views of what politics should be. The opacity and obscurity of the work is, in fact, a function of The Group's politics, which is predicated on a view of history that is not linear or dialectical, but that calls attention to the processual activity of fabricating history and knowledge as a whole. The "responsibility" of the artist (as Nietzsche knew) lies therefore not in replicating the illusion, but in developing a system of exposure that unveils the human labor that produces it. LeCompte's exposures construct the fractal maps that image forth the minute but repetitive links between centers of power in American culture, links that conceal, beneath a carapace of Euclidean homogeneity and stability, an essentially nonlinear shape.

As opposed to Miller's highly serious and moral intentions in *The Crucible,* The Group substitutes an interplay of exuberant theatricality and exposure; and, against Miller's integrated and focused text, The Group interposes deferral and play. But this does not mean that Miller's text is obliterated, as is Eliot's *The Cocktail Party* in *Nayatt School.* Having discovered the importance of texts in creating culture and history, The Group now treats the play as another historical document, another segment of the "tissue of quotations drawn from the innumerable centers of culture." It is, like all texts, something from which we learn about the making of history.

In *L.S.D.* the performers read *The Crucible* as a dance of interpretation, an activity geared toward defining the oscillating structure of Miller's text in the very process of reading it. Each time excerpts from Miller's play are read, a dance follows that comments on the nature of the play's writing. In the first readings, sections from *The Crucible* describing Abigail's character are read. Miller's characterization of the witch-leader is typically that of a white male. That is, given his particular interpretation of the motives for the witchcraft in Salem, Miller necessarily excludes the possible reading that the coven was a persecuted and marginalized group. But in keeping with the ambivalent view, in part 1, of Leary and his paranoid reaction to his "persecution," The Group never gives precedence to this conspiratorial view of Abigail. The associations are never simply ironic (which supposes a closed order of questioning), but speculative, open-ended, and indeterminate.

A similarly playful interpretation of Miller's text unpacked in the performance is achieved by costuming and the distribution of other theatrical signifiers. The women are dressed in period clothes and speak normally, while the men are in more contemporary dress and have their voices amplified by microphones. This really is simply an exaggeration of the authority distribution in *The Crucible,* where the women are primarily "window dressing" and visual images who play off Proctor and the men who persecute them. The men, on the other hand, bear the burden of the play's meaning, hence its "voice" and power.

In each of these interpretations of *The Crucible* The Group seemingly provides its own "readings" of history and of Miller's play. The Group is thus exercising its own "power" and foisting a point of view on the audience. Unlike Miller, however, the performers do not have a single "clear-cut moral attitude," and as a result the meaning of the work cannot be made transparent, since that would only re-create the performance as another form of discourse that nominates moral clarity as a criterion for art. Besides, since The Group has no determinate or authoritative text—only an improvised intertext built from the fragments of its performed "readings"—there is no Presence of the actor, and this inhibits the spectator from discovering in either kind of representation any stable source of authority. This in turn allows the audience to focus instead on the process of representation itself and its collusions with authority (Auslander 1987, 28).

This extreme distancing technique is carried over to the second readings of *The Crucible* in part 3, where the performers stage an earlier reading of the material created while the performers were actually under the influence of LSD. The performance, which centers on the trial scene from *The Crucible,* hallucinates Miller's text and also links the persecution of Proctor with that of Leary. An antithesis to the programmed catharsis of Miller's play, the entire section is kaleidoscopic and seemingly unconnected. The activity of reading has broken down completely, as more and more the performers begin to lose track of what their goals are (*Dafoe:* "Umm, are we staying on the play or are we doing Leary stuff too?"). Amid the confusion of purposes, several performers pick up instruments and begin to play nostalgic acid rock from the sixties, each becoming increasingly self-absorbed. Near the end, Reverend Parris's admonition to Mary Warren to faint in the courtroom is played out by Kate Valk, who tries to hyperventilate herself into unconsciousness in a "Faint Dance." Swaying back and forth, then twirling spasmodically, she finally fixes a tie around her neck and twists it violently. Her attempts, violent and painful though they are, are finally not successful, and her attempts to escape consciousness fail.

Part 3, then, undermines Miller's conception of art, as highly moral and socially "involved," with Leary's. Again, though, the notion of creating art while under the influence of mind-expanding drugs is hardly valorized. In fact, the entire episode is very reminiscent of The Group's work in *Sakonnet Point,* in which self-reflexivity, disconnected activities, and Gray's solipsism were both the strength and the limitation of the piece. Given the movement away from these abstract and self-referential strategies in The Group's performances since then, it does not seem likely that LeCompte is advocating a return to such practices. Instead, as in previous cases the scene seems to focus on juxtaposing disparate modes of reading and writing texts (Miller's, as opposed to Leary's), and on exposing the way that American culture either empowers or marginalizes such meaning-producing processes.

Having delivered in Parts 1–3 a vivid example of what a postmodern political art might look like, The Group turns in the last section to depicting the imagined result of its theatrical endeavor. During part 3, segments of a video are shown depicting Vawter as he drives around Miami. He "telephones" the live performance and reports that, by impersonating a dance/rock band ("Donna Sierra and the Del Fuegos"), they might find a gig for the next night. The scene from Miami evokes ideas and images from earlier sections of the piece. The geographical leap from New England to Florida suggests an escape to warmth and leisure. It is a "back to nature" trek similar to the one taken by Leary, as described in the readings from his son's text, where in the Hispanic culture a sage-mythic male can find the warmth of "those warmblooded little whores" (Savran 1986b, 212). The trip also suggests a flight from the legal difficulties with Miller: LeCompte reported that she fantasized about The Group in images associated with punk performers like Johnny Rotten and the Sex Pistols, as a "troupe of ne'er-do well drug addicts who could never perform in New York anymore. . . . The only place we could ever perform *L.S.D.* would be in a hotel in Miami where Miller would never hear about it" (Aronson 1985, 357). While evoking the Gauginesque quality of such a retreat, the reading also calls up the discomforting reminder of the decadence of the culture, as well as of Leary himself. This in turn is exacerbated by the introduction of another figure associated with the South, G. Gordon Liddy, whose recruitment and training of Cubans around Miami in domestic sabotage is described in the program notes to part 4.

This section opens with both a reading and a dance, the final alignment of the textual and performative activities of *L.S.D.* The readings are excerpts taken from a 1982 campus debate between Leary and Liddy, centered on questions that students asked after the debate. In one sequence, a blind man (played by a performer wearing the "blind glasses" from *Route 1 & 9*) describes how several people under the influence of drugs had fired a shotgun in his face and blown his eyes out. Leary lamely attempts to defend his pacifism, and denounces those responsible. The man accuses Leary of spreading a gospel that gave the people the "false courage" to assault him—Leary's moral responsibility being the price paid by radicals who cultivate a charismatic following and achieve cult status. The blind man finishes by saying, "So thank you, and I hope you can sleep peacefully when I bump my face on the walls, when I stumble and trip. God bless you." When the moderator asks Leary how he feels, he can only answer "I feel very sad" (Savran 1986b, 217).

The passage restates in dramatic form a central concern of the performance: the relationship between an author and her ideas. Since reading has been shown to be a dance of interpretation and misreading, how responsible is the author for the manner in which those ideas are ultimately interpreted? Is Miller, for instance, in any way culpable for what The Group creates out of *The Crucible*? If not, then would LeCompte be responsible for a later deconstruction of *Route 1 & 9*? The performance never answers the questions, because for LeCompte it simply remains irreconcilable. Still, this does not mean that *L.S.D.* fails to respond to the question. Juxtaposed to and overlapping the debate readings is another dance, one that for LeCompte "represents all the work I've done in the last seven years. And it is all the idiocy, all the threat, all the fun, all the violence" (Aronson 1985, 356).

The dance takes place in the trough before the lectern. As Latin music plays, Kate Valk dances a bastard flamenco/ballet. Dafoe and Vawter stand beside and below her under the lectern, chests bared, wearing campy pencilled-in Latin mustaches, and holding pairs of tennis shoes. When Valk jumps at certain cadences, the two males smash their sneakers down on the platform. Behind them on the table is a video monitor showing Parris's own "irreconcilable" question from *The Crucible:* "What is this dancing?" When the shoes crash down, they shake the video cables and momentarily reduce the screen to snow. Like LeCompte's art, the scene is both violent and whimsical, funny and disturbing. The image calls up images of domination and power—the attempt of the men to abrogate the female's performance space, the assault of the real and physical on the artificial representation of it on the television, and so on. The routine also hearkens back to the interactions between what is fixed and enclosed within boundaries (the text, the video images) and what takes place outside those artificial limits (the violent and disruptive gestures of the performers). Yet, as in all of The Group's work, the conflicts are imaged forth unmediated, not reconciled by a "clear-cut moral attitude" external to the activity of dancing. As Aronson notes, the "inexorable repetition of the dance movements at the end of the play became for LeCompte an equivalent to the unanswerable questioning. The answer to 'What is this dancing,' became, in essence, 'My art'" (1985, 356).

That art continues in The Group's most recent works (*Frank Dell's The Temptation of Saint Anthony,* the third piece in *The Road to Immortality* trilogy, and *Brace Up!,* now in production, which will serve as the trilogy's epilogue) in much the same way it began in *Sakonnet Point,* that is, radically deconstructing accepted forms of discourse.[30] The changes that take place between the early nonreferential and abstract work and a piece like *L.S.D.* are mainly due to an altered focus, as the subject of the deconstructive exercises increasingly is discovered outside, within culture instead of solely inside the self or theater. Savran accurately locates The Group's method in a Nietzschean, as opposed to Marxist (or, it could be added, strictly poststructuralist) deconstructionist critique, pointing out that the collective performances "question from a position of doubt" (1986b, 222). For LeCompte and the rest of The Group, truth remains, as it did for Nietzsche in his essay "On Truth and Lie in an Extra-Moral Sense," a "mobile army of metaphors, metonyms, and anthropomorphisms—in short, a sum of human relations, which have been enhanced, transposed, and embellished poetically and rhetorically, and which after long use seem firm, canonical, and obligatory to a people: truths are illusions about which one has forgotten this is what they are."

Still, in its more recent investigations of several significant texts of our culture, The Group appears to be placing more emphasis on adding up the "sum of human relations" mentioned by Nietzsche, rather than on multiplying the radical doubts upon which deconstruction is often based. Unappeased by the image of the free-floating performances that characterized much alternative theater of the seventies (including their own early work), members of The Group have steadily moved their investigations of contemporary society into the texts of American culture, where the culture's meanings reside. This has made them recognize that, for all the fractal and misshapen contours apparent on the surface of American society, there are often patterns of order, usually in the form of power relationships, to be recognized and resisted. For now, The Group seems most concerned with mapping out these matrices of power and domination that have been woven together to form powerful institutions of hegemony and consent. Since the written texts of such a culture are obviously implicated in the formation of its political geography, LeCompte and the rest of The Group have recognized that fruitful deconstructions must be directed against these centers of power. And, though the direction may be new, the use of performance strategies to effect the exposure of dominant discourse remains very much in line with the early stages of alternative theater.

To this point The Group has infiltrated an impressive array of American culture's metaphors and their embellishments. Still, there remains a significant gap in The Group's investigations of the "sum of human relations," that is, the deconstruction of the female texts of our culture. We can only anticipate the effects of LeCompte's sophisticated dramaturgy and deconstructive mise-en-scènes on texts of authors like Virginia Woolf (currently under scrutiny in Wilson's *Orlando*) and Colette (the subject of JoAnne Akalaitis's *Dressed Like An Egg*), or on even more fractured works by Benmussa, Acker, and others. Perhaps even more tantalizing is the prospect of The Group's continuing affiliation with Richard Foreman, in whose writing we see enacted an appropriation of *l'écriture féminine,* continuing the tradition of writers like Flaubert (a source for *Frank Dell's The Temptation of Saint Anthony*), Joyce, and

Marquez. The politics of such appropriations would seem the natural grist for The Group's deconstructive mill.

Recognizing the corrosive and equivocal nihilism of Nietzsche's theories of language, The Group has nevertheless discovered that to confront and expose the operations of language as "a sum of human relations" can be an effective method for understanding how history is written within a culture, and how that acculturated image of history institutionalizes power. Interpreting language in this way becomes an activity that, in another paraphrase of Burke, "does not passively 'see' . . . but constructs a point of view in its engagement with textual events, and in so constructing produces an image of history as social struggle. . . . an image that is not 'there' in a simple sense but is the discovery of the active intellectual soul" (Lentricchia 1983, 11). Thus engaged, LeCompte and The Wooster Group are actually rewriting history, not by imposing upon it another text, but by making its existing texts dance.

Chapter 4

"Of our origins / In ghostlier demarcations, keener sounds": Robert Wilson's Search for a New Order of Vision

The will to a system is a lack of integrity.

—Nietzsche

Lyn: I said to her, "Janet, no one, not even me, knows what's going on." But she says that was the whole point—that *my* not knowing and no one *else* knowing was what it was all about. She makes me feel so . . . so . . . *linear.* See, her theory is if *no* one knows what it's about, it might jolt us out of our normal mode of perceiving, and in having *no* information whatsoever, we'd be forced to confront *new* information. . . .

Of course, Edie cut through it all; she just looked Janet straight in the eye and said, "New information about what . . . ?"

—Jane Wagner, *The Search for Signs of Intelligent Life in the Universe*

Expressing the desire of a number of avant-garde artists and theater critics, Bonnie Marranca asserted in 1977 that the experimental theater groups of the sixties and early seventies had demolished the traditional dramatic experience. "Value," she said, "came increasingly to be placed on performance with the result that the new theater never became a literary theater, but one dominated by images—visual and aural" (Marranca 1977, ix). Tracing the lineage of this non- or antiliterary theater back to Allan Kaprow's Happenings, Marranca suggested that it had culminated in a "Theater of Images," represented by artists like Elizabeth LeCompte (specifically in *Sakonnet Point*), Richard Foreman, Lee Breuer, and Robert Wilson. This move away from the strictures of literary drama marked for Marranca and a number of other critics "a watershed in the history of American theater, a *rite de passage*" (1977, x).

This insurgency against the dominant literary style in the theater, we have seen, motivated a number of consequent innovations. The notion of the orthodox dramatic text that stood invisible behind the performance, ordering its development and creating the Presence of the performers, was replaced by "scenarios" and "pretexts" (the latter often based on remnants of an existing dramatic text), which were highly imagistic and improvisational. Sometimes parodies of the traditional text were created, like the Roy Lichtenstein–inspired comic-book text of Lee Breuer's *Red Horse Animation.* Other times there was simply no text at all, as in performance art. Actors, too, were no longer expected to perform psychologically based "roles," but to serve as icons or *übermarionettes,* ciphers through which the playwright/director expressed concepts and ideas. The notion of the virtuosic Method actor who "becomes" a part determined primarily by the text was replaced by mainly nonprofessional performers whose natural movements and flows of energy became the starting point for a workshop or production.

Perhaps most important for the development of a theater of images were the experiments in time and space. Freed from the Cartesian logic of narrative sequence and unified psychological space that characterizes Western theater, directors found new reasons and methods to slow down, speed up, restrict, and distend the flow of theatrical time and space. Influenced by cinematographic experiments and older or non-Western theatrical traditions, these directors worked with structures of collage, simultaneity, bricolage, and tableau to present a Bergsonian, Einsteinian sense of time as flow, duration, and as relative spacetime "events." These innovations were seldom incorporated into the thematic structure of the performances, acting instead as concrete stage realizations of the phenomenological processes that the actor, and sometimes the audience, experienced in the space and time of the performance itself. Wilson's *Overture for Ka Mountain,* for instance, ran for 168 hours in its Iranian performance, and its length and the fact that it was spread out over several square miles announced its aesthetic, built on a multiplicity of perspectives and on simultaneous action. For these artists, time and space had become, as they had for Gertrude Stein, something to be made presently present.[1]

Although the artists associated with the theater of images often collaborated, they formed no school and never allowed their work to be codified into fixed forms. Still, significant common denominators exist that bind their work together. Partaking of perhaps the most dominant trend in modern literature, these playwrights and directors abandoned the classic text and its ancillaries (conventional language, plot, character, traditional rhythms of action) because those conventions implied a stable and coherent universe, wholly decipherable by the rational mind. Relinquishing control of linguistic signs and their signifieds allowed these artists to defer fixed structures of meaning and cathexis, and to concentrate rather on what precedes such cognitive activity, that is, on the phenomenology of perception itself. And, since the sixties and seventies were characterized in part by a drive to discover the theatrical in everyday life, the concentration was often specifically directed toward theatrical perception.

The natural result was that among directors and playwrights of the theater of images, a tendency toward rather self-referential, metatheatrical investigations—theater's use of space, movement, gesture, sound—prevailed. And this implies a high degree of focus on process, on the notion that how one sees is as important as what one sees. The aim for each artist is to suggest that radically new ways of seeing and perceiving are available; as in Happenings, the point is to "wake the body" of the spectator by making him more aware of the events around him and of their phenomenological significance. Unfortunately, however, we have seen how these emphases also tend to eliminate recognition of the world beyond the theater.

The importance attached to this kind of (pre)consciousness-raising through performance suggests connections to the experimental work of first-generation theater artists like Schechner, Chaikin, and the Becks. And, indeed, Robert Wilson's art has important connections to their theater-as-therapy work, though his methods differ markedly. Perhaps the most interesting thing about these connections, however, is the manner in which Wilson comes slowly to detach himself from them. Like the plays of Beckett and the performances of The Wooster Group, Wilson's work evolves through phases during which his performances move from being strictly abstract, nonreferential deconstructions of orthodox theater or language, toward performance dramas that incorporate both performative and textual idioms, a process that anticipates a return to a more social context for his art. The changes are motivated by a variety of pressures, the most important of which is Wilson's slowly emerging sense of how language functions, both within the theatrical experience and beyond it, within culture. And, while Wilson never directs his performances toward the kind of postmodern political critique of language and textuality adopted by The Wooster Group, he has shown a tendency to dismiss early attempts to do without, or to get beyond, rational language entirely. Instead of disintegrating language and facetiously ignoring the ways that language finds potency within a culture determined text, Wilson's late works confront such linguistic artifacts and use them to investigate not contemporary American or world culture but universal history. Once again, it is the crucial nexus of language, history, and textuality that comes eventually to bring another version of experimental theater out of its oneiric and solipsistic frame of reference, and to turn it somewhat more toward theater's original social context. At the same time, Wilson's rapprochements with conventional drama have infiltrated the dramatic text and expanded its languages, helping to modify what audiences can expect a text to do.

Wilson entered the theater during the turbulent period of the sixties, when the very nature and function of the dramatic experience were being tested and altered. Suffering as a youth from a speech impediment, Wilson worked with Byrd Hoffman, a dance instructor and therapist who profoundly influenced his ideas on performance and perception. While later devoting time to studying art, architecture, and dance in college, Wilson began working with children's theater at Baylor and Trinity colleges. Little by little he found himself aiding brain-damaged children and discovering connections between physical stimulation and mental activity. These experiences naturally intersected with his work in the theater, where he detected affinities between the physical properties of the stage (actor, objects, the audience) and the flows and releases of energy within perceptual space.

Wilson, however, was not interested in the Dionysian body mysticism preached by Schechner and other experimental theater artists of the sixties. C. W. E. Bigsby has noted the crucial distinction that, for Wilson, the

> emphasis on physicality is not just an assertion of the primacy of instincts or the suspect nature of rationality. It is the assertion of clinical theory, the suggestion that rational processes may be restored through a deliberate programme of physical stimulation. The

body redeems the mind by quite literal and physical means; it is not an article of spiritual faith. (Bigsby 1985, 165)

What did interest Wilson in early performances in Texas was the exploration of a theatrical performance in which the important exchanges were between performer, theatrical space, and audience, without the encumbrances of plot, characters, and symbolism. He continued to explore these kinds of theatrical possibilities and alternatives during the late sixties in experimental theater pieces, performance art, and museum installations. He was eventually named artistic director of the Byrd Hoffman Foundation in 1969, and it is from this time that we can mark his emergence as a significant contributor to modern theater.

Between 1969 and 1973, Wilson produced a number of imagistic works that Stefan Brecht refers to collectively as a "theater of visions" (Brecht 1978, 197). These include, most prominently, *The King of Spain* (1969), *The Life and Times of Sigmund Freud* (1969), *Deafman Glance* (1971), and *Overture for Ka Mountain* (1972).[2] These remarkable works constitute a recognizable first phase in Wilson's canon, a phase that—excepting the monumental scale of *Ka Mountain*—anticipates in some respects the early work of The Wooster Group. Elizabeth LeCompte, for instance, saw and admired *Deafman Glance,* and the work significantly influenced, by its use of a nonlinear, imagistic structure and visual language, The Wooster Group's later *Sakonnet Point.*

Wilson's first phase is characterized by an approach built on what Richard Foreman calls "a non-manipulative aesthetic" (Foreman 1970, 1). As wary as Beckett of the preformationist tendency of the classical text, Wilson likes to open up what Foreman calls "field situations" in which each spectator, as "perceptor," is allowed to respond individually to the barrage of rhythms, colors, actions, and images contained in the performance. To achieve this, Wilson uses objects and images at hand, which he maintains are not collected with any specific intention in mind. Performers who have worked with Wilson maintain that these objects are not (as they are for The Wooster Group) objets trouvés, but that they are recommended to him by an absence of conscious control in his reception of them. Similar to the way that The Wooster Group allows themes of a work to emerge only in retrospect as a residue of the textualizing process, Wilson's most crucial or emphatic symbols develop only through the reagents of the rehearsal/production and the spectator.

Wilson's desire, like Beckett's, is for a paradoxical "authorial powerlessness," a disregard for the Presence and power of a text and its creator in favor of a more open-ended and playful dialogue with objects, images, and, eventually, the viewer.

But while Beckett seeks his authorial *via negativa* primarily through a language built on disavowal and abjuration, Wilson's material in the early works is almost exclusively visual. When language is used, it is nonreferential, noncontextualized, dominated by movement, and often senseless: bits of overheard conversation, repeated banal sentence connectives, random speech acts. Other aural elements may be added for texture or contrast. Often, the voices are distorted and separated electronically from the speakers. Generally, language is subordinated to spatial and sonic structures, and especially to image.

And what images. In *Freud,* cave beasts created by the Byrds (the nonprofessional performers associated with Wilson's work during this period) surround the aging doctor, while ladders turn into haystacks and weird shutters are lowered from the blinds. At one point, a young boy thrashes and contorts in gruesome death throes while the Freud figure sits passively at his table. A pair of legs dangle from the flies and walk a beam in *The Life and Times of Joseph Stalin,* as forty black mammies dance below to "The Blue Danube." The *SoHo Weekly News* ran an ad for the performance seeking thirty-two dancing ostriches, over a hundred sleepwalkers (experienced and nonexperienced), various bears, apes, fishing ladies, and an Alexander Graham Bell look-alike. *Deafman Glance* begins with the figure of a darkly clad woman moving with incredible precision and grace, yet so slowly that her movements are barely perceptible. She pours milk, brings it to a boy, picks up a knife, and with absolutely no emotion or change in pace, slowly stabs him, front and back, and lays him down. Raymond Andrews, a deaf-mute orphan whose sensibilities are the center of the piece, moves onstage as the murderous scene is repeated on a small girl. In a weird half-howl, he keens at the sight. When the woman finishes the second murder, the boy walks with her through the backstage wall into a garden party. This constitutes almost the first hour of the performance. Later, there are swamp creatures, a magician, a couple sitting serenely under a burning umbrella, and a frog sipping a cocktail at a party.

As Brecht suggests, the lack of a rational order and of properly objective correlatives for the images in these early works does not necessarily mean that the pieces do not contain a theme, or that they refuse to show a viewpoint. In fact, Wilson's themes recall the early work of The Wooster Group and its focus on the perilous situation of representatives of innocence—children, autistic adolescents, or anyone else uncontaminated by the corruptions of rationality and its languages.[3] For Wilson, as for Wordsworth, the child is in some respects father of the man, and as Laurence Shyer notes of Wilson, "in some ways his is a child's coming to terms with experience in the world" (Shyer 1989, xix). Children, like deaf-mutes and brain-damaged adolescents, are privy to cognitive and perceptual modes that escape the rational mind. And, like the surrealists before him, Wilson wants to tap into these structures to reveal how they interpenetrate rational thought. Like Dali or Breton, Wilson needs both the surreal and its concrete manifestation to create the juxtaposition of images he desires.[4] The result is a s(t)imulation of an alternative mode of perception, with perhaps a sense of its tenuousness and fragility in the face of adult rationality and repression.

Along with a similar conception of the child's sensibilities and of the ever-present threat of their repression, Wilson shares with The Wooster Group a sense of the importance of movement—spatial and temporal—in the overall architectonic of his works. *Deafman Glance* (like The Group's *L.S.D.*) uses references to dance to distinguish its hermeneutic aims from that of orthodox theater. Quoting a passage from Isadora Duncan in the program, Wilson stresses by it "the ultimate aim of freeing the body and the sensibility, the desire to offer method without insisting on content or the authority of paradigm" (Bigsby 1985, 174). This rejection of the fundamental qualities of orthodox drama—social context, moral and psychological conflicts, recognizable content—places the greatest weight of the performance on the formal qualities of the work. As in some of Beckett's later plays and in works by The Wooster Group, the emphasis is less on the decoding of signifiers than on their interplay or "dance."

But we have seen how, in Beckett and The Wooster Group, such work eventually comes upon a margin or seam, something constraining the free play of signifiers in a dance of time, space, and formal arrangement. The loss of the human element itself suggests certain problems, as theater—unlike other, less verbal forms of kinetic art—has always been predicated on the very human interaction among performer, language, spectacle, and audience; theater has thus been traditionally considered a social, and socializing, art. As such, theater (Western theater, anyway) has always been receptive to analysis; and the exercise of power, of interpretation, has been enshrined in theater from its inception. Wilson's art then, at least in its first phase, resists this exercise of power, and thereby retains the anti-intellectual—perhaps anti-theatrical—tendency toward powerlessness so characteristic of performance theater in its early manifestations.

In his flight from orthodox theater and its natural tendency toward creating meaning, Wilson opens himself up to the same charges of sterile formalism and aggressive apoliticality that have been leveled at Beckett, The Wooster Group, and other contemporary artists. In fact, probably more than any other theater artist, Wilson has been singled out almost universally for representing this disturbing trend in recent art. Even Brecht, working with Wilson in early pieces like *Freud* and *Deafman Glance,* was aware of certain conceptual deficiencies. Noting *Freud*'s oblique rejection of the doctor's somber view of existence, Brecht wrote that the performance "hides" Freud's essentially tragic view of man: "It is as though Wilson, stunned by the perception of life as an inexorable rout too swift to allow us to reach out, had glazed it over with acceptance, turning the common tragedy of man against Freud, giving to a vision of defeat the color of beauty" (Brecht 1978, 49 n. 18). This sounds somewhat familiar to Richard Schechner's critique of the abstract dance movements created in The Wooster Group's *Rumstick Road,* in which he claims that Spalding Gray and Elizabeth LeCompte turn their theater into "life for art's sake." So in *Freud* such a coup d'état of modern psychology reminds us of earlier alternative theater's affirmations of ecstasy and its avowal of transcendence of painful events. And, like that theater, Wilson's work yields often a delicious dream of life, but only by ignoring the constraints and amortizations of consciousness and human life.

The same desire for transcendence, masquerading as new perceptual modes, or as powerlessness and the free play of forms, inhabits *Deafman Glance* especially. In the performance, as in most of his work, Wilson tries to conjure up the free play of the unconscious in its dreaming state in hopes that it will stimulate in the spectator a perception of his own epistemological processes, and a newer, higher order of mentation. The search for dream-structures, of course, is not new: as Herbert Blau says, "anything bizarre or puzzling is referred to the structure of dream—as any play can be" (Blau 1982a, 39). But, as Blau goes on to say, many of the claims to this oneiric structure in alternative theater fail to make an important distinction:

> What tends to be forgotten—whether we're talking of the dreamlike in old drama or the oneiric in New Theater—is what Freud never overlooked, that "A dream is in general poorer in affect than the psychical material from the manipulation of which it has proceeded. . . ." It is this material, the *dream-thought* to which both dreamwork and theaterwork are indebted for their staying power, to the extent they really have it. This is another way of saying that whatever the appearances (the manifest content) both play and dream are worlds which in order to appear must first *be thought*. (1982a, 39)

Susan Sontag's landmark 1977 article, "On Art and Consciousness," was among the first to raise questions regarding the thought-lessness of Wilson's theater of visions, which she used to critique implicitly a number of other avant-garde artists who she felt were suffering from a fascination with "the disease of consciousness." She, like Blau, finds it unsurprising that

> an art committed to solipsism would recapitulate the gestures of the *pathology* of solipsism. If you start from an asocial notion of perception of consciousness, you must inevitably end up with the poetry of mental illness and mental deficiency. With autistic silence. With the autistic's use of language: compulsive repetition and variation. With an obsession with circles. With an abstract or distended notion of time. (Sontag 1977, 29)

However, like other performance-theater artists who have passed through a similar stage, Wilson appears to have eventually sensed that the theater of visions represented something of a dead end. His later work reveals a growing need to address in his performances the potency of consciousness as it is expressed through language and by which language constructs reality. However, his initial response to this challenge is not a maturing understanding of the social function of language, but a deepening skepticism about its ability to communicate successfully on a rational level. Brecht (1978, 265–67) points to the works spanning the period 1974 to 1977 as a signal of the decline of Wilson's theater of visions, which, he suggests, is replaced by a theater characterized by an assault on speech. While these pieces were still based on images, Brecht feels they had "become adventitious to other concerns, mere occasions, and their visual development no longer governed structure" (1978, 267).

The problem with Wilson's deconstructions of normal language lay in the fact that, in the very process of laying siege to language, Wilson necessarily introduced it as a component of his performances. He essentially fell victim to the risk of any deconstruction, that is, of "ceaselessly confirming, consolidating . . . at an always more certain depth, that which one allegedly deconstructs" (Derrida 1982, 135). Any use of language poses a problem for theater work built primarily upon images, simply because language represents a more closed semiotic gesture. Implicit in any language act is an act of interpretation: as Beneviste says, language is the only semiotic system capable of interpreting other semiotic systems. When this function of language is joined to its peculiar "grain of the voice" (in Barthes's terms), it cannot help but communicate certain affects. Functioning thus, language will always interrupt the open-ended flow of images and disturb the *jouissance* of free-floating signifiers.

Brecht's suggestion that the next, anti-verbal stage of Wilson's work includes *A Letter for Queen Victoria* (1974) and *Einstein on the Beach* (1976) is based upon his perception that in these pieces Wilson is attacking rational communication.[5] However, the former actively accomplishes this assault, and therefore represents by itself a kind of transitional stage. *Einstein on the Beach,* on the other hand, shows a significant change in direction and marks the beginnings of the Wilson's move back toward a more recognizably theatrical, and hence linguistic, context.

In *A Letter for Queen Victoria,* Wilson shows an inclination to work in something like conventional theater. Still, the move is not toward making the performances function anything like the performance of an orthodox dramatic text. Rather, Wilson uses characters, conflict, plot, and dialogue to create something of a ruse, similar to a strategy we see in Beckett and The Wooster Group, and which appears in Shepard's work as well. This illusion of the dramatic text is used to parody and undermine the nature and constraints of textual representation. In this aspect, then, *A Letter for Queen Victoria* represents an attempt to transgress the confines of orthodox textual drama by inhabiting and subverting it by a kind of performative insurging.

The performance carries over many of the concerns and strategies of earlier work. Images built on straight lines (especially diagonals) are built into several scenes, and they structure most of the formalized stage movement. Aural images created out of nonsense words act as a kind of sonic sculpture within the architectonic of the entire piece. Visual, spatial, and aural images intersect, overlap, and juxtapose themselves in a seemingly random manner. Still, a general thematic terrain is perceivable. The topics of human communicability, murder, civil strife, air disasters, and the atom bomb all form an aggregate theme of a loss of innocence and its eventual expiation and purification.

Yet, as Bonnie Marranca notes, "Wilson's solution to the problem is not an ideological one; . . . it is a romantic, utopian one" (Marranca 1977, 40). In much the same way that earlier experimental theater had rejected the rational closure and interpretive monologism of orthodox drama, Wilson repudiates any attempt to resolve or determine the conflicts that reside in the work. And, as in many performance works from the sixties, the alternative to the determinacy is another species of transcendence; gained, however, not through the rigors and penitent gestures of the performing body, but by rendering language itself as pure gesture.

Language in *A Letter for Queen Victoria,* as in most of Wilson's early works, addresses a fluctuating reality by attempting to render transitive states as substantive ones. By wrenching language from its temporal and discursive contexts, and by calling attention to its phenomenological status through monotonous repetition, juxtaposition to other theatrical elements (images, sounds, gestures), and so on, Wilson draws attention to the word as object and to the theatrical event as existing in a continuous present. But Wilson had more in mind than the evocation of what Stein would call "entity"; for in Wilson's play there is also the effort to use a performative language to privilege that idiom as a preferred mode of consciousness. The early rehearsal process for *A Letter for Queen Victoria* included sessions with Christopher Knowles, a gifted but (it was initially diagnosed) autistic youth with whom Wilson had been working for some time.[6] Wilson asked his performers to imitate and communicate with Knowles in order to learn how to relate vocally without any reliance on the meaning of what was said. In addition to providing a new, nonsyntactic structure for the vocal arrangements of the performance, the exercises were designed to give the sections of conversation "an ineffable formality, . . . [an] air of *ritual,*" and a sense of what "true intercourse" would sound like in its purest state (Brecht 1978, 271). For Lacan, of course, the entire experience of time and memory is an effect of language, and his consideration of disorders such as schizophrenia and autism as language disorders yields significant parallels to Wilson's theatrical strategies. Schizophrenics and autistics do not process language in temporal or syntactic frames (Wilson says Knowles "thinks in terms of pictures"), and so are condemned (Wilson would probably say "liberated") to live in a perpetual present, in "an experience of isolated, disconnected material signifiers which fail to link up into coherent sequence" (Sarup 1989, 134).

Wilson's attempt to invest his performance with such an agenda resonates with a certain familiarity to earlier attempts in experimental theater to escape the literal signifying systems of language. This intent, of course, is present in Wilson's theater from the beginning, but in *A Letter for Queen Victoria* a crucial difference is revealed; here, Wilson is not satisfied to supplement rational language with expanded imagistic and aural idioms, but moves instead toward hypostatizing a certain kind of language and nominating it as a privileged form of discourse.

The work describes a series of social interactions—letters are read, Wilson and Knowles engage in private language exercises within several entr'actes, couples indulge in banal chatter—all of which simulate the structures of normal social interchange. Nevertheless, the function of language and of visual and imagistic elements is directed toward the deconstruction of such bland, rational language as the privileged vehicle for communication and social intercourse. Wilson develops his deconstructions by establishing a series of juxtapositions between what is said and what is done, between what is said and how the words are accompanied by movement, and between what is said and its particular speech-act context. Movement remains independent of speech, for instance, and the dialogue is broken up and distributed randomly. These disjunctions demonstrate that communication can take place apart from conventional hypotactic and semantic contexts, and that what people say is not always the total content of a given speech-act.

In a sense, the themes of Wilson's play dovetail with this attack on language, precisely because both are apocalyptic. Wilson seems to suggest that the same rationality that makes common language a discourse of power and repression is responsible for the disasters introduced suggestively into the performance: murder, suppression of the child, civil war, airplane disasters, and the atom bomb. The implication is that all of these are the inevitable result of a certain kind of mentation, the historical consequences of rationally ordered language and existence. ("I fear we are not getting rid of God," lamented Nietzsche, "because we still believe in grammar.") And, since what Wilson seeks is a return to a prerational state of autistic and disjunct communication, then it is history that stands in his way, and especially history as it is remembered and generated through language and rational narratives. In order to return to a primal state of communication—and by extension to a utopian society—both language and history have to be negated; hence, in *A Letter for Queen Victoria,* the necessary emphasis placed on breaking down rational language, breaking down history (by conjuring up images of war and apocalypse), and then recreating life as primal, ritualized communication. It is no accident that the performance ends with a strange phrase by Knowles ("the angle of the thing angling"); Wilson has written that it was the first line of dialogue given to him by Knowles, but because it represents the advent of a new way of speaking—angular, dependent upon the expressive medium of "the thing angling"—its proper place is at the end of the performance, where it can stand as final testimony to the superiority of the new language built on the ruins of rationality.

The visual and acoustic beauty of Wilson's piece notwithstanding, the assault on language in *A Letter for Queen Victoria* is problematic, in terms of both its effects within the performance and its implications beyond it. As to the latter, the introduction of an attitude toward speech robs the work of a good deal of its "non-manipulative aesthetic" and gesture toward powerlessness. Wilson originally achieved this aesthetic in earlier work by avoiding translating ideas into theatrical terms and evoking specific responses to objects, movements, and sounds. Instead, he simply created situations in which, in Foreman's words, "the spectator can examine himself (as perceptor) in relation to the 'discoveries' the artist has made within his medium, then presented to the spectator with maximum lucidity" (Foreman 1970, 1). But speech is not so easily translated into meaninglessness; both in referential meaning and in its gesture (intonation, rhythm, pitch, "grain"), speech contains the potential for Presence and its investment in meaning and power. The initial problem is that such gestured speech will always be apprehended by the audience as reflecting a state of mind in the character, an attitude toward some action or toward the words themselves. But Wilson's performers are meant to have no "psychology" or personality; they are simply part of what the Bauhaus artists called "ambulant architecture," elements and catalysts of the visual, kinesic, and sonic arrangement of the stage picture/architecture. Once they begin speaking in words, then, they begin to exercise a charismatic power as makers of the song they sing, to paraphrase Wallace Stevens.

The intrusion of speech, then, both creates meaning and retains what Brecht calls "the attributive character of being the speech of *someone*, of a substantial ('real') person or ego" (1978, 283). And this leads naturally to the creation of stage Presence, of the charismatic Other who speaks for the desires and fears of the spectator. The charisma is minimized, to be sure, but certainly not eradicated. Like Spalding Gray's performance styles in works by The Wooster Group, the gesture toward powerlessness and the creation of "field situations" for the audience are at best illusory, at their worst duplicitous. Wilson, for instance, had intended for Knowles to assume a privileged space within both the rehearsals (as a kind of guru/preceptor) and the production. Brecht recalls working with the boy on a bit of dialogue built around Knowles's fascination with the sentence "The Sundance Kid is beautiful." As he remembers it, his own exercise consisted of arguing with Knowles about the movie. But Wilson intervened, angry with Brecht's "critical intellectualism," and replaced him in this scene with another performer (Brecht 1978, 272 n.11).[7] Eventually the central importance of Knowles in rehearsal was attenuated, as was his position within the production. Still, this all suggests that Wilson initially was not willing to trust completely the spectator's open interaction with his materials, but wanted instead to manipulate the audience toward an appreciation of a specific kind of Presence (i.e., Knowles's), its apparent pathology notwithstanding.

Perhaps more troubling than the problem of deconstructing language within the performance, however, are the implications of that problem for Wilson's theater in general. As we have seen before, it is not so much a question of deconstruction per se, but rather of knowing what to do with deconstruction once its basic tenets are accepted; as Heidegger said of Nietzsche's pronouncement about the murder of God, the dreadful thing has already happened. The question that remained, as it remains for contemporary artists aware of poststructuralist notions of language, was what to do with the fallout. *A Letter for Queen Victoria* is disturbing because it hypostatizes language as a ritualized and ahistorical activity removed from the culture that produces it. Modernism created experiments by which language could be rejuvenated by calling attention to words and their ambiguous sediments. The crucial difference between this agenda and that of the postmodern artist is, as Blau notes, that for the modernists "the words were there, luminously. They were not merely fractured or discarded or abused into parody. . . . [I]n the modernist period . . . meanings were *disinterred* through a system of insurgings, rather than merely disintegrated" (Blau 1982a, 88).

Wilson disintegrates language because it represents for him a strictly rational structure against which he wants to oppose the more playful and intuitive modes of perception that he finds in Knowles and others whose mentation is not discursive. For Wilson, reason and language are indistinguishable as expressions of an objectivity that threatens to overwhelm more subjective forms of signification and sense making. Language, from this perspective, limits desire and perception because it signifies and defines; and as Yvor Winters once wrote, we judge definition "the most fierce of crimes."

But Wilson never considers that his own theoretical and conceptual approaches to language are themselves made out of a language that has inscribed its traces within him. He seems to believe that by following the thought-patterns of Knowles, he (or his performers) can stand outside language and take a detached, critical view of it. Anthropologists and linguists (along with Derrida), however, have been telling us that there is no such getting "beyond" language and writing, that whatever we think about these discourses is itself inscribed by the cultural traces that create and sustain language. Too, because language "speaks" us, it enables us to challenge the very ideologies that culture and language have inscribed within us. It must therefore be through language that ideology is challenged, resisted, or transgressed.

If the immanence of language were not alone sufficient to deter Wilson's rebukes against it, there is the further question of the relationship between language and culture. Wilson essentially creates the illusion (common to much modernist art) that his antilinguistic position stands outside, and has not been determined by, culture. Yet certainly Wilson's attitude toward language has been shaped within a cultural milieu that places a great deal of weight upon written and spoken discourse and upon rational communication. When Wilson brings his antilanguage beliefs and practices to his performances, then, his attitudes necessarily contain the forms by which they were shaped, and his importation of Knowles and the mentation the boy exhibits has already been tainted by the earlier appropriation. In trying to speak the language of the Other (in this case, Knowles and his autistic mentation), Wilson is actually only saying himself, even if it is a self partially modified and determined by his interactions with Knowles. Thus it seems that instead of making spurious repudiations of language, Wilson might accomplish more fruitful cultural work if he were to recognize the interplay of differences among words and discourses, and to investigate the psychological and social processes by which these historical accretions obtain relative degrees of power within culture.

Such high linguistic theory may not seem immediately important in the context of the performances, but it connects with the simpler, but perhaps more crucial, point that when Wilson disintegrates language he disjoins the very act of social interaction that is presumably the theme of his performance. For it is language, ultimately, that binds together a community, and by which that community orders its experience and social norms. As Blau says, "language remains the one human activity which undeniably socializes, and most cohesively in its separations" (1982a, 85). The only connections we have to the past (the past beyond *les petites madeleines*) are made through language, and when that language is discarded, so is history, that "experience of Necessity" that refuses desire and restrains individual and social praxis. Wilson's attempts to rekindle the power of nonreferential language and the performative play of signifiers, then, partake of the same atavistic impulse of much experimental theater of the period. And in emphasizing a rejection of rational language and its replacement by new expressive modes, Wilson also fails to provide a critique of what lies behind language, that is, the processes by which its different discourses acquire meaning and stature in culture.

Brecht's final assessment of *A Letter for Queen Victoria* is that its "gesture of contempt" toward language represents a sacrifice of Wilson's theater of visions to the gesture. This is debatable, but the performance does indicate the end of a discernible phase in Wilson's work. Moreover, critical appreciation of his work also changed drastically when, with the arrival of *Einstein on the Beach* in 1976 (revived 1984), Wilson became a well-known artist among relatively mainstream audiences. Marranca's earlier championing of the theater of images as "a watershed in the history of American theater, a *rite de passage*," and of *A Letter for Queen Victoria* as "a grander vision of life than we are used to," for instance, is quite typical of the early eager acceptance of Wilson's new theatrical style. That appreciation, however, gave way in a very short time to a different perspective on his work:

> Wilson's alienation from the realities of contemporary life is precisely the impetus for theater that finds a home in the mythopoeic

> tradition of the American avant-garde. Wilson's recent pieces have used contemporary myths to illustrate his dissatisfaction of modern life. His vision is apocalyptic; he seeks a return to order and peace after the holocaust. Is this not a reflection of Romantic longing for a return to a world that we will never see again? Wilson's handling of contemporary problems is too naive to take seriously.
>
> Wilson's escapism is the problematical element in his theater. The danger is that the audiences, overwhelmed by the monumental settings and beauty of the images, will be passively drawn into the spiritualistic world of his theater. . . .
>
> It is this sense of loss and time and place, the religiosity of the experience, the absorption in images that by their nature are ambiguous, simple resolutions of harsh political realities, and the acceptance of a theater that hypnotizes its devout followers that is disturbing. It is indeed questionable whether Wilson will lead us to higher consciousness. Theater must be more than something to gape at or lose oneself in. (Marranca 1984, 121–2)

I quote Marranca at such length not to reveal a personal critical shortcoming on her part, but rather to indicate how rapidly the negative reaction to Wilson's work established itself among critics of experimental theater. The fact is, of course, that the problems in Wilson's theater mentioned by Marranca were there from the start (and remain in altered form even today). It was primarily a lack of critical rigor due to an understandable fascination for the stunning visual beauty and conceptual grandeur of Wilson's work, that blinded most to the regressive and apolitical nature of his performances. Like the poststructuralist theory that it so resembles at crucial points, Wilson's dramatic aesthetic was undergoing a period of coalescence out of which more socially centered work could arise.

Einstein on the Beach appeared when the critical revision that problematized all avant-garde work of the mid-seventies began, and the work shows the effects. Wilson seems to have anticipated somewhat the new direction, and as a result the performance shows significant divergences from earlier work. Perhaps reacting to the negative effects of paring down *A Letter for Queen Victoria* to the bare essentials of theater, Wilson built *Einstein on the Beach* on a monumental scale reminiscent of grand opera. The performance lasted for almost five hours (not long for a Wilson production, but something of a shock for those at the Met and at BAM), the cast was huge by Wilson's standards, and the production costs ran into the hundreds of thousands of dollars—in part because Wilson was using real (Equity) actors instead of his devoted "Byrds" for the first time. More important, as Marranca points out, Wilson's work was becoming "more accessible" (Marranca 1984, 119); perhaps it is more accurate to say that it was becoming less arbitrary. The seemingly surrealistic images—locomotives appearing on stage, the clock moving asynchronously and backward, figures "swimming" on plexiglass tables, other performers counting fitfully and taking obsessive notes—all relate to the thematic concerns of the piece: Einstein's theories of time, space, and motion (often explained by analogies to moving trains), the tub of mercurized water by which the speed of light is measured, bodies moving in the vacuum of space, biographical references to Einstein, and so on. And, though the images may be arcane, they do seem to indicate, as Bigsby suggests, that "as [Wilson] moves towards coherent themes, so he seems to drift back towards a more familiar theatrical model" (Bigsby 1985, 183).

If this is indeed the case, then it is certainly a theatrical model built on alternative performance, and not on the orthodox dramatic text. The work is Wilson's first to show a strong collaborative framework. Whereas earlier performances were produced in the manner of the Wagnerian *Gesamtkunstwerk* with Wilson bearing the burden of working as director, choreographer, scenarist, stage director, and sometimes performer, *Einstein on the Beach* included choreography by Andrew de Groat (later replaced by works of Lucinda Childs), music by Philip Glass, and "spoken text" by Knowles, Samuel Johnson, and Childs. In addition, the performance was characterized by the collision of rigidly formal structure and rich visual imagery, of objective textual form and subjective, performative content, rather than an explicit accent on one at the expense of the other. This new attitude is similar in many respects to what Beckett (on the austerely minimalist end of the spectrum) does in his later work, and kin to the double-coding of formal clarity and expressive imagery that characterizes Elizabeth LeCompte's work with The Wooster Group.[8]

In terms of providing a thematic core for the performance, Wilson is again closer to experimental theater than to orthodox drama. The central themes seem to cluster around the related ideas of the loss of innocence (familiar from earlier work) and the tension between the rational and irrational, between mathematics and dreaming.[9] But again, since language is not the vehicle for the expression of themes, thematic development is manifested not as in orthodox drama by dialogue and sequential action, but by changes in the work's formal elements, performance rhythms, costuming, and images. The overall structure of the piece, too, follows no linear narrative. Instead, the work is divided into three acts, each relating to one of three concrete images: Train, Trial, and Field. Acting as a prelude, two entr'actes, and a coda are four "knee plays," the joints that hold the primary material together and "bend" the themes in various directions.

Although no clear-cut resolution to these themes is offered, the Field sequences offer images of simplicity, openness, freedom, and relative spacetime, while the knee plays depict images of mechanical gadgetry, constraint, Newtonian absolute space and time, narrative closure, and repression. Wilson characterizes the former as "landscapes" and the latter as "portraits" in terms of their spatial functions, the one keeping the spectator at a hermeneutic distance and the other inviting closer scrutiny and interpretation. The motive thrust of the play, then, is the revelation of a shifting dynamic between life and consciousness illustrated as performative or indeterminate, as opposed to textual and absolute. This thematic structure is not built up by a sequence of conflicts and resolutions, but by contrasts between images that appear and reappear in each act, as for instance the nineteenth-century locomotive and the modern spaceship. Rhythmic movement, too, is used to signal these contrasts, as when the rigid, repetitive movements of Lucinda Childs counterpoint the more natural and expressive movements of the performers in the Field scenes.

Such contrasts help to create a sense of thematic order in the piece, but too close a dependency on them certainly robs the performance of much of its ambiguity and richness. There is no evidence in *Einstein on the Beach,* for instance, that Wilson is "opposed to technology" or "anticontrol"; the spaceship seems to represent for him both the hope of the future and its last gasp, as it carries explorers/survivors into the void.[10] Childs's dance may be controlled, but it is visually stunning and is an example of the beauty inscribed in ritual repetition and physical discipline. Wilson's productions seldom strongly state "for" or "against" attitudes, and in fact it is that kind of rational dichotomizing that he hopes his works will eradicate.

Thus, even with the encroachment of a recognizably theatrical structure in *Einstein on the Beach,* the spectacle still predominates. The work is full of overwhelming visual effects: the spinning Sufi dancing of de Groat, the measured movements of Childs back and forth in the background, the constructivist trial chamber, and the weird beauty of the chorus members brushing their teeth in unison while the Einstein-Player saws at a violin. Art quotations abound throughout the piece, with echoes of Gordon Craig, Adolphe Appia, and the Bauhaus school, and a surprising appearance of a high-tech version of The Living Theater's *Frankenstein* chamber in the final act.

This creates an odd tension between what Marranca refers to as a conflict in Wilson's "classicism and modernism" (Marranca 1984, 121), by which she seems to indicate a dichotomy akin to the paradigms of text and performance. She suggests that the work is somewhat mannerist, and she quotes Arnold Hauser's definition of the term: "a product of tension between classicism and anti-classicism . . . rationalism and irrationalism, sensualism and spiritualism, traditionalism and innovation, conventionalism and revolt against conformism" (121). Hauser might well have been describing contemporary art in general, and especially contemporary performance theater. The mannerist qualities in such performances are due to a crisis in language (verbal and otherwise) and to conflicting ideas about the functions of history and art history in the making of avant-garde art. The crisis produces work that uses these tensions—manifested as another version of the performance/text dynamic—to create an art built as an ad hoc hybrid revealing both distortion and rigid formalism. One result of the unresolved tension, however, is a theater that, although supremely conscious of art tradition and history, is often paradoxically ahistorical.

In *Einstein on the Beach,* Wilson works to agitate various sets of conflicting attitudes and desires: popular and esoteric art, personal vision and social context, thematic coherency and indeterminacy, form and content, sensualism and spirituality, rationalism and irrationalism. This signals an important shift in Wilson's aesthetic, as more and more in his work he seems, himself, caught between the dreamer and the mathematician, between performance and textuality. No longer content to envision a world in which the performance paradigm simply replaces or transgresses the textual, we see that Wilson increasingly comes to want both the powerlessness and the lack of referentiality of pure spectacle, along with the clarity and order of rigid form and significant content. And, without extending the comparisons too far, this suggests the same kind of aesthetic vacillation between performance and text, play and closure, powerlessness and power, that characterizes the work of Beckett and The Wooster Group. Like them, Wilson seeks not a resolution to the tensions but a fruitful dynamic between them, by developing a style that incorporates both performance and textuality within the speculative and interactive space of theater.

While the attempt to discover such a form in *Einstein on the Beach* is therefore significant, it somewhat disables the piece itself. What happens essentially is that Wilson gets caught between the almost pure surrealism of his earliest work and the limited conventions of opera and the Broadway musical. The startling quality of Wilson's earlier oneiric visions gives way to a kind of cultural kitsch that replaces the fascinating juxtapositions of personal data that had made the visual aspect of his work so stunning. In addition, partly to accommodate his new audience, Wilson abandoned the excruciatingly slow movements that had created a tension with visual tableaux in works like *Deafman Glance*. The new approach gave his imagery a static quality, creating a simpler series of unidimensional images, with the result that there is a loss of ambiguity and visual depth. Commenting on the differences between Glass's inspired minimalist score for the production and Wilson's stage direction, Brecht concludes that

> the styles were disparate: cumulative repetition enriched by mutations, a progressive structure that seems itself the work-in-process of its creation (Glass) vs. sustained exposure of major themes subjected to minute fractures, extrinsic structuration of anxiety (Wilson): a naively exuberant vs. an insidiously elegant style. A Beaumarchais spectacle scored by Wagner. (Brecht 1978, 361)

Though the judgment is harsh, Brecht's critique does suggest that Wilson had not yet discovered a method of approaching his productions as a hybrid of his early oneiric and autistic performances on the one hand and more recognizably textual structures on the other.

The slow process of coming to terms with such hybrids is described in the work Wilson has done since *Einstein on the Beach,* including *The Golden Windows* (1982), *the CIVIL warS* (1984), *Death Destruction and Detroit* (*Part I,* 1979; *Part II,* 1987), *Alcestis* (1986), *Hamletmachine* (Paris, 1979; London, 1987), *The Forest* (1988), and *Orlando* (1990).[11] In *The Golden Windows* (which has not been produced in America), Wilson for the first time referred to an existing text as the basis for his stage designs.

Not surprisingly, given the dynamic interactions between text and performance, dream and mathematics in *Einstein on the Beach*, the text was an American book of fairy tales. Wilson isolated the single image of a house on a mountain "differently viewed at different times of the day." Although based primarily on the visual icon, the play is not devoid of language; fractured monologues, repeated phrases, and even small bits of dialogue exist side by side. Still, the concerns with space and movement remain paramount. In keeping with Wilson's implicit desire to wed the visual and linguistic elements, the spectacle and the drama, Bigsby notes that in the work "the urge to reconstruct a complete, logical and coherent narrative is all but irresistible, but there is no model of truth to be unravelled except in its individual moments and the patterns which form, dissolve and reform" (Bigsby 1985, 185). The lack of a shared language or common mythology in the modern world forces Wilson to attempt to renew or reinvent communication entirely. And increasingly, that reinvented language comes to be composed of a stable chaos between the unchained signifiers of performance and the constraints and invariances of the text.

The same agenda is inscribed in the next work as well. Wilson's *the CIVIL warS* was his attempt to effect perhaps the grandest artistic collaboration of all: a monumental five-act opera whose separate sections would be produced independently in five different countries, and brought to be joined together (with thirteen new knee plays) and performed at the 1984 Los Angeles Olympics. The noble effort to achieve a momentary *communitas* across several sections of Western culture fell short of its goals when the U.S. Olympic Committee rescinded funding for the event, leaving most of the work completed as discrete units but denying the many collaborating artists and technicians the chance to see them brought together as a whole. The separate acts have been performed sporadically around the world, but there appears to be little chance that the work will ever be produced in its entirety.[12]

The subtitle of *the CIVIL warS* is "a tree is best measured when it's down," a folk saying Carl Sandburg borrowed for the title of his meditation on the death of Lincoln. The performance juxtaposes the notion of measuring against that of play and deferral. Measuring implies an objective or Newtonian universe, where fixing absolute limits on space and time is the means by which man becomes the measurer of all things. Play, on the other hand, though controlled, functions as a reagent that breaks down and subverts rule-governed activities like measurement (of time, space, reality, and so on). Wilson plays the two notions off one another throughout the piece, "framing the spectator's desire for forms of semiotic finality or closure," in Maria Minich Brewer's phrase, "and radically diverting it to the changing intensities of performance" (Brewer 1985, 25). Like Elizabeth LeCompte and The Wooster Group, Wilson tries to "push two buttons simultaneously" in order to evoke in the spectator a desire for meaning, unity, and wholeness, and at the same time a knowledge that such integrated systems and fulfilled desires cannot be entirely present or stable. The result is a quantum exercise in spectatorship, as meaningful events emerge, coalesce, and disappear in the particle accelerations of the performance.

For Wilson, the opposition never breaks down into either closure/indeterminacy or drama/performance. The pairs exist in order to interanimate one another, to make the spectator become aware of the work as a source of meaning and a process of making a work; as Brewer says of the interpolated *Knee Plays,* "The performers are shown to be *at work* in the process of reorganizing the materials they have at hand" (1985, 26). This activity accounts for the rhythms of the piece, as objects (such as the boat and the book in the knee plays) are found, reshaped, and made into something different, and then are subjected to further transformations. Yet the process is not endlessly recursive; the *Knee Plays* end with the figure of the Reader being directed by Bunraku puppeteers toward the text, which has been created by transforming the boat. And, since the boat has itself earlier undergone a series of transformations (a tree, a cabin, a sunken wreck, a civil war boat being raised, a graffiti-covered wreck in the jungle), it operates as an image of change, but, significantly, change with a history. Some of that history is inscribed (by the graffiti on the boat hull), and the boat itself "becomes" a text of that history. When the Reader sits to look into this text (now an actual book), a tree grows out of the book, bringing us back to the original image, suggesting a cyclical process.

Though there are numerous possibilities to unpack from the series of transformations, the dominant theme that emerges is the evolution of the random object into the text. Wilson at this juncture appears to realize that, despite every effort to undo the text and to escape a closure of interpretive possibility, the activity of assigning meaning and desiring such closure is a fact of spectatorship, perhaps of consciousness itself. Still, he certainly figures such closure as a momentary, unstable phenomenon at best, because one "text" constantly gives way to another in a quantum dance of visual transformations and intertextual reinterpretations. In fact, there is actually a density of texts being created simultaneously and without benefit of hierarchy, with the result that an orthodox hermeneutic impulse (to find either one meaning or another) is "blocked," in Brewer's phrase:

> Theatrical elements are allowed to develop freely without being bound or directed to representation. This is because no one system, be it linguistic, graphic, scenic, musical, or gestural, is allowed to impose its specific order on the others. The open measures of the *Knee Plays* produce a space-time that is perceived as polygraphic, polymorphous, and polyphonic. (Brewer 1985, 27)

Like the standard model of the quantum universe, Wilson's text is bounded, but infinite and interactive, its description embedded within the shifting act of observing it.

Thus, while Wilson continues to search for a new network arrangement of theatrical communication, his earlier animus toward language and textuality is attenuated. Language has become, along with images, gesture, and music, a separate but equal "language" within his performances, contributing to the overall rhythmic patterns of the spectacle. At the same time, the process by which the mind gathers these languages into a bounded but dynamic text has assumed a great deal of importance as a thematic core to the performances. The new approach gives Wilson's formerly static stage tableaux a welcome sense of tension and dynamic movement, and allows him to consider somewhat more closely the fluctuations of history as it is inscribed, erased, and rewritten in various texts.

By the time Wilson comes to *Alcestis,* the tension between the urge to create performance-oriented spectacles and another desire to investigate history and textuality infiltrates the very process of the work's production. The Stuttgart Opera commissioned Wilson to produce von Gluck's eighteenth-century opera *Alceste,* for which Wilson asked Heiner Müller to write a prologue.[13] Robert Brustein, artistic director of the American Repertory Theatre in Cambridge, had worked with Wilson before, and invited him to stage Euripides' play of the same title as "an experimental exploration of the *Alcestis* myth" in preparation for the Stuttgart production (Weber 1987, 21).[14] Wilson was given the irresist-

Robert Wilson/Heiner Müller, *Alcestis.*
Conception/Design by Robert Wilson, American Repertory Theatre, 1986. Photo by Richard Feldman/American Repertory Theatre.

ible opportunity to develop his material, first as a dramatic production based on an existing text, and later as a full-blown opera/spectacle.

The collaboration with Müller, who is "only" a playwright and has no connections to stage design, choreography, or music, itself represents a new direction for Wilson. The choice of this writer, known until recently to only a few readers outside Europe, reveals some significant points regarding Wilson. The two artists are usually described as advocating opposite views regarding the purpose of art: Laurence Shyer, for instance, writes that "one's theater is jagged, dense and angst-laden, crammed with conflicting attitudes, self-destructive meanings and twisted shards of history; the other's glassy, graceful, and self-reflexive" (Shyer 1989, 117). Yet, Carl Weber, Müller's English translator, describes the playwright in terms not unlike those that can be ascribed to Wilson:

> Müller is one of the few dramatists today who could be called a "universal playwright," a playwright asking questions and expressing traumas that concern all of contemporary mankind, not only one group, nation, class or culture. This may sound quite grandiose, yet Müller's view is not a microscopic view. He observes man as if from another planet, through an immensely powerful telescope. He writes with the hope that what he calls "a universal history of man" is eventually going to begin, setting his utopia against the reality of universal misery he sees everywhere. (Müller 1984, 13)

In addition, Müller's texts themselves enact the breakdown of classical textuality through the counterinsurgent dynamics of performance, and thus reflect in some instances the interaction between these opposing tendencies in Wilson's productions. In only one of a series of fantastic coincidences that have occurred between the two artists, Müller delivered in 1977 a paper at a conference in which he defined the term *postmodernism* by reference to one of Wilson's works he had seen, *Death Destruction and Detroit.* He termed the piece "something like a combination of mathematics and child's play," thus elaborating perfectly Wilson's conception of *Einstein on the Beach,* a work Müller had not yet seen (Shyer 1989, 118–19). Also, like Wilson in his post–theater of visions phase, Müller does not fragment his narratives simply to deconstruct language and order, but to investigate the possibilities for new order.[15] Finally, Müller also shares Wilson's sense of an impending encroachment of the technological on modern civilization, and a belief that a change in attitudes, and perhaps of consciousness itself, is the only thing standing in the way of complete destruction. Theater's function at such a crisis point in history is to represent new alternatives to such trends. As Müller writes in his *DESPOILED SHORE MEDEAMATERIAL LANDSCAPE WITH ARGONAUTS,* "[the play] presumes the catastrophes which mankind is working toward. The theater's contribution to their prevention can only be their representation" (Müller 1984, 14).

Although often aligned with Brechtian thought and theory, Müller has said that "it's treason to use Brecht without criticizing him" (1984, 18). What disturbs Müller most about Brecht—as Beckett, Elizabeth LeCompte, and Wilson are disturbed by any classical literary drama—is the linear "A-B-C dramaturgy" that underlies and reifies an aesthetic built on closure and final solutions to the tensions and political conflicts in the plays. Instead, Müller, like LeCompte, prefers to expose the fractal scale of his culture, and to bring to light the gaps, disjunctions, and inconsistencies that make up conflicts without forcing smooth, definitive lines on the material. Müller's world, defined by the same quantum interactions that vitalize LeCompte's and Wilson's, is predicated on the necessity for dynamic change and transformation—that is the theme as well as the form of his art. These parallels to his American counterpart are themselves not so farfetched when one considers that Müller has said he was influenced by the contemporary American avant-garde theater during his stay here in the mid-seventies (Müller 1984, 14). His verbal collages, which sometimes look like the elided texts of Beckett and the self-reflexive "diaries" of Richard Foreman, heighten the sense of slippage and displacement, and also make his radically deconstructed texts appropriate vehicles for Wilson's stagecraft.[16]

Müller's more pointedly political theater also appears to have helped move Wilson, if not directly into the political arena, at least toward a more culturally contextualized and historically informed theater. Wilson's theater has always been directed at reforming or refining perception, but this has usually been restricted to individual cognition and interpersonal communication, or else to theatrical perception. Müller, on the other hand, wants his theater to act as "a thorn in our eye," and to force audiences to recognize that "the first shape of hope is fear, the first appearance of the new: Horror" (1984, 30). And, while neither attitude predominates at the expense of the other in their collaborations, there is growing evidence that the complementary form they are working out may well provide Wilson with new outlets for his impressive directorial and scenic talents.[17]

The American Repertory *Alcestis* provided good direction for this new initiative, since the theme of death and redemption through human effort was a suitably universal one for both playwright and director. The production marked Wilson's first sustained theatrical encounter with an established written text.[18] However, as a descendent of Grotowski, Schechner, and Chaikin (as well as Beckett), Wilson took the opportunity to make substantial alterations in the classical text so that it conformed to his desired notion of an open-ended performance text. As Elinor Fuchs describes the process of elision, Wilson "follow[ed] Euripides' dramatic structure closely, . . . substantially removed the choral passages, cut the text to the bone, broke up some lines of text among different speakers, repeated others, and wove into the text passages of the Müller prologue as well as certain key words to be spoken both live and on tape" (Fuchs 1986, 81). Wilson had not consulted with Müller on the prologue (which was intended for the Gluck opera version), but when the manuscript arrived, "not only did the text respond to the death and renewal theme of Euripides' play as expected, but it uncannily contained major images that Wilson had already installed in his design: a mountain range, the eyes, birds, rock slides, the 'peep-hole into time'" (Fuchs 1986, 81).[19]

Müller's text comprised a single sentence running thirteen typed pages, some of which was cut by Wilson.[20] Originally entitled *Bildbeschreibung* (literally "Description of a Picture"), Müller decided to call it "Explosion of a Memory," the new title indicating some important ideas behind the text. First, the text is an explosion in the sense that it is characterized by frequent fragmentation, distortion of narrative sequence, and a seemingly random interlocking of images and narrative elements. These elements themselves derive from what can be seen as a kind of detonated collective cultural memory. Müller lists his sources in the following order: Euripides' *Alcestis;* the Noh play *Kumasaka;* the eleventh canto of *The Odyssey;* and Alfred Hitchcock's film *The Birds* (Weber 1986, 105). He calls such aggregates "synthetic fragments," and uses them to pursue what Weber refers to as his quest for the Western collective memory: "In his process-oriented dramaturgy, Müller deconstructs classic narratives to quite 'elementary' particles, and then reconstructs from them a text for our age. His radical surgery on revered epics or tragedies goes far beyond mere adaptation, it dynamites their narrative to get at the roots of their meaning" (Weber 1986, 105).

Müller's insistence on the power of cultural artifacts, and on their ability to speak "synthetically" to the modern age, rehistoricizes Wilson's work, and grounds it more firmly within universal human endeavor. While Wilson had once been content to present his nostalgic ruminations on the loss of innocence through the juxtapositions of visions gleaned from personal insight, autistic modes of perception, and the junk clichés of contemporary culture, Müller's text forces him to consider them in *Alcestis* from another perspective, that of the collective cultural history of civilization. And, as in Beckett and the later work of The Wooster Group, the source of that history is discovered within, and expressed by, literary texts. The use of the eleventh canto of *The Odyssey* provides Müller with the motif of the murder of both sexes, and with the idea that resurrection is the complement of insurrection, of change and transformation. The use of the Greek myth recalls, as it did for Joyce in *Ulysses,* that all humankind partakes of the universal, no matter one's station in life. The use of myth, however, is not, as it was described by Eliot in "Ulysses, Order, and Myth," a "continuous parallel between contemporaneity and antiquity . . . , a way of controlling, of ordering, of giving a shape and a significance to the immense panorama of futility and anarchy which is contemporary history" (Eliot 1975, 188). Müller cannot be satisfied with such a reactionary view of history, and so contorts myth in order to make it a source for the desire to change the present, rather than to order history. History becomes not so much a mirror for the present as an affective tool for transfiguring contemporary life.

The effects of Müller's refiguration of the *Alcestis* myth on Wilson's production of the play are both relative and profound. Beyond the inclusion of the "Explosion," there is little in the production that seems radically different from earlier Wilson. Setting the movement came before even looking at the Euripides text; Wilson directed the play in absolute silence during the first week of workshops, "in order," he said, "to see how that was structured" (Fuchs 1986, 86). After reading Euripides' text in rehearsal, he went to work cutting it, before abandoning it again to concentrate on lighting each object in the production and creating the audio environment for these objects. Only after the laying of this groundwork was the text finally incorporated into the design of the piece. By that time, it had been "Wilsonized" (to use Fuchs's term) to break up its organic structure and illusion of mimetic representation: character names were replaced by numbers, live and taped dialogue overlapped, and, most important, the traditional ending of the play was eliminated, including the celebratory lines that close it on a note of restoration and hope.[21]

Startling images again dominate the mise-en-scène: a nineteen-foot replica of a Cycladic statue stands to one side, with a small platform projecting from its midsection. Harnessed there is a smaller figure, wrapped like a mummy, who speaks in a genderless voice the Müller text. A mountain range is built into the backstage area. Embedded in its sides are the artifacts of previous ages—a Viking ship, Chinese funerary figures. Ionic columns standing in front of the mountain later change into smokestacks and break apart, revealing a future city. And, in the most spectacular bit of staging, a laser fixed behind the audience cuts an eye-hole in the side of the mountain. In between these effects, birds cavort on stage, glowing costumes eerily illuminate parts of various actors, and strange half-men, half-spacemen inhabit the realms between life and death.

Still, despite these evocations of past Wilson performances, significant changes take place. In addition to using a text with its own objective substance, and the relative narrative coherency and referentiality this implies, Wilson employs a primarily fixed and built set (actually three different playing areas). And, while many of the images that appear are disarming, few have been made surrealistic or fanciful by Wilson's fertile imagination. Many artifacts and costumes are taken, in fact, from photographs. In addition, as Fuchs points out, "a number of representational 'mood' sound effects, such as birds and wind, function as in a radio score" (Fuchs 1986, 84). Overall, while avoiding to a large degree the constraints of mimetic representation, the production certainly shows Wilson continuing to grapple with strategies for incorporating representational, textual qualities within a presentational, or performative, context.

Fuchs says that the production "suggests an imaginative work-through to the end of western culture" (1986, 85). The cultural references, both in Müller's text and in the mise-en-scène, give the piece a sense of moving through history, not via a linear chronology, but "side by side," as the work's set designer, Tom Kamm, put it (Kamm 1986, 88). Trees become Greek columns, which in turn become smokestacks;

the stage floor is first a mountain; then, moving upstage, it becomes dirt and grass, followed by stone and tile, and then by something that looks like an asphalt road. The effect is to render a relatively specific emotional ambience and mood from the setting, an effect often lacking in Wilson's earlier performances. The overlapping references to the rise and fall of cultures in the setting and spoken text create what Kamm refers to as "a tragedy of culture" (Kamm 1986, 88).

The tragedy, however, is never reconciled within a traditional literary or philosophical framework (i.e., Aristotelian, Stoic, Christian, existentialist, absurdist), but is rather left to exist as residue in the mind of the spectator. Like Müller, whom Weber (1987, 25) describes as anything *but* "the demiurge who creates his own controlled world on stage," Wilson tries to rid himself of the contradictions life forces upon him by giving them body and life through representation, rather than by imposing a solution upon them.[22] Those essential contradictions are built into the very structure of *Alcestis,* as the performance of the main text is followed by a short Kyogen skit, "The Birdcatcher in Hell." Although the skit repeats the themes of death and resurrection and a trip to the underworld, it does so as a broadly comic version of the Alcestis story, and serves to undercut the profound weight of the main act. The effect does not utterly undermine that profundity, but puts the interpretation of the work as a whole into several alternative contextual spaces.

Müller and Wilson have expressed similar desires for a "non-consumerist theater," where signs are not premasticated by an author or director and spoon-fed to the spectator. "Interpretation is the spectator's work," says Müller; "it shouldn't happen on stage" (Weber 1987, 26). What crucially distinguishes this attitude from Wilson's earlier aesthetic is that interpretation, as a confluence of intellectual, emotional, and imaginative activity, and as an expression of spectatorial power, is not being denied or assaulted as an outworn conceptual framework. Previous work had tended to privilege the phenomenological "art" of watching, as opposed to the hermeneutic art. Wilson's current work, on the other hand, seems geared toward the production of performances that engage the spectator in a reexamination of history and culture and of the individual's place within both, rather than in mere introspection. And again, that significant change in perspective is not effected by virtue of Wilson giving up or turning his back on his exciting imagistic style; rather, the new power of the work is released by the collisions between performative and textual strategies. As Müller puts it,

> The first thing in our collaboration was that there was Bob's frame, which is sometimes in danger of becoming a hollow frame—just design. And then there is my material, my texts resisting this frame, and there's a conflict between images and language and this conflict is drama. And so our collaboration can change my idea of theater and his ideas too. There's a drama here and it's not finished. (Shyer 1989, 134)

Alcestis was followed by other works based on literary models—selected texts of Kafka, Müller's own *Hamletmachine,* and, perhaps most indicative of new directions, plans for a version of *King Lear* and for a work based on Virginia Woolf's *Orlando. Hamletmachine,* first produced in France (1979) and restaged almost a decade later on a grander scale in London (1987), brings to the fore many of the most significant unresolved tensions in Wilson's canon. Müller's text for the piece posits Hamlet as a disillusioned contemporary caught between past and present, between history and the desire for an escape from history, and between text and performance. The production mirrors these conflicts, as it leaps from mesmerizing elongations of ritual time to dazzling video cuts and transformations, and from cultural memory (Hamlet's speeches with their infusions of modernist literary fragments, the appearance of Mao, Lenin, and Marx) to a self-absorbed desire for personal transcendence (Hamlet's request to become a woman, complemented by the use of nude females to depict the communist triumvirate). Performative dream-states expressing and eliciting nonrational responses from the spectator are violently interrupted by references to history and cultural texts, ranging from powerful literary evocations (from Euripides, Conrad, Eliot) to mass-culture slogans (references to Andy Warhol, Coca-Cola ads). Neither the performative nor the textual paradigm dominates the other, but their interchanges create a sense of energetic chaos. The effect is not unlike the evisceration of texts and performance ontologies that we see in The Wooster Group's work, especially *Nayatt School,* and, like The Group's piece, *Hamletmachine* acts as a generator to accelerate the oppositely charged particles into collisions (and collusions) that create new and unstable entities.

While *Hamletmachine* (along with other work) was produced outside the United States, Wilson did undertake another collaboration with David Byrne, *The Forest,* which was performed originally at Theater der Freien Volksbuhne Berlin before arriving at the Brooklyn Academy of

Music in late 1988. Based on the Babylonian epic *Gilgamesh,* the work continues Wilson's exploration of the cultural memory through the medium of an ancient narrative. Codesigner Tom Kamm remarked that "what's different . . . is that Bob's really telling a story this time. . . . [I]t's very narrative for his work" (Shyer 1988, 9). The story was of course elided according to Wilson's typical approach, and Wilson still maintained that his purpose in the piece was to destroy language and invent new vocabularies.

Yet the piece reveals the same interactive dialogue between the *épistémès* of vocabulary/language, performance/text, freedom/determinism, innocence/experience, and dreaming/science that occur in earlier work. Also continued are Wilson's attempts to place these seeming dichotomies within an interanimative field where they can be broken down, accelerated, and quantized into new shapes and structures. In Wilson's adaptation, Gilgamesh is presented as a nineteenth-century German inventor and captain of industry, both Einsteinian dreamer and master of commerce. Gilgamesh's sense of mastery over nature and his fellow man is contrasted to the innocence of Enkidu, the "wild-man" befriended by Gilgamesh in the original epic. The environments of both are so similar that they suggest that the two men are mirror images of one another ("We put a lot of parallels into the two scenes," reported Kamm). Wilson again draws a parallel between the world of innocence—hearkening back to the murdered children of *Deafman Glance,* the autistic, prerational language of Christopher Knowles, the Field scenes of *Einstein on the Beach, Hamletmachine*'s victimized females—and the world of mastery and domination: rational adults and their language, technology, and totalitarian political systems. Significantly, however, one world does not dominate or absorb the other. Gilgamesh and Enkidu meet on the common ground of their humanity, and their mutual affinity and complementarity sustain their friendship. When Enkidu is killed in the sixth act by a dragon, Gilgamesh returns forlornly to his city, which he finds in flames. The theme is not especially subtle—the loss of the mirrored Other leading to apocalypse and damnation—but when combined with the stunning visual images and music of the piece, it potently conjures up the archetypal story of the loss of the Other and the consequences of that deprivation for the individual.

Wilson's work, then, shows a consistent tendency to grapple more and more with the substantial texts of world culture, and to reorient his theater away from the simple deconstruction or desemanticizing of

Robert Wilson/David Byrne, *The Forest.*
Courtesy of the Brooklyn Academy of Music, 1988. Photo by Gerhard Kassner.

speech toward a recognition of the cultural work it performs. Writing after the premiere of *Orlando* in 1990, Andrzej Wirth noted that "the staging . . . puts into question" the opinion that Wilson is "fundamentally incapable of or not interested in rendering great literary texts respecting their value as literature" (Wirth 1990, 15). Indeed, Wirth predicts that Wilson's performative strategies and insurgencies within a great text like Woolf's *Orlando* will transform the literary *Sprechtheater* of Europe, simultaneously preserving the "metaphoric brilliancy of Virginia Woolf's language" and amplifying it "in a way unreachable by a conventional literary theater which tries respectfully to translate verbal pictures into visual pictures" (15). We can only anticipate the effect of such amplification on the texts of American writers in whom Wilson has recently expressed an interest: David Mamet's plays, Wilder's *Our Town,* the poetry of T. S. Eliot.[23] As in Beckett, The Wooster Group, and (we will see) Sam Shepard, the movement is toward a radically modified text that discovers in the intervals and lacunae opened up by performance some of the deepest potentialities of textuality itself.

Despite the increasing maturity of Wilson's work, it remains to be seen whether or not his recent theatrical initiatives will find much of a truly popular audience in America. First, it is questionable whether another director or auteur would be willing to stage Wilson's work, since it is so bound up with the processes of its own production and the sensibilities of its producer and his collaborators: one trembles at the image of a Wilson piece being done on a shoestring budget in a regional theater, or at the hands of a well-meaning MFA student at an American university. More significantly, American audiences have seldom showed a proclivity for theater that combines texts and surrealistic performance strategies in a manner similar to that discovered in Wilson's recent work. That is, with perhaps the exception of abstract expressionist art, the brief flirtation with social realism before World War II, and the recent initiatives in theater traced here, Americans have no real tradition of spectatorship for events that interface abstract, deconstructionist form and highly charged content. With rare exception, Wilson's work was originally scorned by mainstream American critics, who generally found it cold and sterile. And although that reputation has been reshaped somewhat in recent years, it is worth noting that virtually every premiere of Wilson's work for the next couple of years is scheduled in Europe. Too, Wilson has yet to win recognition from his American literary peers in the form of an Obie or other such award, although *the CIVIL warS* was the sole drama nominee for the 1986 Pulitzer Prize.

There is hope, however, that some of Wilson's latest collaborations and textual projects might claim the artist a wider following, and more theatrical support in America. That recognition would benefit not only the artists themselves, but American audiences and culture as a whole as well. With American-European relationships recently shifting, and with the realignment of centers of political and cultural power throughout the world occurring at an imposing pace, Wilson's transformational art seems especially appropriate as a viable theatrical language of our time. Wilson, like Müller, shares a typically twentieth-century impulse to balance pessimistic feelings and apocalyptic themes with transcendental urges for political and social renewal. This produces a kind of writing that shows a considerable formal complexity, scale, and richness that is united with significant subject matter. These epic dream-visions express the desire for a radical transformation of the world, and pulsate with the same profound emotions, complex thematic subtlety, and extraordinary visual excitement as does our specular culture.

Chapter 5

The Landlocked Geography of a Horse Dreamer: Performance and Consciousness in the Plays of Sam Shepard

Nothing forces us to be looking constantly for satisfaction that resides only in repose.

—Igor Stravinsky

Even during the height of the nonverbal, nontextual experiments of the sixties and seventies, there were those unwilling to accept unexamined some of the extreme claims of performance and its promise of a theater that could operate as a reality of its own or as the first principle for transcending the burdens of consciousness. However, intrigued by how various performance strategies could operate as a kind of liberating language within the text, playwrights associated with the American experimental theater of the sixties, such as Megan Terry, Jean-Claude van Itallie, Jack Gelber, and Sam Shepard, imbued their plays with ideas and strategies learned in their firsthand experience with the performance collectives of the period. Their innovations, in conjunction with the changes in traditional dramatic structure and logic wrought earlier by the surrealists, the absurdists, and their avatars, have since provided newly emerging playwrights with an alternative to the conventional dramatic text, one better able to express an increasingly frenzied and chaotic vision of American life and culture to new communities of spectators. So it is that today even a text-oriented playwright like David Rabe can attribute a great deal of influence on his own works (*Streamers, Hurlyburly*) to The Open Theater's performances of *The Serpent,* while the work of other authors, most notably David Mamet and Jane Wagner, also reveals benefits from the crossover of avant-garde performance practices into mainstream theater.

The general effects of experimental performance theater on contemporary drama are obviously widespread. The influence of transformational acting strategies (especially as taught by Joseph Chaikin at The Open Theater) on the protean characters in plays by Sam Shepard, Jane Wagner, and Megan Terry has allowed these playwrights to experiment with sophisticated performance techniques that are used to explore gender crossing and the elusiveness of postmodern subjectivity. Theories and experiments in physicalizing the voice in performance at the expense of evoking a transparent referent have exerted a strong influence on the way Mamet and Rabe explore the violence and deceptions that characterize, more so than discursive communication, the thrust of their dramatic language. The increased emphasis on improvisation and indeterminacy, inscribed in the very notion of performance, has infiltrated the structure of a wide number of contemporary plays and changed the nature of the interactions between stage and spectator. Experiments that utilize destabilizing performance strategies to collapse determinate meaning are seen in plays ranging from Wagner's *The Search for Signs of Intelligent Life in the Universe* to more radically deconstructive pieces by Daryl Chin, Spalding Gray, Kathy Acker, Paul Dreschler, John Jesurun, and a host of other authors and performers.

Nor is this any longer a peculiarly American phenomenon. Similar parallels are apparent in British drama as well, where Caryl Churchill, Pam Gems, and other socially active playwrights have politicized the gender appropriations of contemporary culture and the media by the use of transformational acting and other performance strategies. And even a politically orthodox author like Tom Stoppard often gives his plays a nonlinear, open-ended structure by creating characters whose tendency to transform themselves into a variety of performed roles prevents any one figure—or indeed any one through-line of action—in the play from attaining a privileged status. Henry Carr, for example, the befuddled *raisonneur* of *Travesties,* creates multiple realities as his disabled sensorium spins out disoriented versions of history and dada-history. His inability to provide the play with a cogent Presence or center, or to establish recognizable through-lines (who "wins" the art/politics debates, and so on) as he performs his multiple realities deconstructs the very Presence and power of the text he is creating. This leaves the audience, like Carr, grasping for certainty in a galaxy of possible meanings. Stoppard's theater, in fact, has accepted and advocated the notion of a quantum theater more openly than most. His most recent play, *Hapgood,* makes Heisenberg's indeterminacy principle and Bohr's theory of complementarity both the form and content of a postmodern mystery drama.

Perhaps the most significant application of experimental performance in today's theater, however, lies in the awareness of new metaphysics of acting. The theories of Grotowski, Schechner, Blau, Brook, Chaikin, Beck, and other performance theorists of the sixties and seventies laid the groundwork for a more sophisticated understanding of the differences between "acting" and "performing." Acting, as Erving Goffman described it in his influential book *The Presentation of Self in Everyday Life* (1959), symbolizes humankind's entrapment in the constrained roles written by culture. Goffman's *theatrum mundi* was therefore the site of mutual deception and eternal insecurity, where humans attempted unsuccessfully to escape the roles predetermined by an external (and politically suspect) author. Anticipating or building on Goffman's notions, performance theorists of the sixties and seventies constituted the paradigm of the performer, who symbolized for them a constant subversion of the authorial culture, and a reinstatement of the self as the source of individuality, spontaneity, and difference. Beyond its ontological dimension, this distinction has also motivated new permutations for the stage/life metaphor that has increasingly come to characterize the discourse of our mediatized and theatricalized culture. Since, however, in the wake of poststructuralist critiques of origin, few today would hazard the degree of self-consciousness or Presence needed to insist that life is simply experienced or spontaneously lived, the question now is, rather, Is life acted according to some predetermined text, or performed as a series of personality slippages and leaks? Or are the two somehow inscribed within one another, as a constant negotiation and renegotiation between freedom and determinism or between diffracted selves and a stable ego? Without reducing their explorations to pat answers, dramatists have begun to incorporate the tensions created by the two metaphysics into the thematic center of their works. Often, the conflict is expressed explicitly as between the paradigms of performance and text.

Most often these playwrights and performers are investigating different approaches to the nature of reality, as they explore the epistemological and ontological predicates behind the notion of the fixed "dramatic" role of the traditional actor or the text, as opposed to the fluid, transformational relationship of the performer to changing realities that characterizes experimental performance. However, since for many no single paradigm adequately captures the real relationship between self and world, artists have come increasingly to investigate the space between these two existential absolutes. Unwilling to accept either textuality or performance as a reliable master narrative to describe the nature of the self, many writers and performers choose to inhabit the uncertain but dynamic quantum space that divides these narratives, aspiring to discover hopeful alternatives or transformations within the interactive space between them. In essence these artists seek, like anyone intervening in such dynamic ontological spaces, a stable chaos; that is, an image of the self as shifting, contingent, but also constrained by invariances.

Many of the transformations wrought by experimental performance upon the dramatic text are worthy of closer analysis, though most fall outside the range of this study. For rather than simply documenting such crossovers of performance theater into mainstream drama, I am interested in exploring the significant interactions between performance and the orthodox dramatic text that have created a fruitful dynamic relationship between the two, of the kind already traced in Beckett, The Wooster Group, and Robert Wilson. And while a number of recent playwrights have incorporated their experiences with avant-garde performance theater into their work, none has articulated the potentially lively nature of that interaction more vividly than Sam Shepard; and certainly no playwright has aroused more controversy in doing so. On the one hand his turn from the intensely expressive and theatricalized performance medium characteristic of his early work toward a modified domestic realism with *Curse of the Starving Class* (1977) has immensely enlarged the playwright's audience and brought him a recognition formerly received only from connoisseurs of Off- and Off-Off-Broadway. On the other hand, avant-garde artists understandably wary of the monopolizing power of Broadway and its theological stage have posed the usual questions about artistic freedom and the recuperation of the avant-garde by a constraining orthodoxy. Estimations of Shepard's canon often hinge on where one stands critically in regard to this issue.

More thoughtful considerations of Shepard's turn toward a modified realism, however, have suggested that more than popular success is at stake. Lynda Hart's *Sam Shepard's Metaphorical Stages* traces the playwright's career along a line of growing maturity and accelerating imaginative capacity, and concludes that his recent forays into realism have revitalized the form. From a different perspective, critics like John Lion and William Demastes have argued that Shepard has developed naturally toward realism because it represents the appropriately ironic, even "postmodern," means to "illustrate the disintegration of causal threads espoused by the old realism (or naturalism), which simultaneously illustrates the disintegration of the family foundation" (Demastes 1988, 230–31). In this scheme, Shepard's work operates in the same kind of deconstructive mode as, say, The Wooster Group's, in a style designed simultaneously to inhabit and subvert the culturally coded structure of meaning we call (however imprecisely) realism.

Such readings of Shepard's career barometer connect his earlier experimental plays with the more recent realist works, and therefore have the benefit of making us aware of the continuity of Shepard's style and vision, which despite obvious important alterations have retained far more integrity than is usually supposed. Like most significant contemporary writers, Shepard has traversed an eclectic range of sometimes conflicting expressive modes. Hart (1987, 5) even goes so far as to suggest that Shepard's career "recapitulates the major movements in the drama of the twentieth century," though in Shepard's chronology the order is reversed.

The problem here again, though, is that such critical agendas for Shepard's canon seem programmed for gratification; that is, they insist upon a linear evolutionary relationship between Shepard's past performance-oriented work and his more recent realist plays. Usually the implication is that Shepard has somehow "developed" as a playwright as his plays become less expressionistic and experimental, and more realistic. Although such a model rewards us with a sense of progressive direction and interpretive order, it describes adequately neither the dynamic process of Shepard's career nor of his individual plays, realist or otherwise. For example, Felicia Londré attempts to periodicize Shepard's canon as a stately movement from "mindless macho" in his early performance-oriented work, toward an "investigation of his own masculinity" in the plays that begin to show signs of literary order and dramatic craft, and finally to a "mature masculinity" in the works (*Paris, Texas; A Lie of the Mind*) that reveal the male coming to grips with love relationships (Londré 1987).[1] But for Shepard, more than for most playwrights, we need to look beyond this linear pattern for a more complex model that describes how his plays—whether primarily performance-oriented and expressionistic or textually bound and realistic—enact a dynamic relationship between performance and drama, expressionism and realism. Instead of narrating his "development" toward realism and greater textual coherence, then, it seems more fruitful to seek in each play the different fields that create interactions between performance and drama, and to investigate the peculiar energy these confrontations create.

This does not mean that Shepard's career evinces no change or progress, only that the evolution is not strictly linear. For, like Beckett, Shepard often transforms his expressive methods without substantially affecting the core of his dramatic vision. That vision is itself predicated on Shepard's sense of the essential mystery and indeterminacy of existence, and on his need to show us, in Lion's words, "that the world doesn't make sense, can never make sense, will never make sense" (Lion 1984, 12). With that imperative looming over his plays, we should not expect much sense of movement or progress from "mindlessness" to "maturity." Instead, we see the plays oscillating between the contradictory desires for ludic performance and for textual coherence. We can, nevertheless, anticipate that the plays will attempt to impose a transient order upon this dynamic interaction, and thereby create a fruitful tension between indeterminacy and order.

Shepard's epistemological equation is reminiscent of the logic behind Beckett's more extreme anxieties over the need to express something in a world where expression seems not to be possible or meaningful. And, while substantial differences separate the two artists, there remains something in the scope and nature of their dramatic explorations that suggests a certain affinity. The connection is closest when the works of both playwrights are analyzed in terms of the interactions created between performance and textuality within the plays. Both artists, for example, create innovative techniques to deconstruct the orthodox dramatic text in order to expose the prison house of representation, especially theatrical representation, as it is codified within the text and represented upon the theological stage. In this regard they also have a share in the more general contemporary agenda of critiquing the bases of mimetic art and investigating the sources that empower a given textual representation's meaning. But while both playwrights investigate the residua of their deconstructions of textuality, that is, the dispersal of closed meaning into indeterminacy and play, neither Shepard nor Beckett accepts wholly the postmodernist attitude toward the dispossession of verifiable meaning, the breakdown of communicative language, and the improbability of significant action. Unlike most kinds of radically new performance art and performance drama, the plays of Shepard and Beckett are often inhabited by a more pessimistic themata that is grounded in late modernist anxiety. For these playwrights, the notion of performance does not come as a liberating force, but as a kind of false prophet whose illusory promises of freedom and *jouissance* only make the burden and constraints of reality more burdensome.

Shepard thus shares with other contemporary artists a willingness to transform the theatrical experience by exposing and deconstructing, through performance, its various hierarchies of textual power. But significantly in terms of his contrast to more radical exposures of representation, for Shepard the very process of exposure leads him to "preserve," in David Savran's estimation, "rather than transform or supersede traditional theatrical forms" (Savran 1984, 58). In the end, Shepard's deconstructions of character, action, and causality appear to lead, like Beckett's, to paralysis and entrapment, and his plays ultimately seem to affirm the absolute margins of performance *and* drama. The interactions between the two, then, unlike The Wooster Group's or Robert Wilson's, do not result in an endless series of deconstructions that can function as an affirmative response to the politics of culture or the burdens of consciousness. Instead, Shepard's deconstructive strategies eventually seem to fall prey to the risk of confirming and consolidating the very ontologies they try so assiduously to deconstruct; and the results most often derived are feelings of nostalgia and terror.

All of this indicates not that Shepard is outdated or off the track, but rather that despite his use of the deconstructive performance strategies he learned from The Open Theater's workshops and which he has refined throughout his own early plays, Shepard is essentially a modernist, as opposed to postmodernist, playwright. Like Beckett, he has an eye for the problematics of mere existence; and although much of his writing, like Beckett's, is directed toward the dream of a Total Theater, in which sense and object are joined by an incantatory language through the medium of which the weight of the past is leavened, Shepard is also painfully aware that such an escape is improbable at best. As Bigsby notes, "he has the 1960s desire to make fragments cohere and the 1970s belief that truth may ultimately lie in those fragments" (1985, 221).

Thus, when Shepard incorporates performance into his plays as a thematic element, he presents it as a potential means of escape from the confines of the text, one's ego, one's cultural heritage, and (especially in the later work) one's closest connections outside the self, that is, from erotic and familial relationships. Placed in painful existential situations, Shepard's characters try to reach out and find attachments beyond the self. Like Beckett's characters, they choose between isolation and a deeply suspect engagement with the rest of the world. The usual method adopted by Shepard's characters for gaining a selfhood beyond the self, and for attaining some kind of affirmative response to the constraints of consciousness, is through performance. As Florence Falk conceives it, Shepard's characters "try to perform their way out of, or around, disaster" (Falk 1981, 182). That these characters almost universally fail to achieve a proper level of performative intensity, and thereby end up locked into the paralysis in which they begin, suggests that Shepard, like most modernist writers, is consigned to a thematic of "broken immediacy," which characterizes Beckett's plays as well. For Shepard's characters, too—until very recently, I will argue—there has usually been little hope for transcendence and productive action; all that remains is the lingering and illusory image of a time when such freedom was possible, and the feelings of nostalgia, guilt, and entrapment that follow the painful realization that such times are lost. Shepard parts with Beckett only in that the potential for transcendence imbues his plays with a greater sense of hope, though it remains usually a hope unfulfilled.

The central theme in virtually all of Shepard's plays is, as he remarked in a 1981 interview, "the idea of consciousness" (Marranca 1981, 212). In Shepard's plays, this idea is always ambiguous, and in fact exists as what he calls "double consciousness," in which two opposing forces vie with one another for control. The two are predicated on the relationship of performance to drama: on the affinity, that is, between consciousness conceived on the one hand as derived from transformations and transcendence (the *jouissance* of indeterminacy, and the escape from the burdens of memory—and a spontaneous adaptability to find a Presence *within* the present), and, on the other hand, consciousness structured around psychological integrity, a nostalgia for lost grace, the burden of memory, and a claustrophobic sense of closure.

Within Shepard's metaphysics of performance, consciousness exists (or the subject desires it to exist) in a kind of permanent present, as characters attempt to escape the past and live for the moment by improvising a variety of selves and realities with dizzying speed. Intruding into these performances in Shepard's plays, however, are scattered memories and the detritus of a potent cultural heritage—often figured precisely as the broken remnants of past texts—which burden the present and restrict the flow of transformational energy, thus limiting (like a dramatic text) the range and transcendence of the performances. The plays thus enact a double nature of consciousness, which Shepard is unable or unwilling to reconcile. As he remarked to Robert Coe, "It's a real thing, double nature. I think we're split in a much more devastating way than psychology can ever reveal" (1980, 122). The doubly coded schism may be dramatized, usually as a conflict between male and female principles, but for Shepard it lies beyond the scope of performance or textuality to heal the painful breach. Still, Shepard often finds in the space between those poles a potent arena of conflict within individual consciousness and among the essential myths of American culture.

Indeed, this conflict is so intensely realized in Shepard that it reflects even his attitude toward dramatic tradition. His best work enacts an attempt to recall the American past and his own dramatic roots (mainly realism), and also a desire to transcend that past by developing a performance theater that could overcome the traditions that bind him to orthodox textual drama: thus the double-coding of text and performance in most of his plays. His late appropriation of conventional form is consequently best understood, then, not in terms of any linear progression from one "low" or "outdated" style to a more "refined" or "artistic" one, but as permutations of the field relationship in which the same continuous dynamic of attraction and repulsion to both performance and drama, both experiment and tradition, can be traced within most of his individual plays. Here, too, there is through most of Shepard's career little indication of a reconciliation between conventional textuality and avant-garde performance. The two may engage in a kind of interface, and effect a transformation by the exchange, but they are never united.

If there exists any significant turning point in Shepard's career as a playwright, it probably occurs at the point when he stops simply "performing" the writing of his plays and begins to collide them against a more orthodox textuality. Like performances by The Wooster Group and Wilson, Shepard's plays require the tension between both performative and textual elements to avoid the Presence or closure that one or the other creates when it is left unmediated by its complement. For Shepard, the process of bringing the two paradigms into this sort of fruitful collision is revealed over a long period of time, and generates a variety of possible combinations, the recent realist work manifesting only one possible development. The early plays until *La Turista* (1966) are essentially poetic riffs worked over barely established themes, held loosely together with a kind of manic imagism and performative power. Transformational acting abounds in a work like *Cowboys # 2*, revealing the characters to be dispossessed of personal and cultural history. As John Glore described them, these works "gain their life from just such a rhythm of disdainful chaos. They are short bursts of violent creativity, impulsive, totally unencumbered by preconceived strictures. Open-ended and without readily discernible meanings, these plays reflect scorn for the idea of completion, of single-minded wholeness" (Glore 1981, 55). The works are thus oriented toward performance, both as the source for their theatrical power and in terms of the representation of reality and consciousness they espouse. Shepard's regard for the textual coherence of these works is indeed minimal, almost nonexistent; in several interviews during the period he decries the attempt to narrow the richness of the plays by enforcing meanings on them, and insists that the writing was built on "extending the notion of *play* (as in 'kid')" (Marranca 1981, 214). The direction of these plays appears to be toward a deconstructive, rather than textual, gesture as they attempt to accommodate the modern spectator's new ways of making and unmaking sense.

This early avoidance of form and closure, and the rejection of the interpretive power of the text, seems to reflect Shepard's early attitude toward American culture as well. And when his position vis-à-vis that culture begins to turn, so does the relationship between performance and textuality in his plays. The shift is clearly indicated by the writer's (and rock drummer's) stance toward rock music and culture as it evolved through the sixties and into the seventies. As Blau notes, "in his earliest work, Shepard had celebrated music as the nervy embodiment of a restless iconoclasm, the style of risk, 'flying in the eye of contempt'" (1987, 49). The same kind of iconoclastic method inhabits the plays of this period, as Shepard searched for a dramatic equivalent to rock that could deliver the same kind of transcendent experience as had the music. By the time of *The Tooth of Crime* (1972), however, Shepard had begun to sense more acutely the violence and the insipid conceptual frame built into the music and the punk culture growing up at its boundaries: "What he heard was a sound dispossessed of history, savagely, distorting the rituals of liberation by which the sixties were possessed" (Blau 1987, 49). This attitude slowly emerges and matures, eventually becoming distilled in Shepard as a more wary attitude toward American culture—especially the counterculture and its agenda of transcendence through rock music and performance—as a whole. As a result, Shepard's writing, too, though still infused with a great deal of unchained performative energy, becomes less explosive and anarchic, more (relatively) classical in construction and in its use of language. In the same interview in which he professed his expressive strategies of play, Shepard admitted that although for some time he had been "dead set against rewriting on any level," this "holy art concept" had crumbled as he realized the exigencies of the stage performance and the spectator's need for accommodation (Marranca 1981, 212).

Thus when Shepard begins to recognize the need or desire to produce work in which drama and performance act as complements, rather than plays that simply privilege his own diffracted performative consciousness, his writing does appear to change. But the path toward textuality, toward greater emphasis on significant content and clarity at the expense of performative energy, is not a smooth or linear one. In fact, in that gradual process of change, the seeds for a later dilemma are sown. For Shepard never really "learns" (or desires) to inhabit textuality completely, even in his most recent realist works. Operating strongly within his most orthodox "realist" texts are remnants of performance, which haunt the plays as a latent possibility for positive action, acting as an ontological escape valve for the alienation and objectification he sees as the state of contemporary society. His work, though, inscribed as it is within the dramatic text and the hierarchy that empowers it, cannot allow Shepard to grasp such freedom. Existing neither as pure text nor pure performance, the plays usually negate both and thereby create an acute sense of stasis and immobility.

The conflict between the metaphysics of drama and its antithesis performance is perhaps most clearly delineated in *The Tooth of Crime* (1972), a play in which Shepard's uneasiness at the prospect of a culture built on raw performative and image-producing power is rendered, paradoxically, in a classic agon. Hoss thrives in a world where a kind of cross-country "Assassins" game has erupted into the Game, a lethal contest that has subsumed elements of sport, rock music, astrology, and capitalist market venturing. Despite the postapocalyptic, sci-fi setting, with the outlandish camp followers and their stylized surnames (the Gypsy Killers, Star-Man, Galactic Jack, the Keepers), the setting has a curiously post-sixties, Warholian ambience. As the play opens, the characters do not seem actively concerned with effecting a positive or transcendent change in their state; in fact, they seem to embrace, even cultivate, the alienation and overwrought theatricality imposed on them by the Game. Indeed, the names themselves represent a further theatricalizing of everyday existence, an escape from anonymity into an image of radical pop chic that is either produced by the media itself, or in some other ways made unique and "outside" the mainstream. The attitude toward the past exhibited by most characters, too, seems contemporary. There is no attempt, before Hoss's, to reflect on the past and connect it to the present. Instead, there is a studied attempt by most of Hoss's followers to eradicate the past or to jumble it into collages of unrelated images: that is, to recreate the past as a typical postmodern "memory bank"—one thinks of Warhol's Factory-enhanced series of Maos, Jackies, and Marilyns, jumbled together and equalized as cultural icons. This lack of specific history, along with the ability to avoid history's burdens, gives the characters of Shepard's play the illusion that they live fully in the moment, as they perform in the present a series of ever-becoming roles.

Shepard has reported that the impulse for the play began with an image of the character Crow, a "yearning toward violence. A totally lethal human with no way or reason for tracing how he got that way" (Marranca 1981, 217). In his ability to manipulate images without regard for their content, Crow is limned as Shepard's ideal of the postmodern performer freed from all restraint, and his incapacity and unwillingness to reflect on the past become a key element in his character—a standard technique in sixties transformational acting as it moved away from the Method. At an earlier stage in Shepard's career, an entire play might well have been built around this central performative image without much regard for what it "means," but in this instance Shepard realized that the image of Crow "needed a victim, so I gave him one" (Marranca 1981, 217).[2] In doing so, he created a matrix for conflict, the resolution of which cannot help but reverberate with meaning and a certain amount of textual closure.

Crow's victim is burdened with too proximate a memory of his own past, a memory that disables him in the present. Hoss was a loner, a "Gypsy" himself for a time, before the fight at the drive-in when, once he has realized the class distinctions that forced isolation upon him, he finds the power to "kick shit." Once that strength is discovered, Hoss has a Code by which to live. The Code gives him a Marker, a sense of identity and purpose, a connection to a tradition of lethal gamesmanship that has its own internal rules. In the Game, Hoss finds a past, present, and future.

The problem is that Hoss, by assuming the closure of an identity and getting "Inside" the Game, begins to feel trapped by it and its Code, and consequently is discovered on the verge of making a kill before the charts say he's ready. Such an urge to break into the Outside is proof for Hoss that "the game can't contain a true genius. We don't have the whole picture."[3] Since theatrical metaphors and allusions to performance abound in the play, it is not unreasonable to assume that Hoss pictures himself somewhat the same way an actor might when confronted with the confines of a written role or text. The urge to break free of such constraints, to perform oneself into the Outside, the realm of "genius" or transcendence—that moment of Grotowski's "self-penetration"—is a familiar one in the work of the performance groups of the sixties with which Shepard had associated himself. Spalding Gray's emphasis on a "narcissistic" performance style in his work with The Wooster Group is illustrative.

Hoss thus finds himself caught between the Inside (the Game, limits, the text, art) and the Outside (pure play, freedom, risk, performance, life). The Inside means relative security, but at the expense of spontaneity, while the Outside promises risk and greater potential for bigger kills and increased fame, even while it imposes an increased vulnerability. What Hoss has not realized, yet, is that in the hypercharged theatricalism of his world—America in the presumably not-so-distant future—these distinctions have broken down, and "the Outside is the Inside now" (92); no one is watching the Game, because theater (the Game) and life have merged. Escape for Hoss now becomes impossible, as Shepard has subverted the differences between Inside and Outside, thus obliterating both. Hoss cannot play the Game anymore because he is aware of its limits, and he cannot simply "play" on the Outside because he does not, like Crow, have an ability to live without rules.

Hoss is victimized by a sense of tradition as well. He complains that the new Gypsy Markers have "no sense of tradition in the game no more," and reasons that "without a code its just crime. No art involved. No technique, finesse. No sense of mastery. The touch is gone" (218). Hoss envisages the battles and kills as artful, that is, following an integrated pattern that has an intrinsic meaning and is expressive of a larger sense of "honor." For him, they are conceived in terms of well-made artifacts, or texts. Indeed, Hoss, as Falk suggests, is "so beleaguered by fashioned (i.e., commercial) images that [he] can no longer distinguish natural behavior from artificial pose," and so his own style has coalesced into a fixed form (Falk 1981, 186). "Stuck in my image," he laments, already feeling the conflict of his dual natures as his desire for codes, "natural behavior," and tradition begins to give way to an equally potent need for indeterminacy, artificiality, and transformation. And, as in Müller's version of Hamlet in *Hamletmachine,* that crossed purpose of conflicting desires disables Hoss utterly, leaving him (in Müller's description of Hamlet) as an icon of disillusionment and the "petrification of hope."

The word-battle between Hoss and Crow pits the scrupulous textualist against the lethal performer. The conflict is essentially a style match, as Hoss battles to retain his image of self-authenticity and Crow demonstrates his own facility for shifting self-images and roles. Crow gains the upper hand because he is a genius performer, supremely indifferent to an authentic self and its personal history ("I got no guilt to conjure! Fence me with the present!" [241]). Indeed, his only moment of weakness is in Round Two, when Hoss is able to berate him for being unaware of the roots of his music, a possible source for his shifting selves. The embodiment of the Total Theater actor (we remember Spalding Gray's performance ontology of "the many-in-the-one"), Crow has merged his style and performance with his life; "I believe in my mask—the man I made up is me," he sings (234). Hoss, on the other hand, is unable to surrender his desire for authenticity and a stable identity. His acute anxiety at the prospect of losing these—"Nothing takes a solid form. Nothin' sure and final. Where do I stand! Where the fuck do I stand!"—weakens him and gives Crow the necessary edge (245). Hoss goes down defeated, says Blau, "because, unlike the implacable Crow, he *can't* go all the way. He can't live a lying image and he's not an inhuman machine, without blame or guilt" (Blau 1987, 54).

The outcome of the combat is decided by Hoss's indecision and self-consciousness. But as in all plays that touch upon tragedy, this ambiguousness and self-awareness give Hoss a sympathetic edge over Crow, even though they mean his own defeat. When Hoss knows he's beaten by Crow, he first tries to learn the new lethal style; unable to "suss" the protean verbiage, the transformational improvisations, and the shifting imagery, Hoss nevertheless tries to image himself as "a true killer. . . . Passed beyond ache for the world. Pitiless. Indifferent and riding a state of grace" (249). But the image would deny his need for the past, for responsibility, and for a self-confirming authenticity, and so when this realization strikes, Hoss collapses shouting "IT AIN'T ME! IT AIN'T ME! IT AIN'T ME!" (249).

Without a series of roles to perform, Hoss seeks a "genius mark," an act of supreme authenticity. His suicide is a self-affirming gesture that even Crow can admire. Still, Shepard does not weight the resolution wholly in Hoss's favor. Crow is riding in a state of grace, and has revealed himself powerfully as the harbinger of a new kind of consciousness and power. Hoss's ineffectual resistance may draw the spectator's sympathy, but this falls short of arousing any real empathy for what his order of consciousness represents. In the conflict between the modern and the postmodern, between text and performance, Shepard cannot or will not resolve the issues. The result is that, identifying with both, he privileges neither, and this burdens the play with a sense of absolute futility and entrapment. Nothing is offered as an effective means for dealing with the image-making power of postmodern culture, beyond either accepting its suspect claims of pure appearance and play or else committing suicide.

Hart suggests that *The Tooth of Crime* "represents a major departure for Shepard" because in it the playwright "finally has a hero who rejects a theatrical life and a singular image for another reality" (Hart 1987, 53). But is the meaning of the play so narrowly enclosed? Hoss's heroism, as well as the other reality he affirms, is problematic, and his rejection of theatricality can also be construed more as an inauthentic gesture of existential desperation than as a self-affirming act. And to complicate the theme further, Hoss is not the only character whose heroism or victory is in question; Crow, too, appears to have been tainted by his encounter with Hoss. Supposedly a progenitor of the victorious pluralist metaphysic, he nevertheless expresses a strong desire to assume Hoss's territory and fixed standing as a Killer Marker. The result, one could imagine, would be something like a fringe performance artist taking on the role of Willy Loman, and allowing himself to be constrained by Miller's controlling text.

The point is simply that, for Shepard, there is no "point of departure" from a purely pluralistic (performative) thematic toward a purely monistic (textual) one. In much of his early work, the two are inscribed within one another, each effacing the other to the extent that neither can be granted a privileged status. Bound within such a field, Shepard's plays cannot be described in terms of moving from one thematic toward another, only as reverberating painfully within the space that separates one from the other.

The same kind of dynamic informs *Action* (1975), where the presence of some unspecified catastrophe prior to the play has rendered virtually all action, ironically, improbable. The exact nature of the cataclysm is never revealed explicitly, but remains a mysterious obstruction to the characters in the play. As one critic explains, the origin of the crisis has been "misplaced (or more properly, displaced) and the 'crisis' itself has been institutionalized so that it permeates everything in the playworld, appearing solely as a kind of deformed status quo" (Savran 1984, 59). Unable to reclaim the origin of their crisis, and perhaps what preceded it, the characters are cut off from their pasts and left to survive in a world where the only viable alternative is to reconstitute themselves in the present, as performers. Again, like the fragmented figures in *Hamletmachine,* they are insubstantial and incomplete, awaiting with some agony a redemptive final transformation.

Interestingly, as the characters attempt to find a new praxis in the present, they are continually pulled back to a record of their past. The enigmatic "book" to which the characters refer again and again seems to be a historical record of the events leading up to and including the catastrophe. Although the fragments that are read allude only to tangential disasters, they presumably hold the key to understanding the past and its relation to the current scene of anxiety and crisis. The problem is that nobody can "find the place" where they left off reading. Denied the connection to their past, the characters must exist outside the text and its history, in the present.

Once again, Shepard has contrived a situation in which the loss of tradition, history, and meaning—manifested as a text—has left a group performing to save, or at least give meaning to, their lives. The play opens with Jeep's anticipatory line, "I'm looking forward to my life. I'm looking forward to uh—me. The way I picture me."[4] While the line does not ring with the exuberant assurance of Crow's song from *The Tooth of Crime,* it nevertheless reflects the concern with creating an image of the self that can exist both as image and authentic being. And, as in the earlier play, the vehicle for generating this image is performance.

While *Action* does not contain the classic agon between such a metaphysic of performance and another based on the self as text, the tension between the two nevertheless underlies the play. Savran suggests that the alienation and objectification felt by Shooter and Jeep are akin to the split consciousness experienced by the modern Method actor who cedes his own consciousness to the textual character he impersonates (Savran 1984, 61). Within each, there is a struggle for expression of the "true" self and the "performed" self, with the result that consciousness is once again presented as a schism. Even as they try to perform roles, Shooter and Jeep are conscious of themselves, and this dual nature both reflects and generates their anxieties.

The opportunity afforded the characters in *Action* to move away from the text and transform themselves into archetypal performers turns out to be the root of the crisis. The predicament in which Shooter and Jeep find themselves is similar to the one faced by an actor at a moment when the mask slips and the performer is revealed beneath the character. This moment, of course, was a crucial one in the psychology of performance theory that grew up in the sixties, where it was exactly this point that signalled a moment of "self-penetration," or the actor's escape from the confines of the text into the pure, spontaneous, and playful freedom and transcendence of performance. This appears to be the direction in which Shooter and Jeep want to be heading, as they try out transformational acting exercises to free themselves from the text of their past and their own personalities. Shooter, for instance, tries to "act out" a dancing bear, but the results are indifferent. The experience, rather than being liberating, is "humiliating. It's not the rightful position of a bear. You can feel it. It's all off balance" (171). Shooter's performance fails because he is conscious that he is performing. Unlike the bear (or anything else an actor impersonates), the actor is aware both of being himself and of the impersonation he enacts, being at once both the dancer and the dance. The question that confronts Shooter (and one that was never sufficiently confronted by early performance theorists) is whether or not a total performative act—in which self is unconditionally surrendered—can be realized at all. Can self-consciousness be overcome or transcended simply by the intensity of a performative act? For Shooter, the performance "puts me in a different position. A different situation . . . . Performing. Um—Without realizing it. Um—I mean I realize it but the bear doesn't. He just finds himself doing something unusual for him. Awkward" (171). The performance is not liberating, then, but as Lupe suggests, "cruel."

The self-consciousness inscribed in performance reflects the personal alienation that the characters feel constitutes the root of their malaise. Just as the actor is (sometimes painfully) aware of the division between being and performing, so Shooter and Jeep feel acutely the schism between consciousness and the self. Both objectify themselves, to the extent that Shooter feels a terrible fear when he sees the skin covering his body, while Jeep contemplates himself from without and "looks forward" to creating his life. Like the actor suffering from loss of stage presence and the subsequent stage fright, these characters are caught for the moment between being and their performance *of* another being.

Had Shepard accepted outright the claims of Chaikin and other performance theorists, *Action* would undoubtedly have been a different kind of play. But Shepard is unwilling to assent to the panacea of performance, or even to its possibility: like Blau, Shepard feels that the "ghost" is amortized within the performative act, and cannot be made bodily present. Consequently, Shepard's plays offer no solution to the problems imposed by dual consciousness. Instead, as we have seen in Beckett, Shepard can only attest to the schism that divides past and present, character and performer, text and performance. As the characters in *Action* come to realize, cut off from any kind of personal or cultural history, the sense of an authentic self exists only as a vague memory or ghost inhabiting one's consciousness. Unable to grasp this and transform it into a way of being, the two men seek escape from the ghost through performance. They cast off their true selves and attempt to enter completely into the roles they perform. Failing this, they can only end feeling trapped and confined:

> *Jeep:* I used to have this dream . . . I'd have this dream come to me that the walls were moving in. It was a sweeping kind of terror that struck me. Then something inside me would panic. I couldn't make a move. I'd just be standing very still, but inside something would leap like it was trying to escape. It was like an absolutely helpless leap. There was no possible way of getting out . . . For a second I could accept it. That I was there. In jail. That I wasn't getting out. (189–90)

Savran, speaking for a number of critics, feels that Shepard is "obsessed by the problem of entrapment and the impossibility of escape" (1984, 68). Situating the fixation in the playwright's modernist tendency to desire assurance, to sentimentalize the memory of a time when existence contained a sense of immediacy, and to glorify the American past,

Savran ultimately argues that Shepard, like Artaud, is a "failed" theatrical revolutionary. Because Shepard has stayed within the tradition of the dramatic text and the hierarchy of power this implies (with the playwright and text standing oppressively over the performer and performance), Savran insists, he has circumscribed his vision and blinded himself to alternatives. Such alternatives are found, we are told, in performance art, in the works of The Wooster Group, and in other avant-garde activity in which performances are able to image forth "the feminine and . . . the possibility of a future different from the present" (73).

The assessment is a provocative one, and accurately places Shepard's early work in the modernist canon. Having scrutinized more closely, however, the ontological margins that have placed the pretensions of performance into question in the work of the playwrights, performance groups, and auteurs discussed thus far, Shepard's "conceptual prison" seems a more formidable one than Savran suggests. The walls of that cell, after all, are constructed of language, which even in its most deconstructed state still carries traces of the past and the cultural heritage that has shaped its meaning. And we have seen how even The Wooster Group, dedicated to the deconstruction and critique of language (especially dramatic language), has in its recent work been turning more and more toward an appreciation of the power of such language. Besides, their work, while it effectively interrogates the hierarchies of language and representation, has really done no more than Shepard's plays in terms of suggesting concrete future possibilities. Like most attempts in the theater to imagine these, The Group's work, like Shepard's, has reached the margin of performance and turned, willingly or not, back into a radicalized text. If new possibilities are to be discovered, then such work suggests that it will be found within the text, and among its complements of history and language.

A second objection to this common critique of Shepard's position in contemporary theater touches upon the question of the playwright's late turn toward realism. "Shepard's open rebellion," says Savran, "against traditional dramatic structure in his early plays has given way to the more conventional forms of his later dramas" (1984, 69). This not only begs the question of whether or not such "conventional" forms can themselves be reinvigorated to produce the kind of alternative theater Savran describes, but also fails to recognize that, even as Shepard has returned to a modified realism, he has continued to experiment with performance pieces, most notably his collaborations with Chaikin,

Tongues (1978), *Savage/Love* (1981), and *The War in Heaven* (1984).[5] These objections are pertinent because they indicate that Shepard, not content with remaining static within his conceptual prison, is constantly investigating both performance and drama for a way out. And in contrast to the often strident thoughtlessness that goes into attempts at "imaging forth the feminine" and alternative consciousness in so much performance art, these attempts by Shepard to deal with contemporary American culture through text *and* performance remain significant and provocative.

The realist plays are not, as many have suggested, simply a retreat into orthodoxy or the appropriation of the formal designs of family melodrama. As Shepard said in 1974, his realism would not be "the kind of realism where husbands and wives squabble and that kind of stuff" (Chubb 1974, 15). Instead, Shepard felt that attention must be paid to the structures that have traditionally communicated cultural meaning: causal patterns, consistent characters, transparent language, and so on. This does not, however, imply that Shepard intended simply to recuperate these structures without modifying or critiquing them. Indeed, these transformations of realist structures represent Shepard's most provocative attempt—more potent even than the earlier faith in performance alone—to escape the modernist anxieties of his plays.

Some critics have recognized that Shepard's use of realist techniques in recent plays is double-coded, acting as something of a ruse. Like Beckett, The Wooster Group, and Wilson, Shepard invests in the greater textual rationality of orthodox realism in order to critique its limitations and as a way to reinvigorate it into new forms. Searching for a critical term to encompass what Shepard is up to in these works, John Glore invents "nova-realism: a word that suggests not only newness, but also the process whereby the newness is attained—a regenerative decimation of strict, old-fashioned realism in the service of a world behind forms, beneath surfaces" (Glore 1981, 57). Shepard's plays function, then, not as tired reprisals of the realist form, but as a means to undercut those forms and thereby unpack them in order to discover alternative visions to what is found "beneath surfaces."[6] In this sense they share the technique of double-coding that we have marked in other contemporary artists.

Those critical of Shepard's unwillingness to abandon dramatic tradition entirely usually base their arguments on the playwright's continued use of the "theological stage," or what I have termed simply "text," with its hierarchy of power centered on the author, who, according to Derrida, "regulates the time or meaning of the representation, letting this latter represent *him* as concerns what is called the content of his thoughts, his intentions, his ideas" (Derrida 1978, 235). The oppressive presence of the text suffocates the director and performers, and traps them in a scheme where language dominates all other theatrical expression, forcing them to illustrate the text. The Presence of the performance, then, is traditionally not in the actor (as Chaikin and other performance theorists asserted), but in the authority of the text, which is conferred on the actors and disappears behind them in performance.

Shepard's realist plays, however, still inhabited by traces of performance, struggle against the authority of the text and undermine that authority. But unlike what we see in performance art, in Shepard's plays performance itself is never granted a privileged status by default. In true deconstructive fashion, the text and performance are mutually inscribed in one another, each simultaneously negating and supplementing the other. The result is that Shepard's texts, and the various performance gestures that infiltrate them, do not grant a full Presence at all, and leave the spectator with no consensus or center of meaning. This is not to say such plays have no thematic core whatsoever, only that they are not reconciled in an analytical or even emotional framework.

In *Buried Child* (1979), for instance, the confusing blend of what is real and unreal, textually coherent or incoherent, disorients the spectator (and, I suspect, the actor as well). As Demastes points out, however, "contradictions and seeming evasions are not necessarily flaws for Shepard" (1987, 235). The power of such a play likely owes as much to the performance as to any literary structure of meaning inscribed in the written text. This, of course, can be true of any play, but in Shepard's work there is a conscious effort by the playwright to use performance to subvert his own authorial power, and thereby bring attention to the *troué* or natural insufficiency inscribed in textuality itself. As Savran points out, "the recognition of the radical contingency of all these terms [playwright, text, actor, director, character] will lead to one of two possible responses: either to a sense of entrapment and crisis or to a sense of liberation" (1984, 64). We have seen, in experimental plays like *Action* and *The Tooth of Crime,* the degree of entrapment that follows from Shepard's attempts to escape into pure performance; paradoxically, it is in the "realist," more carefully textualized plays that we find Shepard devising a third alternative to the problem, and discovering the greatest degree of liberation.

The early performance-oriented plays usually describe a dramatic world in which history has been lost, and where the "text" or central set of meaningful cultural codes has been displaced. The characters are introduced in the act of trying to use performance to perform their way out of rigidly prescribed roles and identities by enacting a series of improvisational transformations. Failing to accomplish this, the characters find themselves trapped *between* these roles and the desired transformation, in a purgatory where neither stability (often in the form of a Text or "Book") nor the free play of improvisation can be realized. As a result, the plays end on a note of despair and entrapment.

In the realist works, however, the equation is reversed. By starting out with a realist, textually organized matrix, Shepard sets up expectations that the plays will have a transparent, unified meaning and a strong sense of thematic closure. To achieve this, he uses many realist conventions—linear construction, patterns of cause and effect, a symbolic mise-en-scène, psychologically based characters, a wedding of language and explicit meaning—that serve to create a shared fable and form that the spectator can easily accommodate within traditional reading strategies. One effect is that the realist elements can draw the audience into a collectivity, from within which Shepard can then work to resist these reading strategies. That is, having drawn the spectator into such a community, Shepard can then use performance gestures to undercut or ironize the realist framework, and thereby suggest that within even the status quo lies the potential for transformation and difference, the possibility of "another kind of world."

This simple reversal represents quite an effective change, as such irony is impossible to achieve by the deconstruction of what is already a form that resists the spectator's reading strategies, that is, by open-ended and dispersed performance. In essence, Shepard's approach here parallels that of Wilson, who has said that his own productions of Müller's texts represent attempts to "build an agreed language with the audience and then . . . destroy it in order to rebuild" (Jackson 1987, 9). By doing something akin to this, Shepard's later plays convey a hopeful sense that things can, indeed, be rebuilt on the ruins of the realist text.

The "shared fable" that, elucidated through the realist construction of the play, binds the audience into a collective is the same one explored by O'Neill, Miller, and a host of other dramatic predecessors to Shepard: the disintegration and renewal of the American family. Shepard has adapted the theme both to explore its immediate social and cultural impact, and as a vehicle for moving beyond such surface conditions to explore alternative types of coherence. Shepard is often described as following, especially in his earlier work, Artaud's line of theater. Although much of this criticism is misplaced, Shepard certainly shares with Artaud the feeling that "the theater must also be considered as the Double, not of this direct, everyday reality of which it is gradually being reduced to a mere inert replica . . . but of another archetypal and dangerous reality" (Artaud 1958, 48). In the early performance-oriented plays, Shepard's exploration of that second order of reality was paramount, as he examined the archetypal duality of consciousness underlying the veneer of the social mask. The realist plays, on the other hand, combine this investigation of personal consciousness with a new interest in what effects are engendered beyond the self, in familial, erotic, and cultural space. In doing so, they take as their theme both the concerns of realism ("direct, everyday life") and those of performance (that "dangerous archetypal reality" that lies beneath it).

Buried Child is Shepard's first attempt to explore an impulse toward another kind of world. In it, he delineates in a realist vein the family fable, which he uses as an avenue into the play's experiential core.[7] The family's story, with its weird relationships and the overbearing sense of guilt that enthralls the members in spiritual torpor, is recognizable from a number of previous realist works, O'Neill's *A Long Day's Journey Into Night* perhaps most immediately. The first-act dialogue is, beyond a few queer passages, straightforward and expository, and the narrative coherent and organized. The action places the spectator in a community of playgoers well versed (by the television sitcom if not theater per se) in the predicates of realism and the mechanics of the family drama. The only telling deviations from the realist norm are, significantly, not verbal but rather performed stage gestures: Tilden spreads corn husks over Dodge's sleeping body, and Bradley brutally shears the patriarch's head as the lights dim to end the act. Seemingly unrelated to the action of the play thus far, the gestures suggest a deeper, archetypal significance that cannot, at this point, be explained analytically or in terms of an emotional through-line. They disrupt the realistic text developed thus far,

Sam Shepard, *Buried Child.*
Joseph Gistirak, Catherine Willis, Dennis Ludlow, Betsy Scott. Directed by Robert Woodruff, Magic Theatre, 1978. Photo by Ron Blanchette/Magic Theatre.

but do not replace it. As a result, the spectator is understandably disoriented: Is this going to be a realist play, or another of Shepard's imagistic performance pieces?

In the second act, the realistic/textual coherence is further eroded. Vince's arrival should mark a turning point in the family's situation, but surprisingly no one recognizes him. He tries to jog their memories by performing various parlor tricks he once used to amuse the family. These represent performative gestures that act as an alternative to the realistic dialogue. But an important difference exists between Vince's use of performance and that of the other brothers, especially Tilden. For Vince, the performance gestures are a way to ingratiate himself with, and to get back inside, the family; as such, they foreshadow the equally strange account of his mystical vision of his forebears, which he takes as a sign to return home and claim the family patriarchy. On the other hand, Tilden's disorienting performance gestures, we will see, are usually directed outward, toward the disintegration of the existing family and the possibility for a new kind of world.

Throughout the second act the spectator constantly feels the solid groundwork and stable relations of the realist text slipping away. Perhaps the spectator deserves equally Shelly's remark to Vince: "What's wrong with you is that you take the situation too seriously."[8] For such "serious" spectators expecting an intelligible story, the dialogue increasingly becomes less unified, even fragmented and stychomythic in the exchanges between Tilden and Shelly. The plot, too, begins to twist slowly and decompose, as relationships between characters are broken by lapses of memory and an unwillingness to assume fixed familial, and dramatic, roles (*Dodge:* "Bradley doesn't even live here!" [76]; and later, "Stop calling me Grandpa will ya'! It's sickening. 'Grandpa.' I'm nobody's Grandpa!" [90]). These connections are further confused when, near the end of the act, the drowned child is first mentioned: Whose child was it? Has incest been committed? By whom, with whom? The spectator is left wondering, like Vince is, when Dodge asks him, "Between the two of us [Dodge and Tilden], who do you think is more trustworthy?" (99). In this scene of warped domesticity, there can hardly be a correct choice.

The "direct, everyday" reality of the family has been subverted by the attendance of a more dangerous and archetypal world, which impinges on it and threatens its already skewed balance. In essence, these two "worlds" represent the poles of text and performance, the one supposedly fixed and transparent, the other risky and opaque. The first carries the spectator into the drama, as it reassuringly promises a significant beginning, middle, and end; the second, meanwhile, carries the performance into the spectator, as the open-ended gestures and nonrealistic events suggest the deeper, nonrational dimensions of the family's situation.[9] As the text increasingly is unable to assign an unequivocal consensus of truth in the play (in its realist characteristics *or* in the experience of the mysterious gestures and references), the Presence of the text is undermined, and the spectator is left to seek new competencies and types of coherence.

These can be discovered on several levels, as for instance in the intellectual qualities of the play, that is, in the working out of the plot and the resolution of main themes. Or, they may be apprehended on a visceral, experiential level, which we might call "myth" and which Artaud terms the "historic or cosmic" level. Finally (and most likely, given Shepard's dynamics of dual consciousness), they may be resolved in a complex interplay of both. As Hart notes, Shepard has intentionally "set up the audience to follow the tantalizing clues that he exhibits in an effort to integrate the fragments into an accommodating whole," only to undercut these expectations, "frustrating our ability to resolve the action of the play realistically, allegorically, *or* symbolically" (Hart 1987, 76). These are all rational literary structures within the play, but Shepard has also consciously directed the spectator's response toward an irrational, performative, and experiential level.

This ambiguous response pattern is seemingly fulfilled in the last act, where the causal pattern is worked out at the same time that the mythic experience is fulfilled. Significantly, however, the two are not integrated into a single or unified response, but exist in ironic juxtaposition to one another. Vince returns to lay claim to the house and patriarchy, assured that his vision of his progenitors has been a sign for him to carry on the line. On this level, the establishment of a new order and harmony may signal a classical closure of the theme of family disintegration and reintegration. But, again, the indication of closure is a ruse; for just as Vince asserts his violent patriarchy, Tilden returns with the corpse of the buried child.

We may try to arrive at an equivalency of meanings here, trying as Thomas Nash has done to argue that Vince's ascension and Tilden's uncovering of the dead child reflect the culmination of mythic harvest rituals from *The Golden Bough* (Nash 1983, 486). In performance, however, the two strands seem to exist separately, with the domestic drama ending with the suspect elevation of Vince to the family property. This suggests a certain optimism that, in Nash's words, "Vince's rebirth reconciles the antitheses" (490). But Vince's "aria" describing his vision, and his immediate actions following his inheritance, point not to reconciliation but only to another patriarchal cycle of brutality and dispossession. It is true that just as the realist domestic drama begins to merge with the mythic level of the play, we might see Vince as a fertility figure, the new Corn King. His reign, however, will likely follow exactly in the line of Dodge, the Dying King whose bravado regarding his potency ("You know how many kids I've spawned?" [112]) is a shaky front for a real fear of his own sterility and his impending death ("There's not a living soul behind me. Not a one" [112]). Vince's vision (which after all is motivated by his own reflection) suggests he has connected himself to his progenitors and their past world of power and brutality. Dodge has found his appropriate heir, but this reconciliation only suggests that the same cycle is to begin again, as it does when Vince begins to terrorize Bradley and deny the mother-figure, Halie ("My grandmother? There's no one else in the house" [131]). This also coincides with his abrupt dismissal of Shelly, ending any connection to the feminine.

Were this the only response structure operating in the play, the notion of Shepard's work being constrained by a conceptual prison that denies escape and that will "guarantee the suppression both of the feminine and of the possibility of a future different from the present" might be validated (Savran 1984, 73). But this captures only part of the effect of *Buried Child* and denies the presence of the performance gestures inscribed in the text. Many of these disorienting bits of dialogue and stage action, which subvert the realist structure of the domestic drama, are performed by Tilden, Vince's half-wit father. He covers Dodge with the corn ("gently," as opposed to Bradley, who "violently knocks away some of the corn husks" [81–82]), engages Shelly in the fragmented but revealing dialogue that ends act 2, and is described throughout the play as an element of mystery and irrationality. Significantly, he is the prime suspect in the incest, which immediately places him in opposition to Dodge's patriarchy. He is a figure not of brutality and oppression, but of nurturance, weaned by "Mother" (Halie, as mother and mother of his child?). Further, Tilden is described as gently singing in the fields to the child of Halie's incest, and we see him openly communicating with Shelly (opposed to Vince, who treats her like "property"). Finally, Tilden is the only male to see and appreciate the "miracle" of the fields (Tilden = "Tiller"?).

Tilden's strange and disorienting presence in the play subverts the realist action of the drama, throwing mysterious plot strands into it and dis-integrating its naturalist basis. He is not, however, there simply to inject a bit of quasi-absurdism into the play, but to offer an alternative to Dodge's sterility and violence. He represents the "dangerous, archetypal" reality of which Artaud speaks, similar to the domain of performance, which is equally dangerous and irrational, likely to explode the stability of the text at any moment. Yet Tilden's appearance at the end of the play, rotten rags and buried child in arms, does not translate analytically into a "solution" to the problems of family disintegration and alienation. His presence is too passive to represent the vengeance that seems poised to fall on the family, and his actions too tentative to suggest he will overthrow Vince.

Rather, Tilden suggests on an experiential level the promise and potential—attenuated to be sure, but like performance, present, *there*—of a new world built not on patriarchy and violence but on atonement, with a new redeemed order (possibly representing the feminine) arising from it. As Doris Auerbach describes it, "The existence of the child promised a new world order which would have ended patriarchy's violent hegemony. This child had to be conceived through incest. How else are new races founded—with whom did Adam's son mate but with Eve?" (Auerbach 1982, 61). Thwarted in this particular instance by the murder of the potential heir, the new order is still suggested by Shepard as a possibility, a potential future escape from the family patriarchy and from the conceptual prison of the early plays. Even though the patriarchy is not overthrown in the space of the play, the first seeds of pollution and guilt have been sown, and there is an almost classic sense of impending doom hanging over the males at play's end. The conclusion represents another bifurcation point, or moment of singularity, after which the family "system" will move either toward absolute chaos (the continued reign of the patriarchy and its sterility and violence) or toward a higher order of complexity and stability (the other, possibly feminine, world). Rather than dramatizing the outcome, however, Shepard chooses to enact the singular moment and to leave the ultimate outcome to chance and to the spectator's subjective interaction with the material.

Thus *Buried Child* carries, in essence, a double-coded response structure, one operating in a realist, textual framework and another on a deeper, performative level of myth and potential transformation. At the end of the play, the spectator cannot reconcile these structures and thus confer on the text a sense of a determinate resolution and closure and the power over meaning that such closure implies. Instead, Shepard has unchained both the textual and performative signifiers of the play to create a free-floating irony that resists closure and opens up a galaxy of possible meanings. Is the play representing the pyrrhic victory of patriarchy and textuality, and the endless recurrence of male dominance? Or are Tilden's mysterious presence and his unearthing of the child a vision of an alternative to this—an invitation to perceive life as nonrational, performative, in such a way to allow for the expression of openness and "the feminine"? Shepard, always careful to emphasize the immediate experience of the theater and its ability to open up meaning for the individual, has carefully created a structure that resists any exact closure, but that engages the spectator on complex intellectual and experiential levels. Both textuality and performance are coded into the play as one another's opposites to reveal the ultimate inadequacy of simply intellectual or simply experiential schemes in accounting for human experience. What is privileged in their place is the dynamic, unstable interaction between the two, and the quantum order of reality such an interface creates.

Something of the same attitude toward breaking free of the stasis of his early plays informs *True West* (1980), where the confrontation between Austin and Lee explicitly calls to mind the conflict between closure, security, and textuality, on the one hand, and freedom, indeterminacy, and performance on the other. The play not only investigates the consequences of the interaction between the two brothers, but also probes the nature of a transformation between the principles they represent. Austin, the urbanized, postmodern organization man, represents all that has gone awry with the American frontier myth: he is isolated from nature, helpless to confront brute reality (in the guise of the desert), and implicated as a mass-producer of images. Lee is introduced as his opposite, an avatar of the grim and vaguely criminal heroes of American myth, whose special grace was an ability to survive one step ahead of an encroaching civilization by the exercise of an amoral will.

Before long, Shepard dramatizes a grand version of the transformational acting method, whereby the brothers completely reverse their roles and experience the point of view and the desires of the other. What we first learn is that neither was completely accurate in his low estimation of the other in their initial encounter. Lee confronts the special pressures of being creative in a society that imposes artistic (and temporal) limits to the creation of art. After he savages the typewriter, the artifact of a technological civilization for which his desert survival skills are no match, and moves to the telephone, Lee remarks, "I would never be in this kinda situation in the desert."[10] Likewise Austin, despite his collection of stolen toasters, is not yet ready to play Lee's role and survive by himself in the desert.

By the play's end, there is no resolution to the conflict between the principles embodied by the brothers; neither is there a neat synthesis wrought between the two by the transformations between the characters. Instead, the play ends with the two brothers confronting each other in a standoff. On one level, the denouement looks like a prelude to a western shoot-out, with its suggestion of a very terminal closure. But because the scene remains a tableau, the spectator can never be sure. It is just as likely that a chase will ensue, calling to mind Lee's "original" screenplay, with its fascinating open-endedness and its eternal pursuit played out against the limitless Texas panhandle. And while this may not allow Austin and Lee to transcend the roles they play, there is a sense that the very act of their transformation holds out the hope for the necessary momentum, if not the direction, in their quest for another kind of life. In essence, Shepard again ends a play just as the action reaches its bifurcation point, leaving us unsure whether this signals a movement toward continued entropy or a lurching toward a new kind of order and energy.

Shepard's most recent theater work, *A Lie of the Mind,* takes the exploration for "possibilities" to another level. The images of the play—surely the most visually stunning of Shepard's "realist" plays to date—suggest the casual influence of Wilson and the theater of images, but with some important modifications. Although the opening sequences in which Beth struggles to express herself through her brain-damaged language are highly reminiscent of Wilson's pieces utilizing an autistic actor, the rhythm of Shepard's performance is almost antithetical to Wilson's. Whereas for Wilson the fascinating verbal collages created by Christopher Knowles could function as a promising alternative to rationally ordered speech and mentation, for Shepard such agonizing attempts to express the content of Beth's vital psychological desires and needs to others beyond her limited interiority represent the strong need for shared communication.

The direction of the play, therefore, is not solely toward performance, spiraling toward increasing fragmentation and distance from meaning or a center, but toward greater clarity and control, greater textuality. Beth's "victory" is not conceived as the new apprehension of a more anarchic and therefore privileged form of mentation, perception, or communication, but as her ability to cure herself sufficiently to determine her desires and needs and communicate them to those around her. In essence, she *seeks* the amortization of deferral and performance that deconstruction tries to avoid. Her quest for greater transparency and communicability is somewhat similar to Shepard's own search for a more controlled and intelligible form of theatrical expression. Significantly, however, both author and character create in the course of their quests a new form of textuality and communication, one that has been strengthened and expanded by the earlier presence of performative expression. As in nonequilibrous systems, the chaotic flow of energy and matter becomes itself a source of structure and order. The result in Shepard's play is not simply a restatement of rationality or textuality, but a renegotiation of textuality and the formation of a new, ambiguous, and quantum coherence.

To represent Beth's desire for self-authentification after she has been brain-damaged by Jake's beating, and in order to dramatize the struggle this involves, Shepard makes use of strategies and ideas familiar from performance theater. At the same time, he also critiques these ideas to reveal how they have contributed to her violent abuse at the hands of Jake. In her damaged state, Beth shows significant similarities to the theorized ideal performer of experimental theater. She has been brutally cast into a moment "presently present" because she no longer has many memories to draw upon or the speech to form new desires. Her language, like the speech privileged in performances by The Living Theater and in Wilson's antilanguage performances, gains power just *because* it is expressive in its fractured simplicity, and because it allows her to state insights into the other characters that might not be available to those restricted to rational speech. Beth has thus presumably "progressed" beyond her former avocation of acting, to the level of what Grotowski termed the archetypal performer, whose penitent training has stripped away all psychological blocks, and whose "visible impulses" would stand as testament to the naked truth expressed by such a performer. As we have already seen, however, such a performance "artist" does not deconstruct textuality or Presence, but simply recuperates it through the medium of performance. The performer still speaks as the source of the spectator's desires for absolute signifieds and coherency. Accepting such desires, one critic says of Beth that "this former actress, one who had found satisfaction in pretending, is now the essence of simple, direct, spontaneous honesty. Beth has no lie to hide behind and thus no inhibitions to curb her expression of the great truths of the play. . . . [H]ers is a new kind of voice in Shepard's work" (Londré 1987, 20).

The fact is that Beth's voice is not new, nor is it solely representative of the "great truths" of the play, since to accept that formulation implies a world of moral certainty and transcendental signifieds that Shepard is unwilling to accept. She is instead simply another avatar of the "ruse," the center or the voice that provides the illusion of cohesiveness that haunts all of Shepard's work, though here it is enacted ironically in the person of the decentered performer. Like those earlier voices, hers is mediated by Shepard's unwillingness to grant wholly the notion that from even the most simple, deep, and pure springs of primal consciousness, absolute truth, understanding, and Presence can emerge. To endow Beth's voice with such power would be to recreate the theological stage and its monological vision and authorial voice, and if this were the case then Shepard could accurately be described as having retreated into conventional textuality. But Beth's function as the source of the great truths of the play actually undermines and modifies the desires of the audience for certainty, because although Beth appears to speak to our desire for certainty, her voice is mediated by another function she serves, that of a foundation of transformation, uncertainty, and difference.

If after the beating Beth represents, like the Grotowski holy theater performer, the charismatic Other through whom truth is channelled, she also illustrates throughout the play the deconstructive performer whose identity is, like Spalding Gray's, predicated on slippage and transformation, "the many-in-the-one." Beth's voice and Presence are somewhat compromised in the play—and, I would argue, thus rendered more dynamic—by her past vocation as an actress and by her inability to throw off completely, even after the beating, her need to perform a series of transformational roles. In her initial conversations with Jake's brother, Frankie, Beth recalls her reasons for becoming an actress. In fact, for Beth, "acting," in the sense of translating a script, does not accurately define what she was after: "Pretend is better."[11] She explains to Frankie what motivated her need to pretend: "Because it fills me. Pretending fills. Not empty. Other. Ordinary. Is no good. Empty. Ordinary is empty" (75).

Since "ordinary" is "no good" and "empty," Beth fills the void in her existence by performing, as an actress, a series of Others. Yet it is precisely her need, guiltless as it is, to fulfill herself by transforming into various diffractions of the self, and to "pretend" to be other than who she is, that leads to the physical confrontation with Jake. Jake, with the male's monological or textual vision and desire for absolutes, cannot understand the decentered nature of the female, nor her desire for transformation as the means to achieve fulfillment. His reaction to Beth's performative needs is essentially a brutally physical version of Hamlet's critique of the actor: "Is it not monstrous?" Since he cannot distinguish her performed roles from her real identity, Jake assumes Beth is being fulfilled by another man. In a violent confrontation of male Presence, the text, and power against Absence, performance, and powerlessness, Jake attempts to reassert his dominance by physically abusing Beth.

Beth, then, resembles Shepard's earlier female characters in that she never defines a stable identity, but exists as something unstable, intangible. She represents, before the beating, the performative consciousness that finds affirmation in transformation and "pretend." Jake, the typical male in Shepard's canon, needs instead stability and Presence: and the opposition of those needs shapes a confrontation not unlike those found in earlier plays—for instance, between Crow and Hoss in *The Tooth of Crime,* between Tilden and Vince/Dodge/Bradley in *Buried Child,* and between Lee and Austin in *True West.* In these plays, the character dyads often do not describe simple oppositions, but instead are presented increasingly as conjugate pairs that exist in complementarity. They are the embodiment of that perception of an irreducible but dynamic "double consciousness" that lies at the core of Shepard's theatrical vision.

What separates *A Lie of the Mind* from previous work, however, is the degree of Shepard's unwillingness to establish a pessimistic sense of textual closure in the interaction between performance and textuality, and the strong sense that the two are capable of carving out a mutualist space in their interactions with one another. That is, before this play Shepard's vision of an irreconcilable psychological split is most often a source of anguish and entrapment. In *The Tooth of Crime* the outcome of the agon was ambiguous yet determinable, and the result a bleak vision of confinement. *Buried Child,* on the other hand, presents a denouement that leaves the opposition between Tilden and Vince precariously balanced at a moment of singularity, while *True West* envisions that singular moment as potentially violent. *A Lie of the Mind,* however, is built, in the manner of *True West,* around the slippages and transformations between text and performance, as Beth and Jake shift from one paradigm to the other. In doing this, the former lovers discover the space for a tentative reconciliation in the recognition that they are, in a sense, not simply "meant for each other," but actually "interchangeable." Their situation is similar to the quantum "leap" described by Niels Bohr, where particles disappear from one location and appear simultaneously at another without having appeared to traverse the intervening space. The counterintuitive strangeness of the transformational effect results from our language, which has no terms to describe the phenomena of particles acting like waves and vice versa.

Along those lines, Shepard develops in *A Lie of the Mind* a quantum mechanics of character, where Jake and Beth exist not directly in opposition to one another, but as essential complements of one another. So inscribed within one another are their personalities that at significant moments in the play each begins suddenly to enact qualities of the other. This ability of Jake and Beth to inhabit each other, to suddenly "leap" between the spaces that separate them, never indicates a well-wrought solution to their differences, but it does create the dynamic space in which such solutions might be discovered. The play's conclusion opens up, to an extent not previously available in Shepard's canon, the possibility that humans have the capacity to assume the characteristics and affects of the Other and thereby negate alterity.

Beth, in her roles as a spontaneous source of Presence and truth and a representative of Absence and "pretend," is potentially double-coded as a character. She reveals moments when she is capable of the direct, spontaneous honesty that critics admire and privilege as the voice of stable truth in the play. But Beth also retains her need to fill herself by performing other roles, even after the beating, which has supposedly reduced her to the voice of simple, undiluted Presence:

> Now, I'm like the man. *(Pumps her chest up, closes her fists, sticks her chin out and struts in the shirt.)* Just feel like the man. Shirt brings me a man. I am a shirt man. Can you see? Like father. You see me? Like brother. *(She laughs.)* (75)

Wearing Baylor's shirt, Beth transforms herself into the role of the aggressive male, forcing Frankie (whom she calls "my beautiful woman") down on the couch and telling him, "You fight but all the time you want my smell. You want my shirt in your mouth. You dream of it. Always. You want me on your face" (76). Like the typical male characters in Shepard's plays, Beth is here playing out a mass-media definition of maleness; pumping up her chest, making fists, strutting about, and making assumptions about the desires of the Other. She performs, in effect, the male role, and begins to assume the power and prerogatives we had seen earlier in Jake.

It is just these simplified mediatized images that Shepard defines elsewhere as the "lies of the mind" that break down self-knowledge and interpersonal relationships in his plays: "Men turning themselves into advertisements of Men / Women turning themselves into advertisements of Women" (Shepard 1982, 81). That Beth suffers from such delusions as much as the other characters, or that she finds fulfillment in them, hardly negates the vision of love she expresses at certain moments in the play. In fact, her ability to transcend the mind's lying images of the Other renders her accomplishments more poignant. But Shepard never resolves the tension between Beth's contradictory roles in order to reconstitute her as the privileged voice of truth in the play. Such a textual strategy would undermine the complexity of her character and reify the notion that consciousness can ever become stable and absolute. Instead, Beth dramatizes her capacity to enact the consciousness of both female/male and performance/text, as well as her ability to allow the dyads to interact dynamically.

But if Beth can express at some moments her own conscious need to drop her decentered self and to exert power and control over the Other, Jake's character also retains this transformational ability. Perhaps the most startling instance of this occurs at the end of the play when Jake, the Presence-obsessed and oedipally determined male, makes his own quantum leap and suddenly assumes the "feminine" guise (and the fractured language) of the performer who enacts her own transformation:

> These things—in my head—lie to me. Everything lies. Tells me a story. Everything in me lies. But you. You are true. I love you more than this life. You stay. You stay with him. He's my brother. (128–29)

Jake now becomes the decentered performer who recognizes that no stable sense of reality exists within himself, that everything is "lies." Different in quality from Beth's "pretend," perhaps, and certainly not proclaimed with the ecstasy of Crow's song about his image, this still is for Jake essentially a recognition of the need for transformation and for a renegotiation of his desires, and a statement that he has the capacity to enact them. And though no actual reconciliation can take place between Jake and Beth, the final transformation is made when Jake relinquishes his connections to Beth to his more explicitly "feminine" avatar, Frankie (*Beth* [to Frankie]: "Your other one. You have his same voice. Maybe you could be him. Pretend. Maybe. Just him. Just like him. But soft. With me. Gentle. Like a woman-man" [76]). Like Beth, Jake discovers that his double consciousness is inhabited both by the unstable and shifting level of performance and the constant and committed level of the text. The reconciliation of the play, then, resides not in endowing one paradigm over the other, but in realizing the human capacity for complex and dynamic interchange between "pretend" and "be," between "woman" and "man," between performance and text.

For Shepard, real experience does not move in determined lines from states of confusion or disorder toward stability. One's interaction with the world is characterized by strategies of constant negotiation and renegotiation, and these are contained within the mutually bounded spaces of performance and textuality, Absence and Presence, powerlessness and power, transformation and stability: "These twain," said Joyce in *Finnegans Wake,* "are the twins that tick *homo vulgaris.* . . . [H]umble indivisibles in this grand continuum" (Joyce 1939, 419). Shepard, striving for an authentic representation of life's indivisible rhythms, presents his characters as unstable, plural, indeterminate and hypothetical, rather than fixed solely within the prison house of Presence or within a narrow paradigm of the text; at the same time, he does not accept the image of life as utterly performative, free from constraint, constancy, and invariances. The two paradigms exist in a state of constant interface and metamorphosis, forming the matrix for dynamic exchange and affinity. As Tom Stoppard's particle physicist qua triple agent qua postmodern philosopher in *Hapgood* says:

> Yes—no, either—or . . . You have been too long in the spy business, you think everyone has no secret or one big secret, they are what

> they seem or they are the opposite. You look at me and think: *Which is he?* Plus or minus? If only you could figure it out like looking into me to find my root. And then you still wouldn't know. We're all doubles. (Stoppard 1988, 72)

Consciousness is even at its most fundamental level still a double agency of interactive desires and complementary cross-purposes.

If Shepard's plays, then, are indeed moving away from one style toward another, the process does not follow a strict linear path from expressionism to realism, or from male macho to sensitive man. What perhaps separates the most recent work from earlier pieces is simply that, whereas the earlier works usually portrayed the split consciousness and double-coding of textual and performative desires as a source for stasis and anxiety, the later plays reveal a greater willingness to depict that relationship as potentially productive. By resisting the impulse to dichotomize the text/performance, male/female, determinism/freedom sets, Shepard has, like all the artists studied thus far, discovered a rich field of difference and transformation within the interactive space between them. And while the classic reconciliation and closure of the traditional dramatic text have been irretrievably lost, Shepard has joined other contemporary artists in redefining the text as the site of a stable chaos, which when pushed to its moment of singularity might well suggest new and more complex systems of social, erotic, and epistemological order.

Shepard's dramatic canon represents nearly the full spectrum of theatrical experiment that takes place in America from the sixties to the present. His plays enact many of the most crucial conflicts between the orthodox dramatic text and avant-garde performance that arose out of this impressively fruitful period in American theater. If his plays do not always satisfy spectators and critics by synthesizing the discord between text and performance, or between realism and his unique kind of expressionism, they are nevertheless representative of the creative tensions that sometimes result from the interface of the two.

Afterword

The Present Landscape

Wonder is not precisely knowing,
And not precisely knowing not,
A beautiful but bleak condition.

—Emily Dickinson

The last forty years of American theater are characterized by the disarray and eclecticism that have marked virtually every great period in world drama. Still, if one common denominator exists among the few works mentioned here and the many related theater projects left out, it is that all have been motivated by a desire to expose the entrenched workings of traditional literary drama. Instead of representing what is perceived in contemporary culture through the simplified and naturalized topography of the classic dramatic text, these artists have recognized the need to break up that seemingly objective relief map and to scan the landscape in other ways. The work produced aspires rather to a geodesy of our culture, a more accurate (if subjective) model of reality because it takes into account the unexpected curvatures of the terrain, and exposes the warping effects of various unseen or naturalized forces. The function of that exposure, whether it be to dramatize the unconscious desire for expressive order, to explore the politics of representation, to create new perceptual modes, or to investigate the dynamic operations of individual consciousness, varies from artist to artist; but the radical motivating force was and continues to be the thought that theater need not be limited to representing reality in traditional ways. Indeed, among these artists, theater, as a processual and highly self-conscious activity directed toward seeing and speculation, continues to be privileged as the means by which old ways of seeing may be deconstructed and new alternatives suggested.

The aims of many alternative theater adepts—literary or otherwise over these four decades have been at times unrealistically high. Often, as is the case with any significant revolution, the goals of alternative theater have been outstripped by the limited means available. The dreams of Total Theater, theater therapy, and nonsemiotic theater all tend to dissipate under the frictions of practice and close critical scrutiny, though they leave behind a stubborn residue that will doubtless return to haunt theater practitioners and theorists of the future. "Sometimes," muses Derrida, "the most ferocious critics who react vehemently and passionately and sometimes with hatred understand more than supporters do, and it's *because* they understand more that they react this way" (Olson 1990, 7).

These shortcomings in avant-garde theater should not imply, however, that experimental activity during this period has had no long-term effect on contemporary theater. On the contrary, most of the "failures" of avant-garde performance theater will outlive the successes of mainstream textual drama, not as survivors in the canon or in the repertory, of course, but as the sources of important questions facing playwrights, directors, and performers of the future. Experimental performance stretched the potential of theater to its furthest term, and sometimes past that into territories perhaps beyond the horizon of theatrical enterprise. In the end, the experiments sometimes became less a theater of revolt than a revolt against theater, at least in terms of the prevailing cultural definition we normally apply to theater. Perhaps the most enduring legacy of the period will be the sense of crisis that it imposed, forcing those who think deeply about theater to struggle to define their enterprise and mark their similarities and differences from other disciplines and from their own traditions. The experiments in acting method and theory, in environmental staging, in linguistic and textual deconstruction, and in the function of the image within the mise-en-scène demanded that the seemingly inevitable and automatic assumptions behind the nature of representation and its province in culture be questioned and demystified. Like much recent theory, this experimental theater was highly self-reflexive and sentient that it was often undermining the very categories and ideologies it offered to represent. And though the primary impetus for such radical questioning often came from theory outside theater, it nevertheless remained for theater to assume the space—some would say privileged space—of the investigation.

Despite the subversion of the theatrical over the past four decades, however, contemporary theater has managed to survive, even flourish. The paradox owes its existence less to the ingenuity of individual artists than to the nature of theater itself, which survives as a kind of structuration of desire existing quite beyond our analytical interpretations of it. The investigations of theater initiated during the sixties and seventies sometimes ignored this, and based their experiments on scientific methods drawn from anthropology, psychology, speech-act theory, and other areas. Seeking transcendence of consciousness and culture *through* theater, they ignored the necessary reality that theater is itself a structure embedded in a culture that cannot be transcended. The more mature experimental work analyzed in these chapters reveals a common awareness that theater and the culture it represents are linked by dense feedback loops, within which the very hypotheses regarding the intent to get "beyond" theater are formed in the speculative matrices of theater itself.

We thus find ourselves at the margin of theater, and despite assertions that we have moved beyond the theological stage and its locus of power into the disempowering liberation of "performance," "spectacle," "carnival," "play," even "life," the fact remains that every attempt to transcend theater has served instead to restate these margins. As Herbert Blau remarks:

> As other disciplines try to open themselves to a prospective of infinite play, with the theater as a structural model, we can see only the possibilities of a newer theater from the perspectives inscribed upon us by the old, with its inevitable circumscription of play. As we deconstruct the stage or change environments or play in the round, the sightlines are probably ineradicable because indelibly in the mind. . . . The form is ghosted, as we are, by the mental habits of the form, which encrust our habits of perception. (1982a, 74)

Those habits may not be immanent, but they have thus far resisted attempts at transcendence of and through the theater, from the conceptually sophisticated to the simply arrogant.

Still, in the works already discussed, provocative alternatives have been investigated within theater's margins, and exciting new fields of dramatic and performative inquiry have opened up. Such work has grown beyond early attempts at sentimentalizing ritual and venerating performance as the panacea for, or affirmative response to, postmodern consciousness. The new performance drama is grounded more substantially in history, its artists increasingly aware that the past has a hold on the present. Rather than trying to escape history by retrodicting the past or by hypostatizing the present, contemporary theater addresses the past by scrutinizing the role that theater plays in the making of history, whether it be through investigation of past canonical texts by The Wooster Group, of archetypal and cultural myths by Robert Wilson, or of individual consciousness by Samuel Beckett and Sam Shepard. In each case, the artist involved has determined that the fundamental space between text and performance provides a rich source of creative energy, which can be used to create deconstructive dramaturgies for exploring cultural and personal history. In doing so, these quantum artists have both expanded theater's range of articulation and returned it to its social and cultural matrix.

Notes

Introduction

1. I have avoided where possible the use of the term *postmodernism,* not primarily because I believe it has no function in criticism, but because it does not apply directly to what I describe in this study. Whereas there have occurred important cultural transformations between the modernist and the contemporary periods, the nature of those transformations seems less wholesale than is commonly described, and the new forms that may emerge from the disruption of the modernist agenda have consequently not yet been fully articulated. The theater work I describe may signal, as I suggest at certain points, either a manifestation of a new form or a more mature example of what some critics have already described as postmodernist. From this latter perspective, the artists analyzed here have already passed beyond what was becoming insipid and chic in postmodernism, and have since effected a rapprochement between the critical art of modernism and the more playful expressions of postmodernism. If this is so, then their work would stand as another example of the text/performance interaction described throughout this study.

2. Marvin Carlson (1985) provides a useful summary of recent advances in theatrical reader-response criticism, and Blau (1989) has begun to incorporate it more emphatically into his theory. Perhaps indicating a new drift in such theory, Eco's *The Limits of Interpretation* (1990) argues that "in the course of the last few decades, the rights of the interpreters have been overstressed" and defends what he calls "the rights of the text."

3. It is understood that the text can never be unassailable in its coherency and organic structure, despite its attempt to produce just such a structure. Numerous critics have argued that realist texts, for instance, always contain omissions, transgressions, and slippages, and of course Derrida's entire reading strategy is founded on the revelation that the text's conceptual distinctions and categories are doomed to fail by its own use of them. Since, however, I mean to trace definitions of the text as they develop historically in alternative theater, I have adopted the somewhat narrower perception of textuality as it was voiced by artists who were seeking to redefine theater by locating the limits of the text.

4. I will later draw more specific connections between the strategies of performance and those of deconstruction, but for now the type of intersection I intend is captured by V. Leitch (1983, 246): "Deconstruction celebrates dissemination over truth, explosion and fragmentation over unity and coherence, undecidable spaces over prudent closures, playfulness and hysteria over care and rationality."

5. An exception should be made to account for the activities and affects produced in some feminist performance art. Although sometimes formalist, feminist performance art often directs its sophisticated deconstructions against representation and intends its implicit deprivileging of otherness and objectification to act as a powerful political strategy of intervention against male texts and discourses. The interest shown by feminists in poststructuralist theory, similarly, is based on the assumption that if the predicates of representation can be exposed, they can be changed systematically, explicitly, controllably. I will later argue that feminist art and theory have widely influenced the turning away from the type of apolitical and ahistorical deconstruction I describe here in reference to early performance art. For further analysis of the connections between "postmodern" art and feminism, see Jeanie Forte, *Women in Performance Art: Feminism and Postmodernism* (Bloomington: Indiana University Press, forthcoming); Sue-Ellen Case, ed., *Performing Feminisms: Feminist Critical Theory and Theater* (Baltimore: Johns Hopkins University Press, 1989); Arlene Raven, *Crossing Over: Feminism and Art of Social Concern* (1988); and Linda J. Nicholson, ed., *Feminism/Postmodernism* (New York: Routledge, 1990).

6. The breakdown of modernist dichotomies does not, of course, represent a new agenda unique to contemporary art. Among the modernists themselves, the surrealists were certainly devoted to just such a cause. Breton, for instance, writes in the "Second Manifesto of Surrealism," "Everything tends to make us believe that there exists a certain point of mind at which life and death, the real and the imagined, past and future, the communicable and the incommunicable, high and low, cease to be perceived as contradictions" (Breton [1972] 1979, 123). That "point of mind" for the surrealists, however, still signaled a point of transcendence, something on which contemporary artists seldom insist.

7. The terms *adhocism* and *double-coding* are now widespread, but they appear to have been introduced by Charles Jencks in *The Language of Post-Modern Architecture* (New York: Harry N. Abrams, 1977).

8. See especially Bernstein 1980; Simard 1984; and Demastes 1988.

9. Such metaphors are slowly emerging in the critical literature. See, for instance, David E. R. George, "Quantum Theater—Potential Theater: a New Paradigm?" (1989), Delbert Unruh, "Scenography, Postmodernism, and Quantum Mechanics: Toward a New Process of Scenic Design," *Theater Design and Technology* 25, no. 3 (1989): 5–6, 63–65; Bonnie Marranca, "The Forest as Archive: Wilson and Interculturalism," *Performing Arts Journal* 33/34, nos. 3, 1 (1989): 36–44; and Natalie Crohn Schmitt, "Theorizing about Performance: Why Now?" (1990b). Schmitt's *Actors and Onlookers: Theater and Twentieth-Century Scientific Views of Nature* (1990a) was forthcoming at the time of this book's publication. While none of these articles or books apply the metaphors

of quantum mechanics and chaos theory specifically to performance and textuality, their intent to formulate new relationships within various theatrical events links their agendas to my own.

10. The terms *performance drama* and *performance theater* have been used previously to describe emergent forms of theater, but not to delineate a hybrid form. See for instance Timothy Wiles, *The Theater Event* (Chicago: University of Chicago Press, 1980), which introduces "performance theater" to define theater work whose "meaning and being is in performance, not in literary encapsulation."

Chapter 1

1. The Living Theater was the most experimentally active group of the period in terms of exploring new definitions of theater through the plays of Picasso, Cocteau, Jarry, Auden, and Rexroth, and especially in the group's productions of Gertrude Stein's plays in the early fifties. The majority of The Living Theater's later work, however, was devoted to developing experiments specifically within political theater, an arena foreign to Stein. Oddly, few other avant-garde artists worked with Stein's deconstructive texts until the mid-sixties, when first the Judson Dance Theater, and then The Performance Group (under James Lapine), began to stage her work.

2. Recent works detailing what William Worthen calls this "poetics of duplicity" inherent in Western theater include Michael Goldman, *The Actor's Freedom* (1975); Jonas Barish, *The Anti-Theatrical Prejudice* (1981); and Worthen's own *The Idea of the Actor* (1984). Also important in this context are the essays of Herbert Blau, especially *Blooded Thought: Occasions of Theater* (1982a), and *Take Up the Bodies: Theater at the Vanishing Point* (1982b).

3. For a useful synopsis of the philosophical bases for such late modernist art, see Tharu 1984.

4. See Davis 1975.

5. See, for instance, Brown's statement that the "life instinct, or sexual instinct, demands an activity of a kind that, in contrast to our current mode of activity, can be called play. The life instinct demands a union with others and the world around us based not on anxiety and aggression but on narcissism and erotic exuberance" (1959, 308). Similar notions are developed in Brown 1966, Marcuse 1955, and Turner 1982. Huizinga, of course, had written *Homo Ludens* in 1938, though it was not translated into English until 1949.

6. For a general survey of the work appearing in the period, and of the various manifestos that accompanied it, the best sources are the descriptive reviews to be found in contemporary journals like the *Tulane Drama Review* (later the *Drama Review*), *Performing Arts Journal, Theater Journal, Comparative Drama,* and *Theater*.

7. This apparently remains Schechner's view, for in a recent article, "Performance Studies: The Broad Spectrum Approach" (*Drama Review* 119, [1988]: 4–6), he discusses restructuring university curricula around performance studies. In his model, theater and drama would be treated simply as subclasses of anthro-

pology and sociology, that is, as particular modes of performance activity. For a response to Schechner, see the editorial "Critical Positions," by Bonnie Marranca and Gautam Dasgupta, in *Performing Arts Journal* 32, no. 2 (1988): 4–6.

8. I am indebted for this research to Hilary Cohen, whose unpublished dissertation, *Ritual and Theater: An Examination of Performance Forms in American Contemporary Theater* (1980), suggests persuasively that the experiments in ritual were limited by the theatrical matrix in which they were set. Her views support my own regarding the issue, and substantiate Blau's claims that experiments in ritual were, in general, poorly conceived and conceptualized to begin with. For Blau's critique, see especially "The Future of an Illusion" in *Take Up the Bodies* (1982b) and "The Remission of Play" in *Blooded Thought* (1982a). J. Ndukaku Amankulor attempts to find a specifically postmodern use of ritual performance to achieve a combination of the secular and sacred. See his article, "The Condition of Ritual in Theater: An Intercultural Perspective" (1989).

9. Some, like Schechner, found it possible to achieve the level of ritual in the rehearsal process itself, when no audience waited to be accommodated. This in turn led Schechner to begin emphasizing the value of the rehearsal over actual performances, an approach that nettled members of The Performance Group and eventually contributed to its demise in the early seventies and the subsequent formation of The Wooster Group under the direction of Elizabeth LeCompte. See my third chapter for further comment.

10. "The attempt can no longer be simply to change the theater. The attempt must be to change life, and by changing the nature of life it is inevitable that the nature of the theater will change. The Open Theater's esthetic . . . is a witness to a changed life, insofar as its makers have changed their lives and are able to present these changes to the audience. . . . There is a difference between commenting on oppressive situations and turning the actor's body into a testimony to liberated ones—the difference between alienation and community" (Malpede 1974).

11. For theoretical discussion of the powers of performance, see Jean-François Lyotard, *Des Dispositifs pulsionnels,* especially the translation by Knap and Benamou of "The Tooth, the Palm" (Lyotard 1976); Pontbriand, "'The eye finds no fixed point on which to rest . . .'" (1985); and Féral, "Performance: The Subject Demystified," (1985).

12. For commentary on the romantic epistemology behind much early performance theater, see especially the following: Driver 1970; Croyden 1974; Blau 1982b (especially "The Future of an Illusion"); and Blau 1982a.

13. For a thorough discussion of the theoretical implications of Presence in early experimental theater, see Timothy Wiles, *The Theater Event* (Chicago: University of Chicago Press, 1980).

14. For discussion critical of postmodern theater's symptomatic ahistoricism and apoliticality, see for instance Forte and Case 1985; Birringer 1985; Pavis 1986; Auslander 1987; and especially Lentricchia 1983.

15. Lentricchia echoes this notion when he writes that "deconstruction's useful work is to undercut the epistemological claims of representation, but that work in no way touches the real work of representation—its work of

power. . . . Politically, deconstruction translates into that passive kind of conservatism called quietism" (1983, 51).

16. Derrida's own political evasiveness and oftentimes ahistorical approach to texts (an ahistoricism that still pales next to that of an American avatar like Paul de Man), exemplified by his silence on Marx, has been remarked upon by numerous commentators, especially Terry Eagleton.

17. Similar ideas are expressed in David Mamet's remarks to David Savran that "the rules of dramatic structure, redefine them as you will, are based on the rules of human perception and that's what enables deviation from them to work. That's what enables so-called performance art to function. There's really nothing there other than randomness, in a lot of instances, but it works because the human mind will always order randomness" (Mamet 1987, 15). For a semiotic analysis of what Keir Elam calls the "*semiotization of the object,*" see Elam 1980, 8–10.

18. Deborah Rosenfelt and Judith Newton (1985, xv) succinctly state the bases for such a return to social contexts when they speak of seeing relations, rather than disjunctions, between literature and history: "Productions of consciousness, like literature and literary criticism, are also socially constructed, and they too are political. . . . [W]e speak of our knowledge of history, choosing to see in it not a tale of individual and inevitable suffering, but a story of struggle and relations of power. We speak of making our notion of literary texts, choosing to read them not as meditations upon themselves but as gestures toward history and gestures with political effect."

19. Beckett's work, as will be seen in the next chapter, both precedes and continues most of the important avant-garde work I am describing. His significant but ambiguous relationship to mainstream and avant-garde theater is studied by Jonathan Kalb in his recent article "The Question of Beckett's Context" (1988), which was later revised and published as a chapter of Kalb's book, *Beckett in Performance* (1989).

20. In his address to the 1987 American Theater in Higher Education convention, for instance, Blau remarked that "we all love Beckett [now], of course, but I'm sure they're smiling today over something else, probably not a playwright but maybe a piece of performance art or some hybrid of an unnamable form coming into the theater like recombinant DNA" (Blau 1988, 9).

Chapter 2

1. See Hinden 1986 and Whitaker 1986.

2. Beckett's most cogent theoretical writings—*Proust,* Belacqua's aesthetic meanderings in *Dream of Fair to Middling Women,* "Dante . . . Bruno . Vico . . Joyce," the dialogues with Georges Duthuit, the *Disjecta*—often center on just these issues, and reveal Beckett's early interest in developing a theorized impotence in his art.

3. These terms come from remarks Beckett made in an early interview with Israel Shenkar ("A Portrait of Samuel Beckett, the Author of the Puzzling *Waiting for Godot,*" *New York Times,* 6 May 1956, sec. 2, pp. 1, 3).

4. For the notion of postmodern schizophrenia, see especially Deleuze and Guattari 1983.

5. Theodor Adorno, too, is quoted by Pavis as saying that "even so-called absurd literature—in the work of its best representatives—has a stake in the dialectic: that there is no meaning and that negating meaning maintains nonetheless the category of meaning: that is, what both allows for and demands interpretation." See Pavis 1986.

6. See, for instance, Gontarski, *The Intent of Undoing in Samuel Beckett's Dramatic Texts* (1985); Dearlove, *Accommodating the Chaos: Samuel Beckett's Non-Relational Art* (1982); Blau, *The Eye of Prey: Subversions of the Postmodern* (1987); and Keir Elam, "*Not I:* Beckett's Mouth and the Ars(e) Rhetorica" (1986).

7. For a summary of Schechner's use of transactive space, see Castagno 1988.

8. Representative critical views on Beckett's use of myth are found in Burkman 1987.

9. Samuel Beckett, *Not I*, in *Collected Shorter Plays of Samuel Beckett* (1984, 217). All further references are to this volume.

10. Neither Beckett nor these experimental directors were, of course, absolutely original in their intent or practice. The "environmental tradition," as described by Arnold Aronson (1977), evolves from community festivals and fairs, and was a source of scenic inspiration to a variety of modernist playwrights, directors, and designers (Meyerhold, Okhlopkov, and Syrkus, among others). It is hardly a coincidence that many of the best performances of Beckett's plays have been accomplished by actors like Ruth Malaczech, JoAnne Akalaitis, and David Warrilow, whose first theatrical experiences came with Mabou Mines, and whose familiarity with the acting workshops of the sixties has influenced their own interactive and transformational approach to Beckett's theater scores. For an interview with Warrilow on the subject, see Lassiter 1985.

11. For connections between Beckett and Artaud, see Kalb 1989, 147–48.

12. Elam (1986) quotes the following example from *Not I:*

tiny | little thing
out be | fore its time
godfor | saken hole
speechless | all her days
even | to herself
Once or | twice a year
sudden | urge to tell
half the | vowels wrong
nothing | but the larks

13. See Worthen 1984.

14. Samuel Beckett, *Play*, in *Collected Shorter Plays of Samuel Beckett* (1984), 153. All further references are to this volume. I am indebted here to ideas presented by Stephen Barker in an unpublished lecture given at the Scottsdale, Arizona, Center for the Arts on 26 February 1990, entitled "'Am I as much as . . .': Reflections on the 'I' in Modern Drama."

15. See Rabkin 1985.

16. Samuel Beckett, *Catastrophe,* in *Collected Shorter Plays of Samuel Beckett* (1984, 299). All further references are to this volume.

Chapter 3

1. David Savran, *Breaking the Rules: The Wooster Group* (1986). I have made significant use of Savran's text, first, because it is a fine introduction to The Group's work, though it offers no interpretive order for the performances. Also, the book contains useful interview material from the performers themselves. Equally important, his book gives the fullest summaries of The Group's performances to be found in the critical literature, and is therefore one of the only dependable references available for specific dialogue and stage directions for the unpublished works.

Currently, texts for the plays are limited to *Rumstick Road, Point Judith,* and *Route 1 & 9,* which have been printed in journals or on small presses. I have supplemented my reading of those texts by attending performances whenever possible, including productions of *Route 1 & 9, L.S.D.,* and *Nayatt School.*

Marianne Weems, current dramaturg for The Wooster Group, informs me that a text of the plays may be available sometime in 1991, or soon thereafter. The nature of that text will be an interesting indication of how The Group—and other performance groups and artists as well—will attempt to overcome the stigma of having appreciation of their work limited to live performances.

2. Lévi-Strauss's use of the term in *The Savage Mind* (1966) is instructive of The Group's methods. He defines *bricolage* as a process of forming structures based not on causative or cognitive relations but on an ability to form new relationships among disparate parts. In a manner similar to The Group's working method, the *bricoleur* creates these new relations with whatever is available: "His universe of instruments is closed and the rules of his game are always to make do with 'whatever is at hand,' that is to say with a set of tools and materials which is always finite and is also heterogeneous because what it contains bears no relation to the current project, or indeed to any particular project, but is the contingent result of all the occasions there have been to renew or enrich the stock or maintain it with remains of previous constructions or destructions" (17).

3. In addition, Aronson is neglecting the work of other artists, especially Richard Foreman's performances for his Ontological-Hysteric Theater, which show obvious connections to deconstructionist theory.

4. See pp. 50–56.

5. See, for instance, de Man, *Allegories of Reading* (1979), especially the chapter on Rousseau's *Confessions,* where de Man writes that "it is always possible" to excuse historical guilt because "the experience always exists simultaneously as fictional discourse and as empirical event and it is never possible to decide which one of the two possibilities is the right one. The indecision makes it possible to cancel the bleakest of crimes." Amid the recent scandal over de Man's alleged collaborationist writings, Lentricchia has quoted this passage to point out that "in an attempt to undercut politically engaged critics, de Man

writes that whatever you thought about political events is not the case. His mature work is not just ahistorical; it is a principled, intentional, passionate ahistoricism. He didn't just say 'forget history'; he wanted to paralyze the move to history" (quoted in Weiner, "Deconstructing de Man" [1988]). See also Lentricchia 1983, 38–52.

6. For examples of how the depoliticization of deconstruction has affected dramatic work, see especially Sue-Ellen Case and Jeanie Forte, "From Formalism to Feminism," *Theater* 16, no. 2 (Spring 1985): 62–65; Pavis, "The Classical Heritage of Modern Drama: The Case of Postmodern Theater" (1986); and Birringer, "Postmodern Performance and Technology" (1985). Blau's work is also relevant, especially the essays included in *The Eye of Prey: Subversions of the Postmodern* (1987).

7. Critical views on the matter are mixed. Elinor Fuchs, for example, points to The Group's *L.S.D.* (1985) as the initial sign of increasing awareness of the politics inherent in a deconstructive dramaturgy; see Fuchs 1984. Aronson (1985), meanwhile, suggests that *Nayatt School* was the first to reveal such a direction. I think the move was immanent, already apparent in The Group's canon, but did not emerge as an essential concern until after Spalding Gray's influence in The Group waned.

8. This suggests that connections between avant-garde theater work and poststructuralist theory are often too narrow, and that critics have restricted appreciation of performance in general by insisting too closely upon this single perspective. An informed criticism of The Group, and of alternative theater in general, would include ideas from other discourses, most notably from feminist theory, reader-response semiotics, and the sociology/anthropology of culture approach utilized by Peter Berger and others. I have tried to adopt such a multiperspectival view, with the hope that each approach sheds some light on the performances.

9. These notions are staples in the philosophy of Fichte, Schopenhauer, and Nietzsche. Also, for Herbert Blau's meditations on the subject, see especially "Look What Thy Memory Cannot Contain" in Blau 1982a.

10. See the first chapter of this book, especially pp. 44–47, 59–60.

11. "She [LeCompte] is able to give my raw stuff form. She is a classicist, someone in love with form" (Gray 1979, 36).

12. Gray (1979) has described honestly his narcissism and the effects it has on the way he gathers and presents material. His attitude has changed, apparently, as the more recent monologues (especially *Swimming to Cambodia*) combine personal recollection and historical events to describe a process of personal change, in this case a radicalization of his experience, that may perhaps lead to a heightened political consciousness. Thus, his career is paradigmatic of the changes I am describing in collective work and in certain playwrights, from an ahistorical formalism to a kind of postmodernist engaged theater. For an insightful look at this movement within Gray's career, see Demastes 1989.

13. The mass-market co-optation of performance was completed by 1984, when Werner Erhard, founder of the est encounter sessions, reformulated est into a watered-down and more marketable organization called the Forum. The

Forum offers "transformational weekends," where uncertain Heideggerian principles of being and creation of selves through a new language are applied to everyday life. Apparently the weekends are especially popular with the corporate crowd.

14. The illegally bugged conversation caused The Group's first controversy with authority, when the tape's presence in the play elicited a virulent attack from Michael Feingold of the *Village Voice*. Feingold objected because "to make a point of including dishonorable transactions like this is to brutalize the audience, implicating them in the artist's pain instead of offering them a share in its transcendence" (1980, 84). Although Gray responded and tried to explain that the transcendence and pain were intertwined, the Obie Award judges refused to consider the piece for an award in 1977.

15. The Wooster Group, *Rumstick Road,* in *Performing Arts Journal* 3, no. 2 (Fall 1978): 111, 112. All further references are to this text.

16. Xerxes Mehta notes, for instance, that LeCompte's work represents a breakthrough in experimental theater just because she has suppressed the "discursive and analytical" intelligence that he associates with Schechner. LeCompte's work is among the first to forego what he calls a "sense of strain, demonstration, or willed catharsis." See Mehta 1979.

17. For Barthes's notion of transgression, see "On *The Fashion System* and the Structural Analysis of Narratives," an interview with Raymond Bellour, in *The Grain of the Voice: Interviews 1962–1980*, trans. Linda Coverdale (New York: Hill and Wang, 1985).

18. The speech is Sir Henry-Harcourt Reilly's response to Edward's alienation and panic at discovering that his wife has deserted him in act 1. Interestingly, the speech relates Reilly's idea of the subject as a "centre of reality," a notion both accepted and critiqued by the performance. See Savran 1986, 112–13.

19. An interesting sidelight to Brecht's obvious influences on The Wooster Group, and experimental theater in general, is the recent revision of Brecht's plays by critics and directors in Germany. Driven by new approaches by playwrights like Heiner Müller and directors like Alfred Kirchner and Jurgen Flimm, contemporary Brecht performance and criticism is moving toward opening up Brecht's politics and his dramaturgy by introducing the same kinds of performance strategies with which LeCompte has been working. For a summary of these new approaches to Brecht, see the issue devoted to the matter in *Theater Journal* 39, no. 4 (1987).

20. For a description of Gray's continued association with The Group, see Savran 1986, especially 133–57.

21. See Savran 1986, 133–34.

22. In addition to these works, The Group has performed two dance pieces, *Hula* (1981) and *For the Good Times* (1982). The Group has also collaborated with Jim Strahs on *North Atlantic* (1983), and with Richard Foreman on *Miss Universal Happiness* (1985) and *Symphony of Rats* (1988). Currently, The Group is working on *Brace Up!*, an epilogue to *The Road to Immortality* trilogy.

23. The Wooster Group, *Route 1 & 9* (The Last Act), *Benzene* 5/6 (1982): 5. All further references are to this text.

24. LeCompte told Savran, "Maybe once every two or three performances we have a black person in the audience," and Peyton Smith relates an anecdote concerning her fear when, during a performance of *Route 1 & 9*, a black man watched in stony silence and repeatedly reached under his coat. See Savran 1986, 14, 40.

25. Bonnie Marranca attests to the same feelings when she writes that "Wilder is, I think, the unacknowledged early link to avant-garde theater" ("Our Town Our Country: The Wooster Group on Route 1 and 9," in *Theaterwritings* [1984]).

26. In a typically postmodernist irony, Mandelbrot's fractal imaging system has been recuperated by Disney and Lucasfilms, who apply them in creating phenomenally realistic, yet fantastic, landscapes for their films. LeCompte would no doubt enjoy such landscape architecture, though it works in a direction opposite to her own.

27. Savran (1986, 10) gives the following brief summary:

> The New York State Council on the Arts (NYCA), which had been a major source of funding for The Group, judged that "*Route 1 & 9* contained in its blackface sequences harsh and caricatured portrayals of a racial minority" and, as a consequence, cut funding for The Group by forty percent. . . . The Wooster Group convened a number of public forums to discuss the piece's alleged racism and in March submitted an appeal to the NYCA, drawn up by Jeffrey M. Jones, aimed at restoring the funding. The appeal contained a thirty-one page defense of *Route 1 & 9* as well as twenty-three letters of support by a formidable collection of artists, critics, and producers. On June 10, 1982, the NYCA rejected the appeal and upheld the reduced level of funding.

See Dace 1982.

28. For a summary of events leading up to the creation of *L.S.D.*, and a description of the changes imposed on the work by Miller's legal actions, see Aronson 1985 and Savran 1985.

29. This conceptual response to what Baudrillard calls the "mediatization" of subversive acts by specular culture is similar to what Guy Deborg and the Situationists referred to as "detournement." The term is defined as a strategy for diverting cultural elements to new subversive uses, so that the spectacle's power of conditioning is turned toward promoting the struggle against conditioning.

30. I did not see *Frank Dell's The Temptation of Saint Anthony* in time to include it in this chapter, and the review material on the work is generally insubstantial. For a discussion of the piece as a work in progress, see Savran 1986a. *Brace Up!* is at the time of this writing still in preparation.

Chapter 4

1. Stein's influence on Wilson and other elements of the contemporary avant-garde has been largely neglected. Artists themselves, especially Richard Foreman and Wilson, have repeatedly stated their indebtedness to Stein's initia-

tives. For a discussion of the affinities and differences between Stein and the work of these theater artists, see Betsy Alayne Ryan, *Gertrude Stein's Theater of the Absolute* (Ann Arbor: UMI Research Press, 1984).

2. For the auspices of other works during the period, see Brecht 1978, 197 n. 82.

3. Responding to questions about The Group's first piece, Gray replied, "Regarding the movement of the pieces, *Sakonnet Point* was for me the dumb show, the child." As David Savran points out, "If we follow Spalding Gray's conception of the piece as a representation or simulation of 'the development of the child,' *Sakonnet Point* becomes the rediscovery of early childhood" (Savran 1986, 61).

4. After the Paris production of *Deafman Glance,* Louis Aragon wrote an open letter to Breton in *Les Lettres Françaises* (2–8 June 1971), praising Wilson's work as the first true manifestation of surrealist theater. The letter is reprinted in Brecht 1978, 433–38.

5. Brecht also includes *The $-Value of Man* (1975), *Spaceman* (1976), and *I was sitting on my piano* (1977) among the anti-verbal pieces.

6. When Wilson first met Knowles, he excitedly told Kit Cation, "I met this wonderful person who's doing the same kind of thing I'm doing," to which one of the Byrds is said to have remarked, "Maybe Bob is a bit autistic too" (Shyer 1989, 74).

7. "I try to tell my actors not to try to understand what they're doing. They can have understandings and ideas about their parts, but if they try and fix a single understanding it will be a distortion" (Wilson, in an interview with Christopher Granlund [Granlund 1987]).

8. Wilson explained that the new approach was called for by the subject, Einstein, whom Wilson characterizes as both a mathematician and a dreamer. Still, since the fusion of the formal architectonic of a piece and its surrealist dream-content continues to be a factor in later work, it obviously has significance beyond any single thematic concern.

9. See, for instance, Nicholas Zurbrugg's alignment of Wilson's work "somewhere between Beckett's and [John] Cage's antithetical explorations of form, ambiguity, chance, and rule" (Zurbrugg 1988, 440).

10. A similar use of the image concludes *Spaceman,* also performed in 1976.

11. At the time of this publication, Wilson was also due to premiere *The Blue Rider: the casting of the magic bullets,* a collaboration between Wilson, Tom Waits, and William S. Burroughs, in March 1990 (Thalia Theater Alstertor, Hamburg); *King Lear* in May 1990 (Schauspielhaus, Frankfurt); *Forbidden Garden,* with text by Tankred Dorst, in November 1990 (Residenztheater, Munich); and *Parsifal* in March 1991 (Hamburg State Opera, Hamburg). For the complete auspices of Wilson's works, and a list of his minor and solo productions through 1989, see Shyer 1989, 288–317.

12. The *Knee Plays* for the work have also been performed separately, first in America at the Walker Art Gallery in Minneapolis (1984), and most recently at the Civic Opera in Chicago (1988). Discussion of *the CIVIL warS* is limited here to the Rome act and *The Knee Plays,* the only parts I have seen performed (Brooklyn Academy, December 1986, and the Chicago Civic Opera, May 1988).

13. Müller had collaborated with Wilson on the Cologne segment of *the CIVIL warS*, and the two had worked together earlier on the American premiere of that work at the American Repertory Theatre.

14. Brustein has since gone on to become one of Wilson's most vociferous supporters in America, especially in regard to the growing awareness of Wilson's ability to work with established texts. Recently, Brustein wrote that "what's interesting is his attraction to texts, which we will do our best to further in our next joint venture" (Shyer 1989, xi).

15. Shyer (1989, 133) notes that, since beginning his work with Müller, Wilson has even been heard to speak disparagingly of his earlier "pretty pictures."

16. See Teraoka, *The Silence of Entropy or Universal Discourse: The Postmodernist Poetics of Heiner Müller* (1985). Teraoka sees in Müller's aesthetic some interesting parallels to what I am describing in Wilson, Beckett, The Wooster Group, and Sam Shepard. The activity of destroying the original meaning-contexts of written works and fragments in order to overcome the entropy that inhabits them resembles the deconstruction of traditional textuality seen in contemporary theater. More significantly, Müller's ability to use the classic text(s) to open up textual discourse to a plurality of voices describes quite closely what occurs when performance and textuality undergo the types of interfaces I have outlined.

17. There are critics who feel that even Müller's dense texts are insufficient for Wilson's multimedia visual imagination. Zurbrugg, especially, has argued that Müller's *Hamletmachine* "typifies the relatively staid, monodimensional quality of Wilson's Post-Modernity," while Wilson himself represents a "more dynamic, multi-media vision" (1988, 439). Zurbrugg's contrasts result from his own desires for a postmodernism built on a radical eclecticism and on a drive toward representations of "multi-dimensional realities." Such an agenda, of course, accepts the mediatization of postmodern culture and posits transformational energy as the sine qua non of contemporary art. Without pointing to the specific limitations of such a project—or its recuperation by MTV and other mass-market institutions—it still seems relevant to ask why Wilson would choose to continue working with Müller's texts if he felt so circumscribed by them. Müller has said of Wilson's theater, "I am glad Robert Wilson does my play, his theater being a world of its own" (Zurbrugg 1988, 446): perhaps Wilson is equally appreciative of the opportunity to inhabit Müller's texts, which represent a world—historically aware, socially contextualized, politically active—so different from Wilson's own. Again, the quantum interactions between seemingly opposed energies produce the dynamic power of the collaborations. To posit, like Zurbrugg, one or another of those energies as more powerful or dominant (he refers to a split between Müller's "dead-end," as opposed to Wilson's "live-end" postmodernism) is to miss the essential creative tension of the works.

18. Wilson had worked with a text in his staging of *Medea,* but in that production had merely tried to illustrate the existing play. As he has remarked, "I could see the mistakes I'd made in *Medea,* things I didn't like. I didn't like the

question-answer situation, Joe says this and Sue says this. In these Greek plays you have a Ping-Pong match, it's question-answer. It's Medea-Jason, Medea-Messenger . . . it gets boring after a while. And I thought, if I can make it more *one* thing. . . ." (Wilson 1986a, 86).

19. The parallels are even more uncanny when one considers that Müller's text, in his words, "had nothing to do with *Alcestis*" (Fuchs 1986, 95). According to him, the prologue was based on a picture he received years earlier from a young girl, which attracted him because of its "very compelling psychoanalytic surface." Having recently written some text based on it, he simply gave that to Wilson when asked for a prologue.

20. The translated script is reproduced in its entirety in Wilson 1986a, 106–110.

21. In the Lattimore translation, Admetus's last speech is rendered as follows: "I proclaim to all the people of my tetrarchy / that, for these blessed happenings, they shall set up / dances, and the altars smoke with sacrifice offered. / For now we shall make our life again, and it will be / a better one / I was lucky. That I cannot deny."

22. John Rouse (1984) notes that Müller, like Wilson and the other artists under discussion, "is concerned with eliminating, or at least subverting, the authorial subject of his texts—that is, himself as provider of a meaning around which a text can be centered."

23. See Shyer 1989, xi.

Chapter 5

1. What bewilders most in Londré's narration of Shepard's progress is the equivalence of machismo and "adolescent male fantasy" with the performance-oriented expressionism of Shepard's early plays. Most critics, attentive to the breakdown of the patriarchal text and linearity, the emphasis on actor transformations, and the nonrational language in these works, would align them with a feminist project, and indicate their proximity to experimental female writing and to the attempts to discover an *écriture féminine* in the writing of artists like Kathy Acker, Barbara Guest, and most feminist performance artists.

2. Shepard, in fact, insisted that "when you're writing inside of a character like this, you aren't pausing every ten seconds to figure out what it all means. If you do, you lose the whole shot, because the character isn't going to hang around waiting for you. He's moving" (Marranca 1981, 217–18). This explains the development of a character like Crow, but does not really account for the structure of the play as a whole, which shows obvious signs of careful planning and construction. In fact, given the drama/performance debate I am outlining here, Shepard's writing method reflects the tensions perfectly; the character of Crow is "performed" and created almost spontaneously, while Hoss is "scripted" and reined in by the text and his past. The play is built around the interactions that result.

3. Sam Shepard, *The Tooth of Crime,* in *Sam Shepard: Seven Plays* (1981), 69. All further references are to this volume.

4. Sam Shepard, *Action,* in *Fool For Love and Other Plays* (1984), 169. All further references are to this volume.

5. Savran mentions in a footnote Shepard's work in film and the performance piece *Tongues.* While noting that the piece "sidetracks theater's traditional mode of representation," Savran still insists that "the performance itself . . . is not indicative of any major change for Shepard" (1984, 70 n. 24). For further commentary on Shepard's collaborations with Chaikin, see Daniels 1989.

6. Similarly, William Demastes argues convincingly that Shepard ironizes realism in order to demystify its espousal of causality and materiality. Shepard's realism, he explains, is "invaded and rejuvenated by lessons of the 1960's and 1970's and then molded to fit the new perceptions in a manner that the older form was not able to. The search for a causal thread has been abandoned in an attempt to uncover other types of coherence acceptable to a late twentieth-century frame of mind" (Demastes 1987, 231).

7. This may help explain Shepard's reluctance to allow the play, a Pulitzer Prize winner, to move to Broadway. Shepard wrote to Doris Auerbach:

> My reservations about Broadway go beyond the "Commercialism" stigma. I really believe the theater experience of intimacy, a personal transaction between actors and audience. As the audience increases in size, the intimacy is reduced and becomes absorbed in a kind of mass psychology. Reactions sweep through the audience overtaking the individual and causing him to believe they're his own reactions. Sometimes this sensation may even be thrilling but it often has little to do with, and even robs the person of his own response. (Quoted in Auerbach 1982, 53–54)

The emphasis on the experiential level and intensity of the performance indicates that Shepard is consciously aware that the play is operating partly on an intimate, nonintellectual level.

8. Sam Shepard, *Buried Child,* in *Sam Shepard: Seven Plays* (1981), 85. All further references are to this volume.

9. I am using the terminology here of Una Chaudhuri, whose article on Peter Schaffer's *Equus* ("The Spectator in the Drama/Drama in the Spectator" [1984]) has influenced my reading of Shepard. Chaudhuri's suggestion that "the description of how a play works on a spectator—rather than of what it means—can supply the terms our criticism needs to erase the gap between theory and its object" (296) seems pertinent to Shepard's plays, where meaning is often collapsed within the theatrical experience of the spectator.

10. Sam Shepard, *True West,* in *Sam Shepard: Seven Plays* (1981), 47. All further references are to this volume.

11. Sam Shepard, *A Lie of the Mind* (1986), 75. All further references are to this volume.

References

Akalaitis, JoAnne. 1984. *Dressed Like an Egg*. In *Word Plays 4*. New York: Performing Arts Journal Publications.

Amankulor, J. Ndukaku. 1989. "The Condition of Ritual in Theater: An Intercultural Perspective." *Performing Arts Journal* 33/34:45–58.

Aronson, Arnold. 1977. *The History and Theory of Environmental Scenography*. Theater and Dramatic Studies, vol. 3. Ann Arbor: UMI Research Press.

———. 1975. "*Sakonnet Point*." *Drama Review* 19, no. 4:27–35.

———. 1985. "The Wooster Group's *L.S.D. (Just the High Points)*." In *The Drama Review: Thirty Years of Commentary on the Avant-Garde*, ed. Brooks McNamara and Jill Dolan, 345–60. Ann Arbor: UMI Research Press.

Artaud, Antonin. 1958. *The Theater and Its Double*. Trans. Mary Caroline Richards. New York: Grove Press.

Auerbach, Doris. 1982. *Sam Shepard, Arthur Kopit, and the Off Broadway Theater*. Boston: Twayne Publishers.

Auslander, Philip. 1987. "Towards a Concept of the Political in Postmodern Theater." *Theater Journal* 39, no. 1:20–34.

Bair, Deirdre. 1978. *Samuel Beckett: A Biography*. New York: Harcourt Brace Jovanovich.

Barish, Jonas. 1981. *The Anti-Theatrical Prejudice*. Berkeley: University of California Press.

Barthes, Roland. 1974. *S/Z*. Trans. Richard Miller. New York: Hill and Wang.

———. 1975. *The Pleasure of the Text*. Trans. Richard Miller. New York: Hill and Wang.

———. 1977a. *Image / Music / Text*. New York: Hill and Wang.

———. 1977b. *Roland Barthes by Roland Barthes*. Trans. Richard Howard. New York: Hill and Wang.

Beck, Julian. [1972] 1986. *The Life of the Theater*. Reprint. New York: Proscenium Publishers.

Beckett, Samuel. 1983. *Disjecta: Miscellaneous Writings and a Dramatic Fragment*. Ed. Ruby Cohn. London: Jack Calder.

———. 1984. *Collected Shorter Plays of Samuel Beckett*. London: Faber and Faber.

Belsey, Catherine. 1980. *Critical Practice*. New Accents, vol. 9. New York: Methuen.

———. 1985. "Constructing the Subject: Deconstructing the Text." In *Feminist Criticism and Social Change*, 45–64. See Rosenfelt and Newton 1985.

Bentley, Eric. 1985. "Writing For a Political Theater." *Performing Arts Journal* 26/27, nos. 2/3:45–58.

Berger, Peter. 1977. *Facing up to Modernity: Excursions in Society, Politics and Religion*. New York: Basic Books.

Bernstein, Samuel. 1980. *The Strands Entwined: A New Direction in American Drama*. Boston: Northeastern University Press.

Bierman, James. 1979. "*Three Places in Rhode Island*." *Drama Review* 23, no. 1: 13–29.

Bigsby, C. W. E. 1984. *Williams/Miller/Albee*. Vol. 2 of *A Critical Introduction to Twentieth-Century American Drama*. Cambridge: Cambridge University Press.

———. 1985. *Beyond Broadway*. Vol. 3 of *A Critical Introduction to Twentieth-Century American Drama*. Cambridge: Cambridge University Press.

Birringer, Johannes. 1985. "Postmodern Performance and Technology." *Performing Arts Journal* 26/27, nos. 2/3:221–33.

Blau, Herbert. 1982a. *Blooded Thought: Occasions of Theater*. New York: Performing Arts Journal Publications.

———. 1982b. *Take Up the Bodies: Theater at the Vanishing Point*. Urbana: University of Illinois Press.

———. 1987. *The Eye of Prey: Subversions of the Postmodern*. Theories of Contemporary Culture, vol. 9. Bloomington: Indiana University Press.

———. 1988. "With Your Permission: Educating the American Theater." *Theater Journal* 40, no. 1:5–11.

———. 1989. *The Audience*. Parallax: Revisions of Culture and Society. Baltimore: Johns Hopkins University Press.

Brater, Enoch, ed. 1986. *Beckett at 80 / Beckett in Context*. New York: Oxford University Press.

Brecht, Stefan. 1978. *The Theater of Visions: Robert Wilson*. The Original Theater of the City of New York: From the Mid-60s to the Mid-70s, vol. 1. New York: Suhrkamp Verlag Frankfurt am Main.

Breton, André. [1972] 1977. *Manifestos of Surrealism*. Trans. Richard Seaver and Helen R. Lane. Ann Arbor: University of Michigan Press.

Breuer, Lee. 1979. *Animations: A Trilogy for Mabou Mines*. Ed. Bonnie Marranca and Gautam Dasgupta. New York: Performing Arts Journal Publications.

———. 1987. *Sister Suzie Cinema: The Collected Poems and Performances, 1976–1986*. New York: Theater Communications Group.

Brewer, Maria Minich. 1985. "Performing Theory." *Theater Journal* 37, no. 2: 12–30.

Brook, Peter. 1984. *The Empty Space*. New York: Atheneum.

Brown, Norman O. 1959. *Life Against Death*. Middletown: Wesleyan University Press.

———. 1966. *Love's Body*. Middletown: Wesleyan University Press.

Burkman, Katherine H., ed. 1987. *Myth and Ritual in the Plays of Samuel Beckett.* Toronto: Associated University Presses.

Byrne, David. 1984. *Music for the "Knee Plays."* Conducted by David Blumberg. EMI EJ 24 0381 1.

Cage, John. 1961. *Silence.* Middletown, Conn.: Wesleyan University Press.

Carlson, Marvin. 1983. "Theater Audiences and the Reading of Performance." In *Interpreting the Theatrical Past: Essays in the Historiography of Performance,* ed. Thomas Postlewait and Bruce McConachie, 82–98. Iowa City: University of Iowa Press.

———. 1985. "Theatrical Performance: Illustration, Translation, Fulfillment, or Supplement?" *Theater Journal* 37, no. 1:5–11.

Castagno, Paul C. 1988. "Spatial Metaphor in Schechner's Environmental Theater: *Dionysus in 69, Makbeth.*" In *Text and Presentation,* vol. 8., ed. Karelisa Hartigan, 49–62. New York: University Press of America.

Chaikin, Joseph. 1972. *The Presence of the Actor.* New York: Atheneum.

Champagne, Elenora. 1981. "Always Starting New: Elizabeth LeCompte." *Drama Review* 25, no. 3:19–28.

Chaudhuri, Una. 1984. "The Spectator in the Drama / Drama in the Spectator." *Modern Drama* 28, no. 3:281–94.

Chin, Daryl. 1985. "The Avant-Garde Industry." *Performing Arts Journal* 26/27, nos. 2/3:59–75.

Chubb, Kenneth. 1974. "Metaphors, Mad Dogs and Old Time Cowboys: Interview with Sam Shepard." *Theater Quarterly* 4:3–16.

Coe, Robert. 1980. "Saga of Sam Shepard." *New York Times Magazine,* 23 November, 122.

———. 1985. "Palace Revolution: The Avant-Garde Emerges." *NEXT WAVE Festival Catalogue.* New York: Brooklyn Academy of Music.

Cohen, Hilary. 1980. "Ritual and Theater: An Examination of Performance Forms in Contemporary American Drama." Ph.D. diss., University of Michigan.

Corrigan, Robert. 1984. "The Search for New Endings: The Theater in Search of a Fix, Part III." *Theater Journal* 36, no. 1:153–63.

Croyden, Margaret. 1974. *Lunatics, Lovers and Poets: The Contemporary Experimental Theater.* New York: Delta Books.

Dace, Tish. 1982. "Setting the Record Straight." *Other Stages,* 14 January, 5–6.

Daniels, Barry, ed. 1989. *Joseph Chaikin and Sam Shepard: Letters and Texts, 1972–1984.* New York: New American Library.

Davis, Ronnie. 1975. "The Radical Right in American Theater." *Theater Quarterly* 5, no. 19:67–72.

Dearlove, J. E. 1982. *Accommodating the Chaos: Samuel Beckett's Nonrelational Art.* Durham: Duke University Press.

Deleuze, Gilles, and Felix Guattari. 1983. *The Anti-Oedipus: Capitalism and Schizophrenia.* Trans. Robert Hurlet et al. Minneapolis: University of Minnesota Press.

de Man, Paul. 1979. *Allegories of Reading: Figural Language in Rousseau, Nietzsche, Rilke, and Proust.* New Haven: Yale University Press.

Demastes, William. 1987. "Understanding Shepard's Realism." *Comparative Drama* 21, no. 3:229–48.

———. 1988. *Beyond Naturalism: A New Realism in American Drama*. Contributions in Theater and Drama, vol. 27. New York: Greenwood Press.

———. 1989. "Spalding Gray's *Swimming to Cambodia* and the Evolution of an Ironic Presence." *Theater Journal* 41, no. 1:75–94.

Derrida, Jacques. 1978. *Writing and Difference*. Trans. Alan Bass. Chicago: University of Chicago Press.

———. 1982. *The Margins of Philosophy*. Trans. Alan Bass. Chicago: University of Chicago Press.

Diamond, Elin. 1989. "Mimesis, Mimicry, and the 'True-Real.'" *Modern Drama* 32, no. 1:588–72.

Dolan, Jill. 1989a. "Bending Gender to Fit the Canon." In *Making a Spectacle: Feminist Essays on Contemporary Theater*, ed. Lynda Hart, 318–44. Ann Arbor: University of Michigan Press.

———. 1989b. "In Defense of Discourse: Materialist Feminism, Postmodernism, Post-Structuralism . . . and Theory." *Drama Review* 33, no. 3:58–72.

Dort, Bernard. 1982. "The Liberated Performance." Trans. Barbara Kerslake. *Modern Drama* 5, no. 1:60–67.

Driver, Tom. 1970. *Romantic Quest and Modern Theory: A History of the Modern Theater*. New York: Delacorte.

Eco, Umberto. 1979. *The Role of the Reader*. Bloomington: Indiana University Press.

———. 1990. *The Limits of Interpretation*. Bloomington: Indiana University Press.

Elam, Keir. 1980. *The Semiotics of Theater and Drama*. New York: Methuen.

———. 1986. "*Not I:* Beckett's Mouth and the Ars(e) Rhetorica." In *Beckett at 80 / Beckett in Context*, 126–41. See Brater 1986.

Eliot, Thomas Stearns. 1975a. "Ulysses, Order, and Myth." In *Selected Prose of T. S. Eliot*. New York: Harcourt, Brace, Jovanovich.

———. 1975b. "Yeats." In *Selected Prose*.

Esslin, Martin. [1961] 1969. *The Theater of the Absurd*. Reprint. New York: Doubleday.

Falk, Florence. 1981. "The Role of Performance in Sam Shepard's Plays." *Theater Journal* 33, no. 2:182–99.

Feingold, Michael. 1980. "Review of *Rumstick Road*." *Village Voice*, 21 April, 83–84.

Féral, Josette. 1985. "Performance: The Subject Demystified." *Modern Drama* 25, no. 1:170–80.

Foreman, Richard. 1970. Review of *The Life and Times of Sigmund Freud*. *Village Voice*, 1 January, 64–65.

———. 1976. *Richard Foreman: Plays and Manifestos*. Ed. Kate Davy. New York: New York University Press.

———. 1985. *Reverberation Machines: The Later Plays and Essays*. Barrytown, N.Y.: Station Hill Press.

———. 1987. Interview with David Savran. *American Theater* 4:21–22.

Forte, Jeanie K., and Sue-Ellen Case. 1985. "From Formalism to Feminism." *Theater* 16, no. 2:62–65.

Foster, Hal. 1985. "For a Concept of the Political in Contemporary Art." *Recodings: Art, Spectacle, Cultural Politics*. Port Townsend, Wash.: Bay Press.

Fuchs, Elinor. 1984. "Performance as Reading." *Performing Arts Journal* 23, no. 2:51–54.

———. 1985. Presence and the Revenge of Writing: Re-Thinking Theater after Derrida." *Performing Arts Journal* 26/27, nos. 2/3:163–73.

———. 1986. "An Introduction." In "The *PAJ* Casebook: *Alcestis*." *Performing Arts Journal* 28, no. 1:80–85.

Gelderman, Carol. 1983. "Hyperrealism in Contemporary Drama: Retrogressive or Avant-Garde?" *Modern Drama* 26, no. 3:357–67.

George, David E. R. 1989. "Quantum Theater—Potential Theater: A New Paradigm?" *National Theater Quarterly* 5, no. 18:171–79.

Gleick, James. 1987. *Chaos: Making a New Science*. New York: Penguin Books.

Glore, John. 1981. "The Canonization of Mojo Rootforce: Sam Shepard Live at the Pantheon." *Theater* 12, no. 2:53–66.

Goffman, Erving. 1959. *The Presentation of Self in Everday Life*. Garden City: Doubleday.

Goldman, Michael. 1975. *The Actor's Freedom: Toward a Theory of Drama*. New York: Viking.

Goldwater, Robert, ed. 1945. *Artists on Art*. New York: Pantheon.

Gontarski, S. E. 1985. *The Intent of Undoing in Samuel Beckett's Dramatic Texts*. Bloomington: Indiana University Press.

Granlund, Christopher. 1987. "Pinball Ruins." *Guardian*, 23 October, 18.

Gray, Spalding. 1978. "Playwright's Notes." *Performing Arts Journal* 3, no. 2: 87–91.

———. 1979. "About *Three Places in Rhode Island*." *Drama Review* 23, no. 1: 31–42.

Grotowski, Jerzy. 1968. *Towards a Poor Theater*. New York: Simon and Schuster.

Hale, Jane Alison. 1987. *The Broken Window: Beckett's Dramatic Perspective*. West Lafayette, Ind: Purdue University Press.

Hart, Lynda. 1987. *Sam Shepard's Metaphorical Stages*. Contributions in Drama and Theater Studies, vol. 22. New York: Greenwood Press.

Hassan, Ihab. 1987. *The Postmodern Turn: Essays in Postmodern Theory and Culture*. Columbus: Ohio State University Press.

Hinden, Michael. 1986. "After Beckett: The Plays of Pinter, Stoppard, and Shepard." *Contemporary Literature* 27:401–8.

Hofstadter, Douglas. [1979] 1989. *Gödel, Escher, Bach: An Eternal Golden Braid*. Reprint. New York: Random House.

Holmberg, Arthur. 1990. "The Heiner Müller Festival." *Western European Stages* 2, no. 2:58–62.

Holton, Gerald. [1973] 1988. *Thematic Origins of Scientific Thought: Kepler to Einstein*. Reprint. Cambridge: Harvard University Press.

Huizinga, Johannes. 1950. *Homo Ludens: A Study of the Play-Element in Culture.* Boston: Beacon Press.

Innes, Christopher. 1981. *Holy Theater: Ritual and the Avant-Garde.* Cambridge: Cambridge University Press.

Jackson, Kevin. 1987. "Listen with Your Eyes." *The Independent,* 31 October, 9.

Jameson, Fredric. 1981. *The Political Unconscious: Narrative as a Socially Symbolic Act.* Ithaca: Cornell University Press.

———. 1984. "Postmodernism or the Logic of Late Capitalism." *New Left Review* 146:86–88.

Joyce, James. 1939. *Finnegans Wake.* New York: Viking.

Kalb, Jonathan. 1986. "How Beckett Writes." *American Theater* 3, no. 7:32–34.

———. 1988. "The Question of Beckett's Context." *Performing Arts Journal* 32, no. 2:25–44.

———. 1989. *Beckett in Performance.* Cambridge: Cambridge University Press.

Kamm, Tom. 1986. "Set Design." In "The *PAJ* Casebook: *Alcestis.*" *Performing Arts Journal* 28, no. 1:87–90.

Knowlson, James. 1986. "*Ghost Trio / Geister Trio.*" In *Beckett at 80 / Beckett in Context,* 185–205. See Brater 1986.

Kostelanetz, Richard. 1968. *The Theater of Mixed Means.* New York: Dial Press.

Kott, Jan. 1980. "After Grotowski: The End of the Impossible Theater." *Theater Quarterly* 38:27–32.

Lassiter, Laurie. 1985. "David Warrilow: Creating Symbol and Cypher." *Drama Review* 29, no. 4:3–12.

LeCompte, Elizabeth. 1978. "The Making of a Trilogy." *Performing Arts Journal* 3, no. 2:81–91.

Leitch, V. 1983. *Deconstructive Criticism: An Advanced Introduction.* London: Hutchinson.

Lentricchia, Frank. 1983. *Criticism and Social Change.* Chicago: University of Chicago Press.

Lévi-Strauss, Claude. 1966. *The Savage Mind.* Chicago: University of Chicago Press.

Lion, John. 1984. "Rock 'n Roll Jesus with a Cowboy Mouth: Sam Shepard is the Inkblot of the '80s." *American Theater* 1, no. 1:4–13.

Londré, Felica Hardison. 1987. "Sam Shepard Works Out: The Masculinization of America." *Studies in American Drama, 1945–Present* 2:19–28.

Lyotard, Jean-François. 1976. "The Tooth, The Palm." Trans. Anne Knap and Michel Benamou. *Sub-Stance* 6:105–10.

———. 1984. *The Postmodern Condition.* Trans. Geoff Bennington and Brian Masumi. Minneapolis: University of Minnesota Press.

McCarthy, Gerry. 1981. "'Acting it out': Sam Shepard's *Action.*" *Modern Drama* 24, no. 1:1–25.

McLuhan, Marshall. 1962. *The Gutenberg Galaxy: The Making of Typographical Man.* Toronto: University of Toronto Press.

McNamara, Brooks, and Jill Dolan, eds. 1986. *The Drama Review: Thirty Years of Commentary on the Avant-Garde.* Theater and Dramatic Studies, vol. 35. Ann Arbor: UMI Research Press.

Malpede, Karen. 1972. *People's Theater in Amerika*. New York: Drama Book Specialists.

———. 1974. *Three Works by the Open Theater*. New York: Drama Book Specialists.

Mamet, David. 1987. "Trading in the American Dream." *American Theater* 4, no. 6:15–18.

Marcuse, Herbert. 1955. *Eros and Civilization: A Philosophical Inquiry into Freud*. Boston: Beacon Press.

Marranca, Bonnie, ed. 1977. *The Theater of Images*. New York: Drama Book Specialists.

———, ed. 1979. *Animations: A Trilogy for Mabou Mines*. New York: Performing Arts Journal Publications.

———, ed. 1981. *American Dreams: The Imagination of Sam Shepard*. New York: Performing Arts Journal Publications.

———. 1984. *Theaterwritings*. New York: Performing Arts Journal Publications.

———. 1985. "*PAJ*: A Personal History." *Performing Arts Journal* 26/27, nos. 2/3: 23–44.

Mehta, Xerxes. 1979. "Notes from the Avant-Garde." *Theater Journal* 31, no.1: 5–24.

Mottram, Ron. 1984. *Inner Landscapes: The Theater of Sam Shepard*. Columbia: University of Missouri Press.

Müller, Heiner. 1984. *Hamletmachine and Other Texts for the Stage*. ed. and trans. Carl Weber. New York: Performing Arts Journal Publications.

Nash, Thomas. 1983. "Sam Shepard's *Buried Child*: The Ironic Use of Folklore." *Modern Drama* 26, no. 4:486–91.

Nelson, Cary. 1987. "Against English: Theory and the Limits of the Discipline." In *Profession 87*. New York: Modern Language Association of America.

Norris, Christopher. 1982. *Deconstruction: Theory and Practice*. London: Methuen.

Olson, Gary A. 1990. "Jacques Derrida on Rhetoric and Composition: A Conversation." *Journal of Advanced Composition*. 10, no. 1:1–12.

Osinski, Zbigniew. 1986. *Grotowski and His Laboratory*. Trans. and abr. Lillian Vallee and Robert Findlay. New York: Performing Arts Journal Publications.

Oumano, Ellen. 1986. *Sam Shepard: The Life of an American Dreamer*. New York: St. Martin's Press.

Pavis, Patrice. 1986. "The Classical Heritage of Modern Drama: The Case of Postmodern Theater." *Modern Drama* 29, no. 2:1–22.

Pechter, Edward. 1987. "The New Historicism and Its Discontents: Politicizing Renaissance Drama." *PMLA* 102:292–303.

Pontbriand, Chantal. 1985. "'The eye finds no fixed point on which to rest . . .'" Trans. C. R. Parsons. *Modern Drama* 25, no. 1:154–58.

Prigogine, Ilya, and Isabelle Stengers. 1988. *Order out of Chaos: Man's New Dialogue with Nature*. New York: Bantam Books.

Quigley, Austin. 1985. *The Modern Stage and Other Worlds*. New York: Methuen.

Rabkin, Gerald. 1985. "Is There a Text on This Stage? Theater/Authorship/

Interpretation." *Performing Arts Journal* 26/27, nos. 2/3:142–59.

Raven, Arlene. 1988. *Crossing Over: Feminism and Art of Social Concern*. Contemporary American Art and Culture, vol. 10. Ann Arbor: UMI Research Press.

Roose-Evans, James. 1984. *Experimental Theater from Stanislavski to Peter Brook*. New York: Universe Books.

Rosenfelt, Deborah, and Judith Newton. 1985. *Feminist Criticism and Social Change: Sex, Class, and Race in Literature and Culture*. New York: Methuen.

Rouse, John. 1984. "Robert Wilson: Texts and History." *Theater* 16, no. 1:68–74.

———. 1987. "Structuring Stories: Robert Wilson's *Alcestis*." *Theater* 23, no. 8: 56–59.

Sarup, Madan. 1989. *An Introductory Guide to Post-Structuralism and Postmodernism*. Athens: University of Georgia Press.

Savran, David. 1984. "Sam Shepard's Conceptual Prison: *Action* and the Unseen Hand." *Theater Journal* 36, no. 1:57–73.

———. 1985. "The Wooster Group, Arthur Miller, and *The Crucible*." *Drama Review* 106:98–104.

———. 1986a. "Adaptation as Clairvoyance: The Wooster Group's *Saint Anthony*." *Theater* 18, no. 1:38–41.

———. 1986b. *Breaking the Rules: The Wooster Group*. New York: Theater Communications Group.

Schechner, Richard. 1969. *Public Domain: Essays on Theater*. New York: Bobbs-Merrill.

———. 1970. *The Performance Group: Dionysus in 69*. New York: Farrar, Straus and Giroux.

———. 1982. *The End of Humanism: Writings on Performance*. New York: Performing Arts Journal Publications.

———. 1985. *Between Theater and Anthropology*. Philadelphia: University of Pennsylvania Press.

Schmitt, Natalie Crohn. 1990a. *Actors and Onlookers: Theater and Twentieth-Century Scientific Views of Nature*. Evanston: Northwestern University Press.

———. 1990b. "Theorizing about Performance: Why Now?" *New Theatre Quarterly* 7, no. 23:231–34.

Serban, Andrei. 1986. "The Life in a Sound." In *The Drama Review: Thirty Years of Commentary on the Avant-Garde*, 229–32. See McNamara and Dolan 1986.

Shank, Theodore. 1982. *American Alternative Theater*. Macmillan Modern Dramatists, vol. 6. London: Macmillan Press.

Shepard, Sam. 1977. "Language, Visualization, and the Inner Library," *Drama Review* 21, no. 4:49–58.

———. 1981a. "American Experimental Theater: Then and Now." In *American Dreams: The Imagination of Sam Shepard*, 212–13. See Marranca, 1981.

———. 1981b. *Sam Shepard: Seven Plays*. New York: Bantam Books.

———. 1982. *Motel Chronicles*. San Francisco: City Lights.

———. 1984. *Fool For Love and Other Plays*. New York: Bantam Books.

———. 1986. *A Lie of the Mind*. New York: New American Library.

Shewey, Don. 1984. "Miller's Tale: Interview with Arthur Miller." *Village Voice,* 27 November, 123.

Shyer, Laurence. 1988. "*The Forest:* A Preview of the Next Wilson-Byrne Collaboration." *Theater* 19, no. 3:6–11.

———. 1989. *Robert Wilson and His Collaborators.* New York: Theater Communications Group.

Simard, Rodney. 1984. *Postmodern Drama: Contemporary Playwrights in America and Britain.* New York: University Press of America.

Sontag, Susan. 1977. "On Art and Consciousness." *Performing Arts Journal* 2, no. 2:28–31.

States, Bert O. 1988. "Playing in Lyric Time: Beckett's Voice Plays." *Theater Journal* 40, no. 4:453–67.

Stoppard, Tom. 1988. *Hapgood.* London: Faber and Faber.

Teraoka, Arlene Akiko. 1985. *The Silence of Entropy or Universal Discourse: The Postmodern Poetics of Heiner Müller.* New York: Peter Lang.

Tharu, Susie. 1984. *The Sense of Performance: Post-Artaud Theater.* Atlantic Highlands, N.J.: Humanities Press.

Turner, Victor. 1982. *From Ritual to Theater: The Human Seriousness of Play.* New York: Performing Arts Journal Publications.

Ubersfeld, Anne. 1977. *Lire le théâtre.* Paris: Editions Sociales.

Weber, Carl. 1986. "Carl Weber, Müller Translator." In "The *PAJ* Casebook: *Alcestis.*" *Performing Arts Journal* 28, no. 1:104–5.

———. 1987. "A Landscape on the Other Side of Death: Writing against Interpretation." *Theater 3* 3:21– 27.

Weiner, Jon. 1988. "Deconstructing de Man." *The Nation,* 9 January, 22–24.

Whitaker, Thomas. 1986. "Wham, Bam, Thank You Sam: The Presence of Beckett." In *Beckett at 80 / Beckett in Context,* 206–11. See Brater 1986.

Wilder, Thornton. 1974. "Some Thoughts on Performance." In *Dramatic Theory and Criticism: Greeks to Grotowski,* ed. Bernard Dukore, 886–93. New York: Holt, Rinehart and Winston.

Wilson, Robert. 1986a. *Alcestis.* In "The *PAJ* Casebook: *Alcestis.*" *Performing Arts Journal* 28, no. 1:111–15.

———. 1986b. "Robert Wilson, Director." In "The *PAJ* Casebook: *Alcestis.*" See Wilson 1986a.

Wirth, Andrzej. 1990. "Robert Wilson Stages Virginia Woolf and Chekhov in Germany." *West European Stages* 2, no. 1:15–18.

Wooster Group. 1978. *Rumstick Road. Performing Arts Journal* 3, no. 2:92–115.

———. 1980. *Point Judith. Zone,* 7:14–27.

———. 1982. *Route 1 & 9 (The Last Act). Benzene* 5/6:4–16.

Worthen, William. 1984. *The Idea of the Actor.* Princeton: Princeton University Press.

Zurbrugg, Nicholas. 1988. "Post-Modernism and the Multi-Media Sensibility: Heiner Müller's *Hamletmachine* and the Art of Robert Wilson." *Modern Drama* 31, no. 3:439–53.

Index